G000254137

About the Author

After a disastrous (but character-forming) spell at university, then some aimless swanning around, Mike Clarke worked for 38 years in Immigration Control, finally becoming the first Inspector of the elite, discreet and now defunct IS Anti-Terrorist Liaison Unit. He has now, thankfully, retired.

Home Office
United Kingdom Immigration Service

M. Clarke

Home Office   01587

Planes, Passports and Porkie Pies – Slice One

Stirring Tales of UK Border Control
(but not as shown on TV)

Mike Clarke

Matador
9 Priory Business Park,
Wistow Road, Kibworth Beauchamp,
Leicestershire. LE8 0RX
Tel: 0116 279 2299
Email: books@troubador.co.uk
Web: www.troubador.co.uk/matador
Twitter: @matadorbooks

ISBN 978 1785891 571

British Library Cataloguing in Publication Data.
A catalogue record for this book is available from the British Library.

Printed and bound by CPI Group (UK) Ltd, Croydon, CR0 4YY
Typeset in 11pt Aldine401 BT by Troubador Publishing Ltd, Leicester, UK

Matador is an imprint of Troubador Publishing Ltd

This book is written for all those men and women, of every rank[1] and some now dead, who laboured wholly unsung, often abused and largely in vain, in the United Kingdom's old Immigration Service to maintain the country's border controls; but mostly for the IOs themselves, the Immigration Officers who formed the latest thin red line, and to whom I offer my own deepest thanks and admiration. (Well, let's face it: you'll get fuck-all of either, ever, from anyone or anywhere *officially*, now will you?)

Mike Clarke, ex-IO LGW[2] and TN3 LHR, CIO TN2 LHR, Stansted, and Becket House, and HMI (but only t/p) NCU and ATLU. (Oh, and I almost forgot: B.A. failed).

---

[1]   Always providing they'd *earned* it the slow, hard, *proper* way (in this, the first of two volumes, they still did).

[2]   I'll explain all the initials later (except B.A., of course).

SLICE ONE

Which covers: Gatwick 1970 to 1977, when the going was still comparatively good; and Heathrow 1977 to 1988, when we kept going, somehow. But only just.

Contents

PREFACE

What follows is an episodic and spasmodic if not downright erratic account of a career in Great Britain's border control, the first thirty years spent at three so-called London airports – Gatwick, Heathrow and Stansted – deciding which foreigners (almost all) could enter the country, and which (a paltry, unhappy, few) could not: and the last eight on the teeming streets of the great metropolis itself, deciding which of those already (somehow) here could stay, and which (of those we could find), had (at least in theory) to go. Well, someone had to do it. Or try to.

It is also an affectionate requiem, but not so much for the job itself – a necessary evil if you like, and with ever-dwindling effect anyway – as for my erstwhile colleagues, who contrived, God knows how, to form a more or less single, focussed and collective entity out of as disparate a bunch of extroverts, introverts, romantics, pedantics, scholars, general layabouts and devoted alcoholics (not one your average nine- to five-er) as you'll find anywhere this side of Chipping Sodbury.

So then: Immigration UK, a matter of perennial interest if not quite yet fatal fascination to Joe Public, and over the years called many things; bad joke, abject failure, total shambles – all undeniably and ever-increasingly true if you weren't a politician, and even then you could always blame the other side, and usually did – and a subject where polarisation was and remains instant, and visceral, and *no-one* sat on the fence. And who were the few poor sods trapped neatly in the middle, pips (or maybe nuts) squeaking, between the howling fascist thugs and the wailing bleeding hearts? Why, *us* of course, the IS, the Immigration Service, and British to the very core; though now I can say *them*, can't I, because I'm well out of it, and besides, the old Service is long gone.

But don't despair – not yet, anyway. For these two books aren't about the Big Picture (well, not directly and not much), about the colossal and now-irretrievable Kafka-esque cock-up the Control with a big C, *still* risibly so-titled, had drip by drip and year by year and weak by weaker government become, even decades before the West's more recent ventures into the Middle East have left us, and it, with oil on our collective blood-red face.

No, they are just *story* books, or meant to be, and the stories are those of individuals, mostly the ordinary, the little people, Thomas and Leon and the rest, the poor players on the stage who came and went and then were heard no more (especially, if they had any sense, those who *hadn't* gone). They tell too of the eternal battle between the so-called Keepers of the Kingdom's Keys (*us*, if only we still were) on the one side; and of the on-entry refusals and later, internal offenders – rich *and* poor but mainly, inevitably, poor – on the other: and with just a touch, here and there, of domestics.

But "Wait," I hear you ask in probable shocked disbelief if/ when you've read on a bit, "can these stories really be true?" Well, all I can say is that every tale – barring a number of minor changes (like most names, and some nationalities) to protect both the innocent and the part-guilty, not least myself – is as accurate as my fallible memory allows. None need any dressing up anyway and unless I state otherwise, each didn't just really *happen*, it just really happened to *me*. Most are funny – some out-farcing Feydeau, even if the alternative joke had to be cruelly prised from the jaws of some poor devil's personal tragedy with that same black humour which imbues all such tasks. Most, but not all. Because whilst the job was often one to enjoy, it was always one sometimes to regret.

And forget the TV documentaries – expunge them wholly from your seething minds. You don't expect people in them to behave as they would and did *normally* (and doubtless off-camera do still, staff especially included), now do you?

No, this is how it truly was, day in day out, a mere time capsule perhaps, corroded and corrosive, of a *temps* long *perdu* and a now-dead Service, but no less real for that – which also means I'd better warn you again (but directly this time) that it's just about as gently *non*-PC as these days, it seems, you can semi-safely get, or at least I hope so. In other words if you're a fervent '*ism*' or even '*phobe*' -ist, don't read on because you'll only get upset – unless of course you attack *me* instead, and where better for malicious, cowardly, internet spiders – though I rather like real spiders – to hide, anonymously, than in a world-wide web? And if you *do*, despite it all (read on, I mean), and if by the end you've spotted more *Grouchos* or even more *Ernies* than *Clints*, who am *I* to argue?

And one last thing, in case it doesn't hit you from the off, right between the eyes. I'm as proud as Punch to be English. But prouder still to be British.

Cashing *Out*, 1971

So as a brief foretaste if you're still undecided, where better to begin – and only a tad out of order – than with the aforesaid Thomas (who proved in the end to be well out himself – of order, I mean). Black, short, slight, soft-spoken but loudly be-suited and widely be-smiling off the B/Cal[1] Lagos, he copped my recent mentor Paul, sitting right beside me. No hand-baggage at all, which was rare; nothing but that suit, which to the eye was already rarer still, though as yet we didn't know the half of it.

"Hello there, Jimmy," said Paul (so now you've sussed *his* nationality, too). "How long will you be staying?"

"Me, sir?" Thomas replied, laudably politely. "Oh, just one week, two weeks, for a trip, a short *business* trip," and Paul was about to roll[2] him, no more questions asked and his landing-stamp actually poised, when for some reason never explained, maybe simple, honest *joie de vivre* but more likely a premature, wholly understandable but fatally treacherous surge of pure relief at his so-far trouble-free passage, Thomas thrust out his hand – OK, not exactly your average response, but still a welcome change from some of the more common alternatives, verbal *and* physical.

And the only trouble as they shook was that even I heard his suit rustle, a sound so incongruous that it took a moment to engage your senses; and then I looked sideways and saw Paul (who as you've now also sussed was left-handed) slowly lower his stamp.

"Hey. *Jimmy*. What's the matter with yer *sewt* there? What's in it? What the fuck's that *noise*?" he demanded in a rare but fitting variation from the standard interrogative line. And Thomas, twitching a bit now but smiling wider still, said, "Nothing, sir, oh nothing, no, *not at all*." So Paul said, "*OK*, son. *Indulge* me. One more time," and he reached out and took Thomas's hand again, then held it tight as, gingerly, he put out his (own) other one and patted his (you know whose) jacket.

Which crackled and rustled all over, so that what Paul shook next, this time in wonder, was his own wee rock-hard head. And then he took Thomas upstairs to Customs, who first examined the doubly-loud suit carefully as a whole then took it apart, and it had £80,000 in cash badly stitched inside, because Thomas wasn't just a rustler, he was an armed robber who'd cleaned out a Lagos bank right before taking directly, via his twinkling heels like a second Hermes, to the cop-free international skies.

So Paul brought Thomas back down for a *proper* talk, but more of a informal chat than an examination, complete with mutual family snaps and a cuppa or two, and in English without any language problems at all, which reminds me that at that time (and still, for all I know) West Africans in general and Nigerians in particular often seemed to understand Scots speaking English much better than the English themselves, and you can take that either way (which also reminds me that sometimes I used to wonder idly if it wasn't simply a secondary linguistic legacy from the old early days of pistons, steam and empire, and more specifically of ardent and ubiquitous ships' engineers, mainly called Jock).

Anyway, Paul didn't bother to write much down because we didn't then, and at the end when he emerged, he was again shaking his head. "Och," he said, smiling himself this time but wryly, "Yon's a bad, *bad* man. Still, not *entirely*, and *interesting* all the same." And so he didn't roll Thomas but refused him admission[3] instead, and sent him back to Lagos unescorted (those were the days) on the return flight, all done and dusted, and cashless of course. And all *he* (Thomas) said, was '*Thank* you, sir, thank you *very much* for the talk and the tea and for all your trouble,' *extra* politely. And he smiled brightly again as they shook hands one last time. After all, he and Paul were *friends*, weren't they?

Then he went off like a lamb, waving at the rest of us as he left. And we waved back, and the Branch[4] told us later that he was still smiling when the flight landed back home and he was taken off it by the army and chained so that even his last short walk to the beach was loud, and summarily shot.

Well, I was to discover soon enough that there were other odd ways in which a refusal could celebrate his triumphant return home. He might go headfirst down the village well, OK, screaming and shouting, but also at least with the dubious comfort of knowing that – unlike Thomas – he wasn't leaving his family to starve because they'd be right down there with him; or he could get banged *up* instead (with a reduced comparative likelihood of consequential fatality, *instant* fatality anyway, though sometimes after being roughed up here first – not by us, though[5] – and even if he'd left " voluntarily" in the first place).

But all that was yet to come, in the months and years and chapters ahead. Still. *Start with a bang*, they said. So with the unwitting help of a firing squad, I hope I have.

Chapter One

IN

Well then: still with me? Right, your choice, and here we go. So: Immigration? Not exactly the hub of my world at the time back then in late '69, nor even the extreme periphery. No, me, I was dozily floating along, head just above water, in a placid sea of sex and booze (just once a week though, the booze I mean), vaguely waving and ever so slowly drowning – but *happily*, you know – when it all changed forever. And *I* blame Aunt Syb, because she sent the *Telegraph* advert through 'in case I was interested', always the diplomat. 'The Keys to the Kingdom,' it said, 'A' levels only required; and it asked pointedly, Kitchener-like, whether *You* could handle the control of the UK's borders, deciding which foreigners could and which could not enter the country. Well, how the hell was *I* supposed to know, in advance, the answer to *that*?

But it sounded like fun – a kind of *responsible* fun – so I applied, only just in time but that didn't matter because I was only going through the motions – a university reject, positively *thrust* and not just *dropped* out and after *two* years not one, each circumstance then fairly uncommon in itself and in combination truly rare, *and* it was a bloody fit-up in the first place (well, I would say that wouldn't I, but you can make up your own minds later). And next? A succession of dead-end jobs, that's how Dad would have put it anyway; but he kept his eternal disappointment to himself, a deep and solitary shameful sorrow locked away – at least, it was from *me*.

Bar man, Bread man, Milker man, everything in fact *except* Thief – though once, when aged fifteen I'd spent a long hot summer working for peanuts on Walton pier, I *had* been accused of pinching pennies from the slot machines. It was a slanderous, outrageous, *cheap* claim – *pennies*, for fuck's sake, the *old* ones – but they took no prisoners in pier-land and mindless violence was well on the cards until I pointed out – a tad incoherently as I was choking with righteous rage at the time (and the thick hairy arm round my neck didn't help) – that no *half*-competent thief would so gratuitously weigh himself down with his pitiful booty as to turn one major potential escape route into a swift, wet, deep and inevitable grave instead – " Well, 'e sank like a 'kin *stone* when 'e jumped, and I reckon it was them *coppers* – naah, not *you* boys, the bleedin' *coins* in 'is *pockets*."

So with that background I knew the Home Office wouldn't look twice but it would please Syb, and Dad's view of me could hardly get any worse. And it was a big surprise when the call for interview came – in fact it made me feel so good I decided I'd actually *go*, even though it would be a waste of everybody's time.

And suddenly there I was, in the hot seat, and it didn't take long. There were three of them and the chairman was a woman, quite charming; like a lot of women then, she *knew* she was innately superior and didn't need daily to *prove* it, and in my memory she did most of the talking. The other two, both male, laughed a lot though, at times almost hysterically – a really good sign, I thought. Or bad. So I'd introduced myself and we all shook hands, and then Madam and I talked about cricket. And cricket. And cricket.

Cricket. It was one of the few subjects then on which I still felt eloquent, no, actually *enthusiastic,* and on the day I truly was, just lucky I suppose unless Madam was even more skilful than I thought and somehow drew me out. I don't know whether she really did love the game but she seemed to, and she knew more about it than I did. Anyway, I left thinking that I'd put on a pretty good show for an occasional twelfth man, I'd actually *enjoyed* myself, and when the acceptance dropped through the letter box, it was a hell of a shock – an umpire's thumb's-up even, if you like.

Later though, after I'd been there a while and started to get acquainted, I thought I'd sussed it. They wanted men who had the brains to *get* to university, though you didn't actually have to have *gone,* especially if you were older; and if you *did* go it was all right if you left prematurely or got ejected, providing it wasn't for something criminal or really disgraceful, naturally. In fact an early academic exit could even be a bonus because it might leave you better equipped to spot the mirror of your own failings, whatever they were, in others – to wit, in foreigners seeking UK entry. Set a thief to catch a thief perhaps as long as there was no real history of theft, and I've already covered that. And the dead-end jobs, especially the bread and milk, had all involved meeting the public in a variety of situations, some a bit iffy[6], which was precisely what the new job was going to be about.

Oh, and before I lose yet more readers through my apparent disparagement of female equality, let me explain that when I referred above to 'men', I meant it: at that time and for a few years to come, the job was exclusively male. And when I refer to the 'Branch' in a purely immigration context, that's what it was then called: IB, the Immigration Branch of the Home Office, later to become the IS, the Immigration

Service, though as of April 1st 2008 – and what date of *any* year could be more fitting – that title ceased also and the whole shebang, arguably including the last shreds of any coherent, realistic, informed and *committed* control, was consigned, for now if not forever, to the big, leaky and infinitely flexible bin of history.

Anyway, there I was, a budding Immigration Officer, *in* the Branch though not yet *of* it: and I was to report for work on January 29th 1970, at LGW, London Gatwick, the new-ish second airport of old London Town. So I did.

Chapter Two

GATWICK

Where the first person I met was Paul the aforesaid, a rough, tough Glaswegian and thus perfect for mentoring the bloody English. Because if you *were* bloody English and had to learn about foreigners you couldn't do better than start with a Scot, which was handy since they were *everywhere* in IB in a kind of fluid human reverse-role mutation of Hadrian's wall. And the first thing you learned was to watch them carefully and constantly, especially Glaswegians – they could be *very* touchy.

For example: you'd be out together having a few, and sooner or later you'd say the wrong thing (although none of *us* could ever work out later what it was and *they'd* never tell us, *if* they even knew), a silent fist would come flying out of nowhere (shades of Prestonpans), and you'd be flat on your back shocked, stunned and Cope-like, or at least highly alarmed by the near miss. But at least it was always a fist and not a glass, because like Paul and Thomas we were all friends really and they meant nothing by it – except at footie-time of course; ah, *then*: talk about two-legged short-fused McMolotovs deeply disguised in ancient, vengeful rage and cheap malt – but I'll come back to all that later. Maybe.

So anyway, no big deal. It was after all a free country, or free-*ish* compared to most whatever the rabble-rousers thought, and no-one cared if, still a sprog, you went for a pint afterwards along with the rest, just so long as you sat at a separate table – as *close* as you liked, but *apart* – and said nothing to anyone because sure as hell none of *them* would say anything to *you*. It may seem strange now with all this hypocritical bright welcoming crap, but it was standard treatment then, the dying howl of the all-male pack, and not just in the Branch. It had the great merit of being natural, of being how the world really worked – *there-you-sit-mate, a-bloody-little-sprog-who-knows-fuck-all-and-don't-ever-forget-it* – and if you were normal it wouldn't last too long, in my case and those of the two other bloody-little-sprogs who started at the same time, some six weeks as I recall.

Then, one day seemingly no different from the others, you'd be sitting there in solitary splendour sipping your fizz as if you were truly fucking invisible – or there might even be two of you, two lonely lowly silent sproglets nursing your glasses as you listened shyly to the next table's banter and review of the day, the day in which you too had been involved – you *had*, you *knew* you had, and they'd talked to you *then* all right – and you were starting to wonder what was wrong with you and when if ever this would end when suddenly you clocked a brief, expectant, illogical lull in the conversation. And out of the new silence you heard first what sounded rather like a resigned group sigh, orchestrated and almost theatrical, and then a single sentence, again illogical, something like "Right then, gentlemen, let's have them over," and then your names, as if from nowhere, across a crowded room.

It was all done quite formally – "Mr. Clarke? Mr. McQuinn?" – and somehow you sensed that you weren't meant to join them, not yet, but simply to reply "Yes?" politely so we did, and then the response was, "What are you drinking?" and you told them (no clever stuff though, just bitter), and somebody brought it over and *then* the invitation, "Come and join us," in that order, and you were in as if you'd always been, *right* in with no transition. And now *you* could peer idly at the *next* new poor sods in the hot seat, serving their time before the great day came. Now too though, you'd better bloody well buy your round when it was your turn, afford it or not, because if you were excluded for not doing *that*, you'd *never* be invited back.

Anyway, by now I was getting to know the place. The *new* terminal it was then, recently completed and part of the Gatwick South of today, so largely unrecognisable. A lot of people thought it would be a white elephant – how wrong can you be – and it was regarded with deep suspicion if not downright derision by our colleagues at Heathrow, or *The* Airport as *they* called it, the superior fuckers. *They* also sometimes called *us Gay*-wick, in reference to a rumoured preference by a few of our number for the company, off-duty also, of fellow men to that of women. But it was a cheap shot – perhaps, who knows, spoken in hidden, dubious envy so far as the hetero rest of us were concerned and certainly no truer of Gatwick, if true at all, than I found it to be of Heathrow when in due course I went there next. How's that then for careful phrasing and besides, now, who the hell cares?

Gatwick, then. It had grown from the almost-standard Nissen huts and tents to the new solid Airport in no more than five years, and was the home of a number of British airlines which couldn't or didn't want to get into *The* Airport, where BEA and BOAC effectively had a stranglehold on all the slots available for UK airlines.

So we had BUA (British United Airways) with the girls in light-blue throughout (from skirt to skin I mean, and there was a 1970 girlie calendar, airline-issued, hanging on the wall, progressively (or regressively, depending on your point of view) to prove it. January to May helped a lot but December didn't, though as a last provocation she might *just* have kept her light-blue heels and hat; then Dan-Air with the girls in red, at least on top; and Caledonian Airways with the girls in tartan which soon amalgamated with BUA to form B/Cal anyway, again wholly ditching the blue; and give or take, a good time was had by all, not least in the absence of uniform or so I heard. (We of course wore plain clothes and maintained reasonable, generally be-suited and slightly-flared standards, oddly enough until the moment when the first of our own girls appeared, after which it didn't take long for them to drop – the standards, I mean.)

Most of the foreign scheduled carriers – effectively, the national airlines from each country which had one – were based at Heathrow too, and *we* were the undisputed kings of the ever-expanding British charter market which, since the passengers were themselves almost exclusively British, was of no interest to us whatsoever. But we had BUA scheduled flights to several European countries, we were growing like Topsy and we already had the Loftleidir, the Icelandic national carrier. It provided the gentlest of introductions to the kind of traffic that *did* concern us, it stayed at Gatwick for a while until it moved to *The* Airport and all I'll say for now is that it was *fun*.

So far as the local IB staff were concerned, the youngest was nineteen – he'd started the year before me, when the Home Office had a brief flirtation with direct school-leavers – most were in their twenties or thirties from a variety of backgrounds (one ex rock-star, several ex-National Service or regular forces, one or two mainstream Civil Service and at least one literal layabout), and a few had been in the War and were close to retirement. Almost everyone was Brit-born and bred but two originated from the (Indian) sub-continent and it's as easy as it's unfair to say now that they both tried a bit too hard in their different ways to fit in, especially when the rest of us didn't go anywhere near far enough *out* of *our* way to help.

Many of the IOs had a few (more) drinks after work as you know already; and most got on pretty well, especially amongst the younger unmarried set (which at once excluded me, poor sod, firmly hitched – or so I thought – and with two small children). But there wasn't much external socialising, airline girls apart, because 24-hour shift work distances you from 'normal' life (anyone who's done it will know what I mean) and our world was therefore artificial, but no less real for that.

So what exactly *did* we do? Well, if all you want are the stories or if you think you already know, say perhaps from those same TV programmes (though you already have my view of *them)*, this is where you can pass smartly (or smart-arsedly) on to page 16. But the following may just give even *you* a better insight.

So: the *Telegraph* advert had pretty well summed it up. All we *could* do with Brits (unless they were in the SI, see below) was to confirm that that's what they were, and in the early days that was no problem at all. A quick glance up, down, up – face, photo, face – was enough: there was no need for any verbal exchange nor could we require one, though a rare muttered, 'Thank you,' might even more rarely elicit a muttered 'Thank you,' back (from the passenger, I mean). So far as most were concerned we might just as well have been robots but you soon got used to it, and a barely human silence was still better than the merry quips of the occasional half-pissed comedian (I'm still talking about passengers, naturally).

But where Brits were concerned, other parties were involved: Customs of course, but they had their own Hall upstairs and generally kept their distance, only rarely coming down to look over our shoulders to identify anyone of particular interest. No, the ones we worked with all the time were the Police and not just your average plods but Special Branch, with an SB officer in the seat by your side and he – and again in those early years, it invariably *was* he – would have his own targets: criminals of course, Brits as well as foreign; terrorists (at the time the Irish, SB's historical prey, were the only regular game in town); those of other security interest (i.e. IC – Iron Curtain – connected), who were as likely to be Brits as anything else; and people of particular occupations. I remember that for a year or two antique dealers were right in the frame, because some of them – but only a dastardly, fiendish, unpatriotic few, surely? – were working some kind of import/export scam.

But back to us. Each IO had two books – one thick, one thin, one greenish black, one blue – which he took everywhere on the Control, both arrivals and embarks: the SIs we called them, the Suspect Indices, issued annually with the already-known and perennial recidivist identities pre-typed in, the thin book for Commonwealth Citizens including Brits and the thick one for Aliens – *human* Aliens of course – who were all the rest. The SIs were as personal to an officer as his own uniquely-numbered set of landing and embark stamps because he had to update them manually from ILs, Interport Lists sent out daily, detailing in the main the most recent nationwide RLLs – Refusals of Leave to Land as we called aliens who were bounced, and RAs – Refusals of Admission to Commonwealth Citizens, Brits apart, similarly treated. And if he was lazy and didn't, he stood to be summarily sacked after the occasional surprise check. And one or two officers were, and you couldn't argue with that.

Everything on the ILs had to be entered, and apart from the refusals there would be security and Customs cases and all kinds of odds and sods – including the occasional '*Not to be confused with…*' and when you read *that*, you knew some poor innocent unlucky sod had precisely the same details as a suspect, had already suffered for it once and despite (or because of) the warning was likely to cop it again. And I nearly forgot the endless Wards of Court entries, strictly for embarks, where you looked up any single adult travelling with a child lest it was an abduction. But that was just a joke because whilst the action in our book was 'Refer to SB', the action in theirs was 'Refer to IB', and I can't recall anyone ever being caught at it anyway.

As for the rest, anyone who wasn't British (or for practical purposes Irish, but I won't go into that right now) was fair game: *anyone*, because this was three years before the onset of the EC (European Community as it was then) and the border began at the coast, Wogs began at Calais, everywhere beyond it was foreign and the Control was essentially an economic one.

So if you wanted to come to the UK to live and work and you lacked the right permit or if you came here with so little money that you'd *have* to find a job, you'd be sent back; and we sent back Frenchmen and Italians and Spaniards and Portuguese, mostly waiters, in twos and threes daily, and – waiters largely apart, but for the same reasons and from time to time – pretty much every other nationality you can think of, Americans North and South, Asians, Africans, Aussies and Kiwis and even the occasional West German and Dutchman too. (But not many IC nationals, because the Curtain was far too efficient for that, both in *and* out.)

The mechanics of it couldn't have been simpler. If you were a foreigner seeking entry, the onus was on *you* to show that you were genuine, and the standard of proof was the civil one – not the criminal absence of reasonable doubt but a simple balance of probabilities, so achieved easily enough; but if the IO *wasn't* satisfied to the same standard, back you went, no appeal, no argument. We had the same power as Customs to search baggage, if there were no Customs Officers about we'd happily do it ourselves and in case anyone these days is still confused about the difference between us *and* Customs, we are interested in people as people and essentially they are interested in goods, and in people only as carriers. It's as easy as that.

All foreigners were subject to examination which meant to questions, and the first one was in essence invariable – if you asked one at all that is, because if the whole flight was made up of middle-aged red-faced bermuda-shorted Yanks from Tampa who had to confer with their wives before they even knew where the hell they actually *were* on the lightning two-week European Tour, it became at best academic and at worst – say, if there was another flight about that you *did* want to get your teeth into – a complete waste of time.

"How long will you be staying?" or, "Just a Holiday?" or, "In the group?" it went, or if it *was* a red-shorted bermuda-faced Yank and you were feeling ill or hung-over or generally pissed off or just plain mischievous, a put-on icy *"Been alors. Velcome to Paree, monsewer,"* in bad, *bad* Franglais, a signal for your colleagues on either side to start gabbling away at their own Yanks in real fluent French if they could and in false fluent bagpipe if they couldn't, to the invariable, inevitable, wholly unfair but still highly satisfying confusion of the New World.

Most people said, like the Yanks, that they were here for a short visit. Most of them, like almost all the Yanks, were telling the truth and most of the time it was easy to spot the ones who weren't. You'd start with nationality and age and job and funds and (sometimes) appearance – can someone from *there*, *that* old (or young), doing *that* (if anything) and paid *so little* for it, *really* want, *or* afford, to come *here* just on *holiday* ? – and go swiftly on. 'D'you have a return ticket? How much money have you brought? What d'you do in Fairyland? Got a leave letter? How much d'you earn? Married? Children? – *How* many? *Lucky you!* – Know anyone here? No? So that's why you're staying at the bloody Ritz?'

And there you have it. A thirty year-old married man earning a tenner a month as a waiter in you-name-it where the holiday season has just ended, with five children and a sixth on the way – *Congrats again!* – coming for two weeks to see Big Ben and to stay in an expensive hotel because he knows absolutely no-one here, using the family's life savings to do it. *Bollocks! Do I look like I was born yesterday?*

And you'd take him up to Customs and at first and for a while, until it became depressingly routine, it was rewarding to find, neatly laid out on top in the bag of the man who you reckoned was really coming here to be a waiter, *Blow Me, a waiter's outfit!* And it got even better when despite his repeated and vehement denials, you fished out the letter which told him where and when to start work here or at least where to look, and which as often as not would say somewhere, usually underlined or in capitals but not necessarily in English, *'Remember! Whatever you do, don't bring this with you!'*

And sometimes they'd half-listened, so it wasn't in the bags or the diary but you were bloody *sure* that they had the UK address written down *somewhere* because they couldn't simply *memorise* it. And different nationalities hid it in different places – yep, it did work like that, predictable, stereotypical even, or almost racist you might say today, as if that negates or excuses the fact – some on a note inside their socks, the ones they were wearing I mean, some inside their underwear or trousers, *written* inside that is, and thankfully usually on the spares in their bags though not always; sometimes written on themselves and, twice in my experience, on chits inserted in places where if Customs really wanted to look they were welcome but otherwise they could *keep* the bloody things – and if chummy hadn't had the sense to use a condom to wrap it in, you couldn't read the words anymore anyway, but then *he* couldn't either.

And once in a while they'd brought no papers at all so they thought they'd cracked it, but then you'd ask Reception on the Concourse to broadcast a cunning British message, 'Would the person meeting Jose go to the Information Desk,' and you'd wait a minute or so, standing off to the side and semi-invisible whilst Jose cooled his heels airside, but then there he'd be, Juan looking for Jose, his brother. But according to Jose he didn't *have* a brother or if he did, he was back home in Fairyland; and you'd talk to Juan and tell him he might see Jose later but right now he, Jose, was in big trouble.

Then you'd go back to a now-worried and sometimes-shaking Jose and say, 'Are you *sure* you don't have a brother here?' to give him a chance – natural justice and all that – but usually he just dug himself a bigger hole and really whatever he said you'd got him and back he'd go, occasionally protesting but mainly philosophically, his passport endorsed with the refusing IO's landing stamp containing a prominent ball-penned cross[7] to indicate his refusal, the pen pressed down so hard (until they stopped us) that it went through several pages to defeat the obvious response of simply tearing the offending one out, and that's why it was important to get the details on the IL quickly, because there was a fair chance that Jose would simply turn straight round to try his luck elsewhere (or maybe even with *us* again, when he'd likely be the obvious one head-down in the queue, with permanent problems with his laces) after attempting to hide the refusal stamp, either by the aforesaid page removal or by covering it with foreign postage stamps or by going for broke and obtaining a whole new travel document, the tell-tale old one having been conveniently 'lost'.

But all that's mostly about aliens and would-be visitors, because at the time there was a loophole which made our efforts with Commonwealth Citizens a joke. In those years there was no internal control whatsoever (barring deportation, which was technical, court-related and not for everyday use[8]), the desk literally *was* the frontier and once past it you were *in*, full stop. A few – a very *un*lucky few (or just plain stupid) – took the obvious practical athletic option (or just panicked) and simply *ran* at us, hurdling any barriers in the way. But that wasn't cricket and we'd recover them, physically, within moments – after all, it was quite hard for them to remain discreet. The *cunning* method was much, much better though; all you had to do was to be from the Commonwealth – or at least to produce a Commonwealth passport – and then simply change spoken economy with the truth into physical extravagance with the lie – you just fiddled your apparent age!

A silver-haired (say, Sikh) gent would come shuffling up to the control, bent double, leaning on his stick and looking every day of his passport-proven sixty-seven years and you admitted him because when he was *that* bloody ancient, under the law you had no choice. Then he'd shuffle past you and maybe limp another yard or two for form's sake and you'd be dealing with the next passenger when you'd hear the crash and turn round and there he'd be, upright, straight as a rod, stick thrown away and shaking the flour out of his hair to reveal a laughing, strapping twenty-five year old who vaulted athletically, nay, triumphantly, onto the escalator.

And OK, his instant elation would turn to instant panic because he'd never even seen one before, and he'd clutch at some non-moving part and cling on like grim death and topple backwards as his legs remorselessly continued, and finally skittle anyone behind him; but however perversely satisfying that might be, it wasn't the same as doing the job properly, was it? Toppling happened every other week anyway, and I only saw the age trick once. But once was enough for me.

FIRST BLOOD

So: story time again, but properly this time. And let's start with Leon, also aforesaid, a young black Yank off the Loftleidir whom I met briefly and only once, in the usual way. But I still remember him as clearly as Thomas, not because he was the first passenger I ever refused though he was, but because the decision was one I've always wholly regretted. And I can see now that he was a real victim of circumstance and just unlucky to wind up in front of me, a brand-new IO only two weeks in post, on a day when the duty CIO was himself not just newly promoted and newly arrived at *his* first-ever *air*port but also out to impress the two Box (Security Service) liaison ladies, down for a visit.

Our usual Loftleidir customers were hippies as you'll shortly see, but Leon was different, a 'retiree', which meant an ex-conscript who'd just finished his US military service. And as he presented his passport he told me that he was only passing through on his way to his old US Army base in Frankfurt where he was to start work the next day, but this time as a civvy in the PX, the on-base Yank equivalent of the now-dead British NAAFI.

Anyway, he showed me his ticket and appointment letter and I was all set to roll him when a hand gripped my shoulder, a voice whispered fiercely, "*Stop!* He's a *refusal. Knock him off!*" and there was George the new man, with the two Box girls wide-eyed close behind him. I asked why, to be told that Leon needed a German work permit. So I asked him if he had one. No, he had not. Well then, said George, loudly, the Krauts would doubtless refuse him if *we* didn't, and they'd bounce him straight back to *us* as his last port of call, not the US, where *we* would then have to send him, perhaps at public expense – it was all part of the border game. And all that sounded reasonable, despite Leon's protestations that he didn't need *German* permission to work *inside* a sovereign *American* base.

Well OK, what *Leon* said sounded reasonable too, but at the end of the day I was still a sprog (part-time invisible) who knew damn-all and the CIO had to be right surely, with all his years of experience albeit at a seaport, so I did as I was told. I already knew from watching others that refusing someone entry face-to-face wasn't pleasant, and that first time it certainly wasn't. But it got easier with practise, and perhaps that one was so bad not just because it was my first but because a part of me felt even then that somehow it was wrong – or if it wasn't, that *I* was in the wrong job (although another part of me thought, *That's probably what everyone thinks, the first time*).

I didn't understand then, though I was told bluntly enough by my colleagues very soon afterwards, that what I should've done was to remind George with equal bluntness that *his* job as a Chief was to consider any case *I* referred to *him* as a potential *refusal* but that it was *mine* to *land* people, and that if I chose *not* to refer to him in the first place, then that was the end of it. They weren't commenting on Leon's individual merits, just on the general principle of the thing, and when shortly though not without some trepidation I told another inquisitive CIO much senior to George to fuck right off and he duly left with a surprised grin but without demur, I must say it felt good.

None of which helped poor old Leon who really was a nice guy, and overall he took it pretty well. He did however shout a bit, no more than a general rail at fate – *Why me?* – and although nothing serious, enough to earn him a two-man police escort to the aircraft (a rare thing indeed in those Thomasian days and ostensibly a simple, sensible precaution set up by a wise and prudent George, though now I think about it, maybe he was *still* just out to impress the ladies). Anyway, no-one laid a hand on Leon because there was no need, and we all walked along the finger chatting companionably, four old mates together, as far as the top of the steps where suddenly it all kicked off. But even then it was just handbags, a symbolic, harmless scuffle at which Leon himself seemed surprised and at what he saw as a clear injustice and perhaps even racism too (though it was still just 'prejudice' then). And I stood back in the high confined space, to let the uniforms do their job.

Which they were doing with typical good humour – "Come on Leon mate, be a good bloke, you *know* this won't help, and it's nothing personal," – and with a true minimum of force so that it would still have been a total non-event, had not Leon's flailing Spanish Archer done a spot of knocking off of its own, to wit one of the copper's flat hats. It was clearly a potential game-changer, and for an instant everybody froze. Then we all rushed to the side-rail, Leon included, to peer over mesmerised as the errant titfer sailed down. And with only some twelve feet to fall it was well on its way to a perfectly safe, soft and clean landing, right way up and no harm done, when it seemed to catch a little puff of wind and promptly overturned, side-slipped shyly, paused perversely as if consciously choosing its spot, then plopped neatly into the only patch of oil on the tarmac – and a small, hat-sized, one at that.

I heard one copper give a horrified gasp and the other a choked giggle, and I *thought* I heard an odd third gasp as well, one which seemed to fill the air as if nature herself were astounded, a *universal* gasp far louder and more intense than could have come from just *our* few throats, even though they now totalled six because the two stewardesses inside the door had stuck their heads out to watch. And then as his colleague, now helpless with laughter, draped himself over the side-rail, the hatless one gave way to his own emotions and sternly propelled an un-resistant Leon on board like a bullet from a non-existent gun.

Each party having well and truly shot its bolt, there was no more trouble and that seemed to be the end of it until, both coppers having regained a semblance of composure, the three of us turned to descend the steps, only to be met by what now sounded very like distant cheering and applause. And then when I looked up, I understood that earlier extravagant gasp. Because every terrace was thronged with onlookers, bloody *thousands* of them, all young, almost all female and almost all looking our way. Oh, they weren't there to see *us*, they were waiting for the Beatles to return from their latest American tour. But they were early, and excited, and there was nothing else but us *to* see.

And so whilst one copper ruefully retrieved his slippery hat, the other removed his with an oily smile and bowed low to his audience, milking it quite disgracefully as the crowd began to stamp and shout and the applause spread and grew to muffled thunder. Which was when, despite my concern at the way the Yank had been treated (and Leon, if you ever read this and recognise yourself, I'm *still* sorry for what it's worth), it first really struck me that this might be my kind of job.

ICEFLIGHT

The Loftleidir: up and over the Pole, the cheapest flight from the States and brim-full of gentle hippies, most of whom given half a chance would have just *loved* to put a bloom on your cheeks as well as in the barrel of your landing stamp, flower power in action, or is that just me? Why, even the refusals, Leon apart, were gentle – '*Hey* man, *c'mon,* you don't have to do this. What, you mean you really *do*? OK then, g'bye now, have a nice day,' – and I exaggerate only a trifle, peace, peace… The standard cases fell into your lap – no money, no return ticket, seeking work or just begging and more often than not they'd even tell you so straight out when you asked, '*Hey man*, is that a *crime*?' And it wasn't, nor did it necessarily make you a bad person; but it was still enough to see you on the first flight home: 'Do *not* pass Go'.

Drugs too were involved, naturally, and we had one or two in-house specialists who got it down to a fine art, their first question not the standard 'How long..' but '*Tell* me, mate, *have you ever smoked cannabis?'* said *sotto voce*, companionably indeed almost conspiratorially with a shifty sideways glance, born of a genuine albeit disguised professional interest which in the early days would as often as not elicit an instant, honest *'Man, who hasn't?'* and on occasion, from the truly naïve, a generous 'Sure man, why, d'yuh wanna joint now, I've got one, *right here.'* And in either case their spruce goose was well and truly cooked because they'd be referred to Port Health, to the famous Doc, the Port Medical Inspector (PMI), who had clear, immoveable views on the subject and would forthwith issue a Port 30, a notice authorising – no, *directing* – us to refuse entry on medical grounds, at the drop (coppers apart) of a hat. After all, they were *addicts*, weren't they?

But the rest of us thought that that was not quite playing the British game and we'd take them straight upstairs to our waiting, slavering Customs colleagues, which soon enough was the only route anyway because they rapidly wised up and realised that we weren't *quite* the nice guys we seemed to be – well, maybe *at heart* but not *professionally* – and if *Customs* found drugs or the standard letter, *'Now remember, don't…'* we'd knock them off, gently. But otherwise, if they had money and a ticket, they'd be on their way, no harm done. Whatever their rose-coloured plans, *we* knew they wouldn't stay here too long because the winters were a bit harsher than those on the West Coast and despite all Hari's very best acquisitive efforts, they soon killed off every single one of those flowers in your hair….

Then off the Loftleidir went, to *The* Airport where else, never to return and soon to be replaced by sterner stuff. And we were truly sorry to see it go.

FRONTIER GAMES

Even then, the night duties were real bastards. They were long – 1900 to 0800 hours – and wore us out, particularly the second of the consecutive pair we did at least once every two weeks and sometimes much more often. But they were fun too, in the early years.

Usually soon after midnight we'd manage to snatch a break to get over to Eddie's, the big on-site Italian greasy spoon, for a huge meal served in a pre-stressed concrete bowl and fairly glowing, if not *quite* ticking, with cholesterol – 'Curry and rice *with* chips too please Ed, and make it *triple* grease,' only one of several culinary combinations which later in the small hours would predictably provide the essential fuel for a major, *major* farting competition, wholly impromptu and indeed mainly involuntary but still, once invoked, highly competitive (triple-judged on the qualities of volume, tone and malodour) which – though naturally embraced with enthusiasm only by its participants, the rest remaining passive observers nasal *and* aural until they finally staggered retching from the reeking Ready Room – would in terms of comparative petomanic invention have reduced the infamous future has-bean scene from *'Blazing Saddles'* to the level of a routine documentary shot in the reading room of the Bodleian on a quiet day.

And before that in the interim smallest of hours with our stomachs tight, starched, as yet still fully retentive and no doubt slippery to boot, we'd sometimes spend a while listening to the musings of the duty CIO. (I remember one particular night when we got Bertie onto his own fifties' past – 'Then there was good old Operation Post Report[9] and the DPs,' he said, his eyes half-shut. 'Busy all right, but fun. Most of the chaps were fine, of course, and d'you know what we wrote on their files?' No, Bertie, we said. 'Have a guess, then.' We can't, we said. 'Oh. All right. PPSP, that's all. And d'you know what that stood for?' No, we said again, naturally, and even at the time I thought Bertie's response encapsulated two vital components of standard British-ness, the first a prevailing, lasting and sublime arrogance, but the second as if to balance it, an inherent dry self-parody of equal longevity and perhaps only identifiable if you *are* British, 'Why, a Pleasant Peasant of Security Purity, of course.')

And after that, our national pride suitably renewed, or restored, we'd take advantage of the gaps between flights to organise short sprints down the deserted fingers. But when the same person – that aptly-named bloody shit Browning (of whom more later), who must have been an extreme hyperthyroid as well as extra fucking fit – won every time, we changed them to wheel-chair races instead and only packed *them* up when one contestant, travelling at high speed, hit an obstacle which stopped his conveyance stone dead but not him, so that he continued alone, briefly and horizontally, before head-butting something even more solid, the old Nelsonian-oak British desk, leaving it unmarked and losing little actual blood but sustaining a concussion which could have put him permanently in a wheel-chair.

Then, in the eerie stillnesses of dawn, we'd close all the gaps in the barriers and stand back to wave cheerily as a flight emerged from one finger and marched obediently across our front, its passengers staring at us blearily from just ten yards away, so near and yet so far, before disappearing with despairing looks over their shoulders down another.

Oh, and talking of diversions and at the other extreme, I almost forgot the occasion on which one exhausted officer, snatching a quick (but still formal, because he was by nature a very orderly man) forty winks in the aptly-named Black Hole, our foul and airless sleeping accommodation at the rear of the Control, slept right through his alarm and was woken only by the knock of the airline girl with a flight close on her high heels, so that he was forced to adopt some small degree of instant informality and clear it *in situ*, still in bed but at least sitting bolt upright and wearing clean striped pyjamas, as the passengers – all Brits, Thank God – filed slowly past, holding up their passports with one hand for his swift scrutiny, itself severely hampered by the handkerchiefs necessarily held over their noses by the other…

One night we set up a Special Nightshift to celebrate Sam's birthday – he was the second youngest on the staff, but still eighteen months senior to me. And the team *was* special – hand-picked weeks ahead, all eight and including Sam himself, naturally. But *he* didn't even make it to midnight because he'd come in early to get a head start and collapsed, pissed, at about 2200 hours. And whilst we'd never expected to get any work out of him or that he'd last out till the end, we still felt a tad let down as we put him gently to bed. After all, not even making it to the *start* of your twenty-first was a pretty bad show.

At any rate and whatever the holes in the rationale, we took it upon ourselves to make up for his shortfall. And in the small hours, with no flights showing or expected, someone decided to make a symbolic gesture, a Statement of Who and What We Were, and taped up the Control from end to end with several thicknesses of bog roll (government-issue it's true, but only because it was all we had; we weren't trying to show that our action was official, or to imply that *all* passengers were necessarily shits; we hadn't intended the symbolism to stretch *that* far, or the paper).

No, 'England is *shut. You shall not pass,*' that's all we meant (though looking back now, perhaps on the contrary it was only the perforations that were truly prescient). And it was only in emphasis of the same original message that in due course someone else set fire to the flimsy barrier at both ends, and then again as the flames caught hold, two things happened at once: out of fucking nowhere a flight entered the Hall, and the Night CIO – by chance another new promotee and lately from the same port as George – emerged in all innocence from his office across the way.

It was one of those little things that made you perversely proud to be British – made *me* proud, anyway. The Boss took one look at the smoke-shrouded Control, part smouldering and part still in flames, and his jaw dropped. Then he saw the approaching flight, and his re-action was commendably fast and wholly decisive, as you'd expect from a Senior Officer. *"Jesus Christ,"* he muttered, and disappeared back into his office, firmly shutting the door just as the first passengers glimpsed us dimly through the pall: a small group, somewhat white-faced but dedicated and determined, soldiering on bravely despite the obvious unnatural physical hazards around it – at least that's what I assume they *thought* they saw, because they proceeded *ultra*-rapidly past our desks and up the escalator to Customs without a single query or backward glance, or choking cough, *or* offer to help, and without a single later complaint.

And why? Perhaps they were simply too tired, or were all equipped with asbestos underwear, or maybe it just shows what people will routinely put up with, or would then. Because there was the same total lack of response when on another day a year later and with my first marriage now in tatters, I had a momentary reflective rush of blood and overturned my own heavy oak desk in front of a full arrivals hall with no trouble at all and one hell of a crash (to any eager Jungian aching to believe, the total proof of noisy spirits but in truth the precise opposite, a silently-consumed half-bottle of scotch, and only 70-proof at that). Anyway either way it showed that the new CIO's judgement had been right, all along.

Which brings us neatly to booze in general. Strong liquor, as you may already have gathered, played a regular part in our daily doings, though in more manageable quantities of course. It was always welcome but always, *always*, came a poor second to work, and though it always (well, mostly) appeared on the scene unplanned, it was never unexpected. Because we had an ART you see, not an Armed Response but an Alcohol Recovery Team, or more accurately since that implies specialist training, an ARK, an Alcohol Recovery *Kit*, always afloat, ready to hand and useable by *any* amateur enthusiast, which worked like this.

At least every other day a fair few returning holidaymakers, Brits naturally, would reach the Control a little wobbly or a tad tipsy or even pissed out of their tiny brains; and clutched tightly and unopened in their hot sweaty hands would be their then ultra-rare and extra-precious Duty Frees. But the Floor was hard thick marble and the DF bags soft and thin, and destructive percussive collisions between the two – which happened regularly enough through a moment's inattention, even when you *weren't* pissed – could have only one outcome.

The resultant sound of breaking glass was unmistakable, and soon became familiar music to an ever-attuned ear. And as if that wasn't notice enough, a volley of oaths would routinely follow and on occasion punitive half-cut intra-familial fist fights break out as the ultimate alert. But usually everything after that initial impact was superfluous, because from a door behind the British desk a man – suited, booted and still smart-ish albeit invariably jacket-less, who didn't look at all like your average cleaner but nonetheless with mop and bucket in hand – would briskly emerge, pausing only to say something like, "Oh *dear*. *All* broken? Then *I'll* dispose of *that* for you, sir," (or "madam," as the case might be), before seizing the clinking bag, always authoritatively and by main force in the event of any resistance, then popping it in the bucket and vanishing back through the same door as swiftly as he'd come. (The mop was only a prop, of course; if we'd done the *genuine* cleaners out of a *real* job there would've been *real* trouble.)

And the rest was routine, because the simple working element of the ARK – a filtered paper funnel inserted in a large glass container – was as I said, always ready; and the mess from the bag, once deposited carefully inside, would be left to drain and settle for an hour or two, then usually filtered again. But on days when we were especially thirsty and in the event of a timely breakage, the wait could be cut drastically by dispensing with the second filtering – normally *de rigueur* for the more sensitive – entirely. And whatever the delay, the resultant brew wouldn't last long, notwithstanding its strength – its composition routinely a mixture of the then almost obligatory DF twins of scotch and gin, but with brandy and/or vodka sometimes thrown in. The texture varied too, from the pleasant lubricant of the lovingly double-filtered to the raw abrasion of the hastier alternative, the latter's extra bite doubtless due in part to the still just-visible element of finely ground glass. Nor can I pretend that there was no commensurate contrast between the varied effects of the two brews on their consumers – well, on *me,* anyway – because whilst with one my subsequent questions flowed with greater smoothness (to the point of being downright silky), after a glass or two of the other they became by comparison distinctly harsh. And cutting.

But it couldn't last, and eventually Jim and I were caught red-handed by BAA[10] security expanding the dying Empire in the middle of the night, with me wobbling precariously on his shoulders whilst reversing the directional signs far out in the fingers. (None of it was done with malice though because all the fun was in the preparation, and we always called off the joke as soon as it began to work.) Anyway, this time when challenged we ran, but were finally cornered giggling foolishly in the place where sooner or later they were bound to find us: the airside bar.

Sadly, the two middle-aged men who caught us there, chests heaving, faces red and they looked even worse, proved strangely to have no sense of fun whatsoever. But there was nothing they could do on the spot – a couple more pints, and they would have been in real danger of arrest – and we parted with a brief mutual exchange of rude lewd gestures and general verbal abuse. But at 0900 hours the same day, feeling much less cheerful – like total shit, in fact – we found ourselves standing smartly to attention before the ACI, the Assistant Chief Inspector, one grade up from our erstwhile beloved HMI[11] and now our local Big Boss because the airport had grown. And when he asked whose idea it had been we both answered 'mine', the way one should, to be duly dismissed with a short, mild dressing-down whilst with a resigned sigh he reached for his pen to issue a Local Instruction forbidding the Consumption of Alcohol when on Duty. Again.

Still, drink was a two-edged weapon and once in a while we had a chance to do the right thing. One night I emerged stone-cold sober onto the Control to find a half-drunk Libyan who *would not* stop making loud and obscene suggestions to a lady from the Office of Statistical Surveys (something *we never* did, not loudly and in public, apart from BAA security anyway). He also ascribed his athletic – nay, superhuman – proposals to the fact that she was not only female but British, a claim somewhat ironic given that she was manifestly South African, but I like to think that that had no effect on my reaction.

So I warned him once but he carried on, buoyed up by the admiring laughter of his half-drunk companion. Then I warned him again but he still wouldn't stop, and in the absence this time of any police I deposited him neatly on a bench at the rear of the Hall. I didn't use much force, not really – it was a push rather than a punch, and without any *deliberate* acceleration through the blow – but his teeth did rattle as his head struck the barrier. Anyway he shut up then all right and so did his companion, and that was when I noticed too late that a flight had stopped to watch. These days it could have got messy, what with the blame-game and especially with CCTV. Then, they all stood and applauded, and that was the end of that.

A CUNNING LINGUIST

Mid-1971 by now; slow, patchy beginnings, but the work steadily growing. Technically everything counted as an examination, even half a dozen words, and sometimes it was the short ones that threw up a cracker. Take the day early in the year when I was leaving the control for a discomfort break and as I passed Pat I caught first his tone, the vibrant venom in his voice, and then his actual words. And I stopped.

"*Listen*, you," Pat said. Venomously. "You've been here *before, haven't* you?"

"*Eh? Che? No!*" (Italian for, '*Eh? What? No!'*) said the young man in shades, decisively and obviously Italian himself, although I can't tell you why.

"*Oh yes you have*; *and* you *speak English*, speak it *well* too, *don't* you?"

"*Eh? Chi, Io? No!*" ('*Eh? Who, me? No!*')

This last was said earnestly, passionately and apparently from the very heart. But that's how they say everything, and I for one couldn't tell whether he spoke English or not; he might just have reached the stage of total denial. But Pat was getting angry, a man on a mission, and he leant forward across the desk to employ his best, his subtlest, his *ultimate* technique.

"*Yes*, you *can*. I *know* you can. You're a *fucking bustard liar, Eyetie*," he said in his natural broad Geordie, and the Italian visibly jumped. Then he leant forward in his turn, and took off his shades, and smiled. And as his eyes crinkled and his improbably-white teeth flashed, he waved both his arms in the air, nodded vigorously and proved them both right as he shouted, "*Si*, ('*Yes*,') '*e vero*,' ('*it's true*,') '*fucking*', ('*fucking*,') '*I know 'fucking'!*'" ('*I know 'fucking'!*')

Pat however was momentarily rendered speechless by the degree and precision of his success. His mouth opened and closed in the usual way, but no sound came out. It was the first time I'd ever seen anyone 'doing the goldfish,' as Ron called it years later at Terminal Two, the phenomenon which always followed the killer question and was an unerring indication of guilt, so this time the biter bit. But he pulled himself together enough to stamp the Eyetie up in heavy silence and to send him on his way with a peremptory and very continental jab of the thumb. Then he turned in his chair, still breathing deeply, and saw me.

"And what are *you* grinning at?" he demanded.

"Who, me? Nothing at all, mate," I said hastily. I could almost *taste* his residual ire and to change the subject, really nothing more, "and where exactly is he going here, anyway?"

Pat stood up, advanced as if to deck me and looked at me closely. "You really don't know?" he asked.

"No," I said. I really didn't.

"The *fucking bustard*. New*castle*," he said, and I controlled myself with an effort.

"Oh," I said. "The girls are beautiful up there, *and generous too, especially* to *foreign fuckers* – or so I've heard." And I left him and it, rapidly, at that.

PERSONATION

I missed my first Home Office Sports Day, a big event for those so-inclined, but I heard about it later. Every section of the Department which could raise a team or even a contestant or two took part, some simply because you got an extra day off, but the Branch and HM Prisons took it seriously and one or the other always won. Competition within IB was fierce too, and as usual Terminal Three, Dover and Gatwick were the main rivals.

But soft, that was not all! Miracle of Miracles and Ring Out Wild Bells, the Home Sec. himself had turned up, to present the prizes – he always *tried* to, or *said* he did, and this year something somewhere must have gone badly wrong, because he'd *actually made it*. And now the sports were over, his own big moment had arrived as he arose to address the expectant and adoring crowd.

"Good afternoon, ladies and gentlemen," he began with an unctuous smile, and looked quizzically up at the blue and cloudless sky. "Well. *Excellent weather* for another *excellent day* which has again brought us all *together*, and I am *delighted* that *so many* of you could come.

"And now it is my sincere pleasure to present the prizes. First, the One Hundred Yards for Men (he had to be sex-specific because the Home Office at large employed women, lots of them, even if IB still didn't): and the *winner*," – he paused for a second as an earnest aide whispered in his ear – "the winner *again*," and he smiled, *again*, "is Mark Browning, from Immigration Gatwick," and that rapid shit Browning (remember him?) came forward to receive the Cup, *again*, amidst the cheers of his home port and the tepid applause of the rest, not least Terminal Three who always fancied themselves as sprinters. Well, they always just fancied themselves.

"Next," the Home Sec. continued, "the *Two* Hundred Yards for Men: and the winner this year…" – as he looked at his paper, he frowned momentarily because he *did* like to share things out and perhaps it was a typo anyway – "is…" (pause again, whisper to Ernest, *no* mistake,) "is *yet* again, Mr. Browning," and yet again Mark came forward, to a further port-related mixture of hearty cheering and less hearty, even reluctant now, general applause. Anyway this time The Great Man, who learnt quickly, consulted his paper anxiously before he continued, and his brow cleared. *Thank heavens there's no more of that Gatwick fellow*, he must have thought, as he went blithely on. And on. Until -

"*Right*," he said finally, as he looked down to see the last name, which *again* made him smile, then to check the relative standings of the competing sections and the final result at the bottom. "And so to the final and as it happens the *decisive* prize both in the departmental and in the individual team" – he paused, frowned, contemplating his audience briefly as he gauged its re-action like the professional he was, but finally couldn't resist it, "- *individual team*? Bit of an *oxymoron* there I'd have thought, but never mind," as the IB, most of whom by definition *could* speak *some* English, tittered in mild derision and the rest, detecting a possible insult (especially the larger Prison Officers), stirred uneasily, so that he knew he'd really dropped one and hurried on, "as I was saying, in the individual team competition, which is for the Men's Obstacle Race; and the winner *is…* " – he paused once more, this time expectantly, knowing he was on a clear winner himself now and smiling a particularly big and generous smile, not just because it was nearly over but also because he really *did* like to be able to demonstrate the good old British senses of *fair play* and *tolerance* and *equality* (the latter a forerunner of *diversity*) and that afternoon, until then, as it happened and given the year, there hadn't been too much opportunity – "the winner is, er, *Effie Oloboto*, from Immigration Gatwick, which means also that the IB is the *Departmental Section* winner and that Immigration *Gatwick* have won the *Team* Cup. So. Mr. *Oloboto*. *Please step forward*."

So what next: a late last extrovert sprint for the political line from a rampant Mr. O? No, indeed. There followed instead a strangely-pregnant hush in the Gatwick section of the crowd, which like the Home Secretary went on and on (the hush, I mean). And when, finally, it parted (the Gatwick crowd, I mean) to allow its de facto hero to emerge, he did so swiftly, abruptly, almost in fact as if forcibly propelled from behind; and shyly too, and suitably humbly, his head down. But he had to look up to receive his medal and the Cup, and if the Home Secretary was surprised as he presented them, he didn't show it much. Perhaps his mind was already moving ahead to his next meeting or perhaps he really didn't notice though I doubt it, or perhaps he'd just had a lot of relevant practise.

"Well. *Congratulations, Mr....*" the Home Secretary said, and paused once more, almost as if reluctant to continue or perhaps just seeking inspiration, for another quizzical glance at the sky. For a long moment he seemed to be on the verge of saying something else, something perhaps (for a change) of real moment, but in the end he simply shook his head. Then, "Congratulations, Mr. *Oloboto*," he concluded, the name seeming still to stick somewhat in his throat.

And as Effie turned, himself almost reluctant now, and raised his trophy high but briefly – and almost it seemed a little unnaturally, so that it tended to obscure his face – to the crowd in general and to the Gatwick group in particular, there was a burst of convulsive laughter from the latter, verging on the inappropriate but seemingly involuntary, and polite applause from most quarters; but a noticeable silence from all the other Immigration teams and supporters except for one loud growl of "*Oloboto, my arse!*" from the general direction of Terminal Three.

It was a remark which might have been considered gratuitously and even racially offensive, had not appearances given it some immediate credence. For although Mr. O. walked – or rather scuttled – back to the close-packed body of his local followers at a speed surprising even for a champion before disappearing totally into their protective midst, there to be loudly toasted – '*Effie! Effie!*' – it had nonetheless become readily apparent during his brief time in clear view that there was little in his colour or features consistent with the ethnicity already then routinely associated – at least by Immigration Officers – with his name. In fact, he didn't look in the least African, and that was because he wasn't.

Oh, he was a Gatwick IO all right. But his real name was James, and he was a Devonian, from darkest Devon. Someone had however suggested the pseudonym as a joke, and he had adopted it and entered the race in that identity, blithely and meaning no offence. After all, who the hell, then, would have expected a *Nigerian* to *win?*

TEARS FOR FEARS

The Biman came from Dhaka in Bangladesh, created on a shoestring as the national airline at the same time as the nation itself, in early 1972. It flew into Gatwick for a while before moving to Terminal Three, and after missing every bloody one of the doubtless plethora of forged documents on the first flight because we'd never seen anything like it (and thus unwittingly encouraging others yet to come), we wised up quickly and began to refuse passengers by the dozen.

It was, literally, child's play: you were already generally suspicious, even before (say) Abdur Rahman reached the desk to present you with a well-worn nine-year old UK passport. And sometimes you saw from a first swift look that the year, just the year, of birth had been changed (but badly, blame the poor brake fluid); and then, whether it had been forged or not and whether you'd spotted it or not, you saw from a swift look at *him* that he still had on the same shirt and tie as in the supposedly contemporary photo, and that he hadn't aged at all, not even by a *single day* – well, that's not quite true, he *had* aged by *exactly* one day, because that photo had only been taken and inserted yesterday and you confirmed that it wasn't the original by sticking a pin through its embossing and finding that it came out at a different part on the other side of the page. Oh, the simple, humble pin: we all carried one in our lapels and called it 'The Forgery Kit'. Then it was all you needed – pretty cheap too, and never broke down – happy, simple, pre-IT days, even if now and then you were still bound to feel a prick.

But that's not what I remember most about the Biman. I remember the Bangladeshi whom someone else had already refused and who was set for a swift return, who suddenly appeared unbidden in the entrance to our Ready Room. First he leant against the door jamb, somewhere in his thirties and a small, thin unremarkable man as you'd expect, who just looked at us dully, silently, beseechingly as we lowered our newspapers and looked dully, silently, indifferently back. Then after a while he slid slowly down the wall and collapsed on the floor inside the door, beside the ticker-tape. And then he started speaking in bagpipe, and although the interpreter was busy elsewhere and we couldn't understand a word we all knew that he was pleading because he wept, and we could guess what he was saying too (which the interpreter confirmed later).

He said he had come here to earn money to send back to his wife and children because they were starving, and he had borrowed from the village money-lender to do it because *he* had told him how *easy* it was to get in. And now his family would die anyway because the same money-lender would throw them down the village well when he returned home owing all that debt but unable to repay it. Or something like that, ending always with what must have been *"Please, oh please,…"*

And the weeping man didn't have a handkerchief so after a while tears began to run down his nose too, which itself began to run, and then the only thing he could find to wipe it on was the spewing ticker-tape, a half-inch wide, and all *that* did was to smear snot all over his face. And no-one helped him, we all just laughed quietly, collectively, almost gently but without great interest as he wept quietly on the floor; and eventually we carried on reading our papers. But later, when he'd been taken away, we were all *extra* quiet, and if my Dad had seen it he would've been very, *very* angry with everyone, especially with me, but I never told him about it because I knew that, and soon enough he himself was dead.

I've tried often, sometimes involuntarily and always in shame, to analyse why we behaved as we did that day. I've considered the people in the room, all of whom by then I knew well; and if any one of us had been outside looking in I know he would have leapt verbally and probably abusively to the weeping man's defence, or at least he would have wanted to; and perhaps even then some of us did, yet all seven or eight of us kept quiet. The group, the pack, the mob instinct? Maybe, in part. Or racism then, pure and simple? No, I don't think so, unless that always began at Calais which it only did sometimes and then mostly in jest, and it was certainly nothing personal. So I don't know the answer: the Collective Beast that lurks in us all perhaps, Brits included, ever waiting for release; but that's no excuse.

For myself, I was as arrogant, as conscious and as proud of my British-ness as the next man, and maybe that was an attitude that the job was bound to engender anyway. I was also part of the last generation that, for a while at least, still clung to the residue of Empire and besides, the IB was as near as a civil servant could ever get to *living* the life of Sex, Drugs and Rock'N'Roll – well the first and the last at least with a lot of hard work thrown in, but with Booze in place of Drugs because the only poor sod I ever saw in the job who tried *them* was newly transferred to us from the DHSS[12] and loving every minute until he was picked up with his first-ever spliff at the first-ever Glastonbury and kicked straight back to his parent department like a dose of salts, once inevitably bubbled by the two-faced local fuzz.

And finally, apart from all that, I for one still believed – still *knew*, with due apologies to the thus unintentionally-excluded various Celts – that as an Englishman I *had* won first prize in the lottery of life and that nothing could ever, *ever* change that, even if we *had* finally managed well, truly and irrevocably, to lose the collective bloody ticket.

But along with the supreme British arrogance went the instinctive automatic British support for the individual, especially the underdog – remember Bertie? Yet on that day we had edged a little closer, dangerously close perhaps, to the group *silence*, positive and beyond mere acquiescence, and to the Death's Head and the Hammer and Sickle, the two identical extremes and both symbols which, because of Dad, I hated with all my soul. At least I never saw anything like that again, anywhere, and after all, we were *British*, so *it* couldn't happen here. *Could* it?

BAD MEDICINE

1000 hours, already a hot, dry late summer's day and already weary because I knew it was going to be a long, dry shift, an extra long (*and* extra dry) one, and the African Safari passengers from Nairobi needed Port Health[13] so we stood chatting in our usual huddle, idly watching them on the other side of the barrier, doing its proper job this time, before dispersing to our desks as the first of them re-appeared heading for us and I looked at them more closely. We didn't get much off the Safari – there should never have been much *to* get, as it was a UK-originating charter – but there was always a chance and now was the moment to get a first impression, before they were right there in front of you.

The queue was forming, the presenter was starting to filter them and I was still waiting for mine when there he was, straight out of nowhere, not in front but right beside me, almost landside already, and I'd never have seen him at all otherwise. *How the hell's he done that,* I thought as I looked down, *It must be his height,* though what I meant was the lack of it as he looked back and up, up at me, silent and unblinking (him I mean), a tiny old black man about three feet tall, barefoot and in full tribal dress with a stick longer than he was which he didn't seem to need in the first place because even without it he was ramrod-straight. And under his gaze I averted my own – yes, averted is the only word – and picked up his passport which somehow was lying on my desk though I hadn't seen him put it there, and I wasn't sure he could have reached up that far anyway.

So I opened it and read his name, and I'm not going to invent a false one now because I can't remember what the real one was and you never know, I might strike lucky. Then I turned to his other details, and two entries stood out. Against 'Date of Birth', no day or month, just '1845', which for some mistaken reason made me think of Culloden and which by my quick correct calculation would make him some 127 years old. So, *Bollocks*, I thought at once and contemptuously, a trained officer, and interested now as I glanced at him again, composed, compact and still silent (*him,* I still mean). Then, against 'Occupation', there it was, *'Witchdoctor'*, handwritten which gave it more credence. And my response was again instant, but this time at the other extreme of emotional belief. *Oh, shit!* I thought. Well, I've always been somewhat sensitive about these things.

He must have known what I was looking at and perhaps what I was thinking too, and I thought I saw a shadow of a smile cross his face and linger in the depths of those deep black eyes as I turned to the back because we stamped all Commonwealth passports from the rear end forwards – the opposite of what we did with Aliens, since we had to show that there was a *real difference*, remember? It contained several UK stamps already and it was clear that he came and went every two years or so, on a short visit each time. So, "Same again?" I asked, as if he wanted not another stamp but another pint, and perhaps too in an absurd unconscious effort to disguise my *own* occupation, and I got a brief nod in reply. Then, "Thanks," I said, politely, as I bent to hand the document down to him after rolling it, and I got another nod, slightly deeper, as he turned away.

It was only after he'd gone that I realised that *he* hadn't uttered a single bloody word, and later I asked myself whether my approach had been influenced, or even God forbid dictated, by his stated career. Well, I'm not sure of the answer to this day. Maybe I was just deferring to his age, whatever it really was, or maybe that's what I'd like to think and at least *he didn't* stop to throw away his stick and shake the flour out of his hair. Anyway, I never saw a witchdoctor again, not knowingly, and finally I told myself that he clearly wasn't an immigration problem. And it was true, he wasn't, and besides, why *invite* trouble? *Well out of it,* I thought with relief. *Prat!* Just how wrong can you be?

SHELTER

2230 hours now on the very next day, but noxious night at last, and finally, finally heading homeward. Noxious? Well, only in hindsight, and now I'll tell you why...

But first a bit of background. In late 1970 we'd moved to Uckfield, still twenty miles plus from Gatwick but a lot closer than Hastings. Three other IOs lived there already, so at least two of us could often car-share and sometimes we'd even manage to get all our shifts, if not quite our fourfold collective shit, together. And then on the drive home after that bastard second night the trio of passengers, truly exhausted, would swiftly fall fast asleep in the magical, slumbering depths of Ashdown Forest where soon, under the persuasive combined heavy breathing, human and tree, the driver's head too would sink in weary surrender, only to jerk violently awake within milliseconds – or was it a nightmarish half-minute – as the car began first gently to meander, then to swerve, and finally to leave the road, and *everybody* woke up.

But we all did it, each in turn, so there was no real rancour as the rest roundly abused the chauffeur of the day. And the great thing was that it only ever happened once on a trip because after that the residual adrenalin (or latent panic) would keep the driver going till the end. He might drive badly or madly or both, and usually did, but he was certainly wide awake. Often though, we just couldn't fix the shifts, day or night, to fit in the first place, certainly not for all four of us because the bosses tacitly preferred it that way, and you could see their point of view: if, say, we crashed and burned and all died together, and especially on the way *in*, they'd suddenly be a whole half-shift short.

Anyway, where was I? Oh yeah, 'Noxious', 2230 hours as I left the terminal, my Peterson tight-clenched but unlit and staggering slightly (me of course, not the pipe) after yet another double shift, an early/late like the day before, which enabled local management to prove but quite falsely that they had it all under control. I got a couple of odd silent looks as I passed Eddie the Spoon's but took them as no more than sympathy until I reached the car park where I fumbled in my pocket, found my Balkan Sobranie Flake (I must have been a prize pretentious prick at the time) and went to fill the pipe bowl, only to find that it wasn't fucking there.

It must have fallen off after leaving the office, i.e. somewhere in the last half mile, leaving me thereafter to swan erratically along whilst apparently deriving deep pleasure from sucking what must have appeared to be a commensurately bent, spent, empty, effete and at best flaccid cigarette holder – so much for the odd silent looks. Anyway I dimly reckoned I could narrow the search a bit by starting from where I'd noticed the first odd glance. But it could wait – it would damn-well *have* to – till tomorrow which, as everybody knows, is always another day.

And progress: actually inside the car now, sitting there lifeless, slumped like a sack of spuds, totally creamed (though not quite *fully* mashed) and wholly dispirited to boot. Thirty months in give or take, and just starting to feel that I could *really hack it* until the day before when *he*, black fucking

Merlin, had come as a salutary shock to my nascent seen–
done arrogance. 'Ten years,' they'd said on the course, '*ten years*
before you're really on top of it,' and that had already seemed
optimistic even before The Case of the Dangling Pipe, which
had never happened before and seemed to my addled mind
to have surely been conjured by the witchdoctor whom after
all, despite my best unconscious efforts, I must somehow still
have contrived to anger. *Punishment? Retaliation?* I speculated
vaguely. *OK, but finished, done now, anyway.* Because it never
occurred to me that it might be no more than a precursor,
a portent, of worse things to come. Or even the immediate
bloody overture.

Then I pulled myself together. *OK*, I thought as I began to
revive, *First things first and the only question now is what to play on
the way to keep me going, come what may*, a mere throwaway line or
so I thought because I *never* learnt, and which still left me right
on the horns of the proverbial Welshman[14], torn between the
melodic extremes of the 'Cello Concerto' and 'Let it Bleed'.
But the mid-summer night was warm, as warm and cosy as a
thick rug, *so* warm in fact that perhaps a storm *was* threat'ning,
and I opted for the rock. Besides, that was the tape already in
the bloody deck and I had neither the will nor the strength to
change it.

So windows down, volume up and off I set with twenty
miles to go and the Stones for company, and you can't do much
better than that. And soon there I was again, softly cruising,
alone but not lonely, back deep in the dozing, ancient forest,
its trees arched protectively overhead like old friends with
nothing to see but the cone cutting the canopy and nothing
to hear but Mick and Merry and the rest, interspersed briefly
every four and a quarter minutes with a short burst of the low
burbling fart of the mini's exhaust – height apart, not unlike

me I suppose – because I couldn't get my brain past *'Gimme Shelter'* and kept re-winding the tape.

Then, suddenly there *they* were, two figures caught in the act, one man, one woman, pinned like merth[15] full in the headlights, crouched as if consciously guilty against their own unlit car in an all-too-familiar position, and strangely enough with a small dog on a lead by their side. No, no, they weren't *at it*, just trying to pour fuel into the car's tank from a can – which condition, though one may seem at first thought to be distinctly analogous to the other, was in fact in this case a very different, indeed a wholly contrary, thing unless immediately *post*-coital, because it seemed clear from the spout's now-near-vertical and almost desperate angle of inclination that the can too was dry.

Fleetingly, as I passed, I wondered whether it was a set-up for a mugging or hijack, or even rape or murder most foul, just a shot away: but on a by-road in the middle of nowhere where you might see no-one for hours, *and* with a small dog? *Come on*, I thought, then pulled in with a squeal (of brakes, I mean) and backed up.

"Hello," I said brightly as I got out. "Need any help?" And the dog saw me and barked and pulled at its lead as they both straightened. A young couple, no longer spout in hole now, but hand in hand instead.

"That we surely do, mate. No juice, and the bloody jerry's fucking empty." Kiwi perhaps? No, Aussie for sure, but the bark had sounded almost Pom.

"Ah," I said, a lofty Samaritan, and I don't mean 'tall'. "Then I'm your man," *For All Seasons* of course, and I opened the back of the mini-traveller and got out *my* trusty can.

"Fair dinkum," or, "What a beaut,"? No, none of that Strine literary bollocks, he just said, "*Great*, mate," and then

I shook the can because it felt ominously light, and *it* was fucking empty too. "Aw, *shit*," we said together in international English, beautifully synchronised as the dog sighed, and now I *couldn't* leave.

"Sorry," I said. I meant it: I was deeply embarrassed. "Look, there's an all-night garage on the A22 and I was going that way anyway," – well, I wasn't exactly, but it wasn't far out – "so you can fill the can there, then I'll bring you back. OK?" and when they looked at each other, I knew exactly what they were thinking. But on a by-road in the middle of the forest, with odds of three to one including the dog, and with *two* empty cans *and* the Stones? *Come on.*

So, "What a beaut, mate, fair dinkum," he said, like an *ultra*-jolly swagman, and the girl and the dog both smiled, their teeth shining in the light reflected off the trees. And that was when I noticed too that the girl didn't have much on and as I looked at the pair of them – him and her I mean – I envied their extreme youth but not for long because I wasn't *that* much older though opaquely dressed, and a clear image of my own wife, young and beautiful (still the first, to avoid any confusion) sprang suddenly into my mind, snug in bed by now, maybe wearing nothing but a faint smile herself and probably asleep but surely soon wake-able. And, tired as I was, love was just a kiss away.

Then, "OK. Get in," I said, somewhat stiffly. So they did, all three of them in the back and I could see them in the rear mirror, the dog in the middle, settling down comfortably as we drove off.

"Where are you from?" I asked, just for starters and in an effort finally to rid myself of the vision of my wife, which was still physically distracting me (and indeed, affording a potential second gear lever).

"Australia, mate – Perth, both of us. D'yer know it?"

"No. Sorry," I said. I didn't, truly, because I've always been crap at geography. And I didn't tell them what I did for a living either because it could be an instant fractious show-stopper with foreigners, especially Aussies for some reason, even though it was still a decade before Mad Mel[16]. But the ice on the billabong had been broken – he was Steve and she was Raelene and I was already Mate – and we chatted away happily as I drove past my normal right turn and headed deeper into the forest.

"Stones," Steve said. "Great." He knew his rock all right.

"Yep," I said, and to demonstrate my own English versatility, "It could've been Elgar. D'you like him too?"

"Can't say I know him, mate," he said. "What does he play?"

"Oh, *Steve,*" said Raelene, embarrassed herself now. "Elgar. *Elgar*, *you* know. 'God save the Queen,' and that."

"Oh yeah," he said vaguely. It sounded to me like *he* didn't know either, any more than *she* did, and that he couldn't give a glad fuck anyway, but what the hell. Perhaps he was ahead of his time, or just wasn't a royalist.

So, "Not far now," I said to change the subject, seeing the map in my head and then in the darkness driving skilfully round the expected sharp bend, the mini at just the precise speed to maintain adhesion whilst pushing it – *God, I really knew that car* – and suddenly it wasn't a ninety at all but a true bloody U, still wet and greasy from a recent shower, and having safely negotiated the expected angle, I lost it. The car didn't spin or anything but just seemed to shoot off the road like a slingshot as early minis would sometimes do, and careered into the trees at a considerable speed.

I was conscious of the engine's sudden roar, of dark shapes

rushing past, of Merry's voice cracking with terrible[17] timely effort on the third *'Murder!'* and of the headlights' crazy rise and fall as we mounted a bank, then sank and rose again. Another crack but this time mechanical, and we decelerated abruptly and stopped with the car's nose in the air on the up-slope of the second bank, far steeper than the first. The headlights still shone, if only at the stars, but the engine had stalled and in the rear-view mirror I could still see an image of two haloed Aussie heads. The silence was almost total because the Stones had sensibly self-ejected. And all I could hear was a soft whimpering, but at least it was only the dog.

"Everybody all right?" I asked, in the stillness. I noted that it was no longer just warm in the car but suddenly hot, and that I was right back to the standard solo gear stick, and I knew what embarrassment *really* was.

"You OK, Rae? You, Bonzer?" Steve asked, so perhaps it hadn't been a British bark after all, and when they both nodded, he said "I think so," – no 'mate' this time I noticed, and I remembered how Aussies were pre-conditioned to despise any Pom failure. Then I got out, sinking deep into the leaves, and tried to assess the damage. Outside the zones back-lit by the beams I couldn't see a bloody thing but I knew that the road had to be some thirty yards behind and somewhat above us, as overall our passage had been downhill. I knew too that we weren't going to get out of there under our own steam that night but I got back in and tried the engine anyway, and it started. I didn't even bother to re-insert the tape, though. Christ, things were bad enough already and why again tempt fate?

So, "I'll just give it a go," I said, engaging reverse, and to my amazement the mini backed slowly but steadily out of the forest with no trouble at all, down, up, up and down again until it stood once more on the road. "OK then," I said, "sorry about that. Let's see if we can make the garage," and in the absence of any response whatsoever we set off. But as soon as I put the car in forward gear I knew something was seriously wrong. OK, it still steered, but only like a barge with great corrective circles of the wheel so that I found myself beginning to hallucinate and to think the mini's big speedo was a binnacle, and I had to go very slowly to maintain any control at all. And the road proved to have several more long sharp bends, so that I needed all my wits and any residual skill to stay on it. But there was a bright side, because I barely noticed the continued total, censorious absence of the previous easy conversation, as if the ice-breaker had turned into the *Titanic* but at high temperature.

Still, we got there eventually, and as I drove gingerly onto the garage forecourt the owner appeared from his office. "G'day, mate," I said – Stone the bloody crows, *I* was doing it now. "Can you fill the can, no, both cans, up – my friends have run out in the forest. Oh, and before I take them back," – at which Steve burst into frantic life with a clear pre-emptive strike, "No, no, we'd like the walk," as I continued – "can you have a quick look at the car too please, the steering seems a bit slack." (Typical whingeing pom understatement now, see?)

So the cans were filled and the garage man took a quick peep down under, and that was all he needed. "You *drove* it here?" he asked in clear disbelief. "How far?"

"Oh, three or four miles," I said, bashfully.

"Jeez," he said. I doubt he'd ever used the word before in his life, it was becoming a fucking epidemic. Then, "God knows how. Your bloody steering rack's clean broken, it's in two parts."

"Oh," I said, as the young couple exchanged glances. Perhaps they were unemployed mechanics and knew what he was talking about or maybe they were just relieved, but either way it was all automotive Greek to me.

"Well," said the garage man, "*this* won't be going anywhere tonight. I'll run you two back, and the phone's inside so *you* can arrange a cab, or a lift." "*You?*" He meant *me*, so the traitorous bastard was *already* on *their* side! They stood there in a close, defensive, accusing group, all four of them, and he said the word as if it was all *my* bloody fault, and I suppose most of it was. Well OK, pretty much *all* of it, if you insist.

"Yep, no probs," I said, inevitably, and phoned my wife. I didn't want to do it. *Now it's really late and she'll be right out,* I thought. But she wasn't, the line was engaged and after I'd listened to the tone for a while I rang off and stood outside for a moment, shaking my head to clear it because I suddenly felt sick, then went back in and forced myself to dial another number which belonged to a colleague I'd always considered a friend despite the growing whispers, and that was engaged too. And as I listened again to the same tone I just stared mistily up at the stars because that's when I first *knew* that our marriage was in real trouble. So I rang off again and called one of the three car-sharers who lived nearby, and he got up and came and got me.

My farewell to the Aussies was brief. "Goodbye," I said, and again, "Sorry about that," and they muttered a brief response. Even the dog wouldn't look at me but I barely noticed, and the next morning my wife drove me back to the scene and I found where we'd left the road and traced the tracks into the forest. Not far in, when we would still have been travelling at some speed, they neatly bisected a large tree and a massive boulder, the only one in sight and the gap a foot wider than the mini.

"God, Mike," my wife said, and she took my hand. "You could have been killed."

"Yes," I said, and I suppose she meant nothing particular by it but I wondered for a self-pitying instant whether that wouldn't have been better all round, apart from the Aussies of course, and Bonzer. If only I'd been even ruder to the Witchdoctor – clearly I *had* been rude somehow, but not quite rude *enough*.

A shot away? Or, perhaps, perhaps still, a kiss? I never asked about the phone calls, because I knew now that it could be very foolish to venture into a dark place with someone you didn't know, or even sometimes with someone you thought you did. We divorced two years later, and I found the pipe bowl untouched in the gutter on my next day in, exactly where I'd expected it.

SUPPLICANT

More Africans, to wit the first flight (no pun intended) of Ugandan Asians – the only refugees, genuine or purported, we were destined to encounter in numbers at Gatwick in my time. And *they were* genuine, all of them in terms of their manifest fear, and most too – though not *quite* all – in their claimed level of Amin-enforced destitution. The plane had been on the ground, full, at Entebbe and then in the air, for an eternity so the passengers, especially the women and children, were truly exhausted. We had a lot of sympathy for them as individuals if not necessarily for the reported situation that had forced them here, and I turned equably enough when someone tapped me on the shoulder from behind. It was a young Asian man.

"Yes?" I said. Politely. And then I saw the brimming hatred in his eyes.

"*We'll* be running this country in twenty years, you'll see," he said, in perfect if accented English, and although that may be a familiar, even passé refrain now, then I couldn't believe it.

"*What?*" I said.

"You heard me," he said, but then he repeated it anyway and instantly the red mist began to hammer unbidden in my brain, like the drum of somebody's doom – Drake's, if this bastard was right. But for once I mastered it, and pointed to the escalator. "Welcome to Britain, your chosen sanctuary. That's the way in – and out, and I suggest you take it *now*," I said, still politely, as I ached to wring his fucking neck. At least, that's what I hope I said, I can't precisely remember, but whenever the incident comes back to me – and it has, over the years, though less often than Thomas and the Weeper – all I feel is a great and raging anger, and an impotent and indefinable shame – oh not *that* again, no, shame that I *didn't* wring his neck, and this time with Dad on *my* side. After all, it might have afforded him a better sense of perspective, or even of gratitude. The passenger, I mean.

AN UNCOMMON COMPLAINT

The Biman again, and another Bangladeshi in his mid-thirties; but this time I'd refused him myself and although the case was stone cold I felt somewhat sorry for him, perhaps in belated compensation for the weeper because I couldn't get him out of my mind. This one though seemed quite philosophical about it, and once I'd done the paperwork I walked down to the aircraft with him and the security guards, Leon-style. I took an interpreter too, as we chatted away I felt much better and as he boarded we shook hands and he even smiled – shades of Thomas again but without the waiting beach or clearly, the way it turned out, the village well either, and with no ill feelings whatsoever.

Or so I wrongly thought until I found the package lying inert in my pigeon-hole, some two months later. It contained two letters inside one envelope inside another inside a transit bag, the whole therefore very like a flat soft Russian doll and all sent via what to us was already another riddle wrapped in a mystery inside an enigma and still growing, to wit the bloody Home Office. The outer envelope was addressed to me by name, 'From The Office of the Prime Minister' and one of the letters within the inner, from the same source, invited my comments on the other, also written in not wholly unreasonable English, which was from Shahnaz Begum – the professed parent of Ali, my late seemingly-cheerful refusal – and addressed generally to Number 10, Downing Street, England and more specifically to Mrs. Edward Heath, to whom it spoke woman to woman, and mother to mother.

Mrs. Begum began with the hope that Mrs. Heath was well and not weighed down by her husband's fearful responsibilities; and continued that she was writing only reluctantly, to protest at the treatment her son had received at the hands of Gatwick Immigration Officer Stamp Number 47 – *me*, though she didn't know *that* – whilst on his first short visit to the UK. Said officer, she said, had for no reasons *at all* chosen not to believe her dear Ali. He had in fact gone so far as to *refuse him the English door,* and had sent him straight back to her, his mother, in Bangladesh, *his tale between his legs.*

But that was not all, *not by any mean.* Because Ali had taken with him, to show in England, his *very own* Second World War medals of which he was so proud, won for fighting with the British against the Japanese,: indeed, he *had* shown them to the .first person he met there – *to whit,* Officer 47. But when later *he* (that same Officer) had been taking him (Ali) back to the airplane to send him so unjustly home, he (me) had suddenly and without warning jumped on his (Ali's) back, *bare-ing him to the ground,* and had then seized the prized medals and destroyed them, ripping the ribbons up before his (Ali's) very eyes and shouting out, *'This is the rain of Elizabeth II. Georgey VI medals no good.'*

And so, in the light of this, said Mrs. Begum, she now sought three things: first, compensation (though in what precise form, she *didn't* say) for the wrongs done directly to her son, including his medals destroyed; second, an *insurance* that when he came again he would be admitted at once and without difficulty; and third, a further *insurance* that the *miscreant* Officer 47 would be severely punished. So now the Prime Minister's Office wanted to know what Officer 47 himself had to say, before it composed its reply.

Well. *'Fuck me,'* was what Officer 47 said, briefly and precisely, in initial response as he read. And he said it out loud, involuntarily and with a degree of real foreboding, not because the complaint had any substance but because it was his fourth one in three years' service – the norm was one every ten years, so he'd now already had a full career's-worth – and although he had answered each satisfactorily so far, mud finally inevitably sticks.

This time again though, I was lucky. There were colleagues

to say that I had not been rude to Ali in any way on the control – I hadn't – and the security guards and interpreter to deny that I'd later jumped (on) him and torn his ribbons up – strangely enough, I hadn't done that either, in fact I'd never even *heard of*, still less *seen any* ruddy medals and, my alleged decorative violence apart, my claimed harangue on the matter, necessarily conducted through the interpreter, himself crouching referee-like whilst we'd scuffled noisily on the floor, would itself have proved rather hard to keep discreet.

But a biased observer – and there were already beginning to be plenty of *them* – could have pointed out that all my witnesses were inevitably – no, better still, what's the word these days, *institutionally* biased – and/or that I might simply be concealing my sublime linguistic skills (of which, more later[18]) under the proverbial bushel. So it was as well that a quick calculation in *anyone's* arithmetic showed that in 1945 when the war ended, Ali the much-decorated war-hero, whose passport for a change had *not* been altered in *any* way, would have been just nine years old.

I duly pointed all this out in my reply, and heard no more. And throughout the rest of my service I had only one other personal complaint, years afterwards at Terminal Two, which I'll describe in detail later. So in the end, complaint-wise, I wound up pretty much what I generally considered myself – Mr. Average. And how the Office of the Prime Minister contrived nicely to point out to Mrs. Begum that, the facts of the case apart, her impassioned maternal appeal was bound to fall on the double-deafest of uxorial ears, I still don't know.

KRAUT CONTROL

1ˢᵗ January 1973 signalled the start of the Immigration Act 1971, the last fully effective and thought-through piece of relevant legislation we've had (or *ir*relevant, come to think of it) – the *only* one in fact since the Aliens Order 1914; and it was the date too of the UK's entry into the European Community as it was then known. For practical purposes any real routine oversight of full nationals of the Member States ceased at 0001 hours on the day, and for a short while afterwards (months, I mean) until we expanded the old British desk to form an inclusive overall EC Control for Brits *and* most of the rest of Western Europe, the Arrivals Hall was bedlam, and we were in real danger of going under as we tried to cope.

It was a fascinating historical insight into the way things and people – or even nationalities – just don't change, not overnight anyway *or* in two hundred years. The Dutch for example behaved impeccably from Day One. They were relaxed and polite, but then *they'd made it* up the Thames before. The French however approached in doubly-dubious depth, their standard formation when confronted by the thin red line, and with ill-concealed suspicion about their new-found *liberté* (and fuck *egalité* bro), their drums this time silent and, having learned by their fatal mistake, ready to duck the moment *we*, Maitland's successors, suddenly stood up. The Italians however advanced *Al Duce* style, naturally – grandly, gloriously, *and* without losing a single further yard of ground.

Which left the Germans. Who just came on and on and on, panzer grenadiers legally toothed now but Thank God physically tiger-less, with shouting groups besieging each desk, the EC-riders round the UK wagon train. And us, the Brits ourselves? *We* just shrugged our shoulders, *stood firm* and *took it*, took it *all* as per bloody usual – OK, mildly irritated, but at the end of the day it was no more than you'd expect, and who better equipped to cope with god-awful foreign muddles when perforce we coped every day with ones home-grown?

Still, most of them (the foreigners, I mean) soon saw the problem and quietened down, self-organising without any help or advice from us. *All* of them did, in fact – *except* the Germans, the most natural self-organisers of all, who continued perversely to run riot instead in a joyful, aggressive, Germanic *schwer-punkt* kind of way and wouldn't listen to anyone – it was the Munich Festival every weekend, only now and then without the Beer. And I suppose we should have expected nothing else – after all, it was just Sea Lion thirty three years late – but that didn't make it any less tricky than it would have been to swat the buggers off the beaches in 1940, only a tad less dangerous.

And thus it went on until the night when the Germans first encountered Chris. Chris was one of the oldest and most senior IOs, in his mid-fifties perhaps, and he looked every day of it, plus some. He too had come to Gatwick from a seaport and he hadn't been with us that long. But he had already established a reputation for touchy eccentricity, for friendly irascibility, of being someone with a heart of pure gold whom you crossed nonetheless at your peril, and his standard dry cry (now of course, wholly *verboten* and even by then somewhat outré) of '*Wogs Up!*' over the newly-installed tannoy whenever *any* flight entered the hall, was something even the Inspectors didn't challenge.

Anyway, it was late on a Friday night, the Krauts were

in the hall in *gruppe* force because several flights had arrived almost simultaneously, and we had given up all pretence of politeness and were simply yelling at them in English in the time-honoured way, but to no avail. Then the magic happened: a few fluent words in German from an open doorway, a dozen at most, not shouted but rapped out, guttural and authoritative, their origin a vague hunched shape which loomed against the light. And the mob, both young and old, swiftly quietened, drew back airside and began to mill around uneasily.

And Chris appeared. He walked straight into their midst head down and silently, walked a bit haphazard, lopsided, ramshackle-like, walked the *English* way, shuffling almost – *you* know, the very *opposite* of a goose-step. Yet the effect seemed mesmeric, and then when he raised his head and spoke again, he still didn't shout. But he looked a number in the eye and his voice echoed clearly through the Hall as we watched in awe, and again he didn't say much but in no time they were formed up in orderly, wary, silent lines and they showed us their documents one by one and went through like lambs. Thus was Op. Sea Lion cancelled for a second time, or even reversed, and later it came out that Chris had been a P.O.W. in Germany and had been very badly treated.

After that, it was a madhouse every Thursday and Friday night as before – unless *he* was on, and then somehow word of his presence seemed to precede the arrival of the Germans in the Hall because they came in as docilely as they left (thinking perhaps, *When is he coming, when,* who knows?), even if he didn't say a bloody word. Chris: a dear man. His approach may be unfashionable, even unthinkable now, but only because times have changed. And I'll say this: unlike some, he *had balls.*

CHANGE OF HEART

Freddie Laker was another card, and I recall the officials from The Board of Trade who'd turn up on embarks now and again, and again, as they tried with increasing desperation to break the so-called 'Affinity Groups', his ingenious way of beating the large carriers' cartels. But he gave *us* a few headaches too, long before Sky Train, because he began to run big charters to Mauritius and although we'd naturally assumed that that meant *Brits* going on holiday *there*, it didn't work out that way at all. It was the Biman all over, and the worst night-shift I ever did at Gatwick still remains hideously clear in my mind.

The Port Louis passengers had entered the Hall at 2000 hours, and we'd worked on them non-stop and were close to completing the first sift at 0745 the next day as the shift ended. We had about forty sat down, most of them cast-iron refusals, and having been informed by my last one, yet another beaming bogus returning resident, that London buses were green, our policemen's helmets white (though perhaps that was just taking the pith) and that they (the police) always carried guns (in those days, they still didn't), I was just putting the icing on the cake by showing him a hand-full of coins from my pocket and asking him to identify them when I realised that I was so tired *I* couldn't recognise them either.

The drive home was an interesting one too, even by our normal standards: for once the group shift theory had worked, all four of us having been on our second night, and the adrenalin notwithstanding we all sensed that *this* was the one we really were unlikely to survive and so took turns talking nonsense to the driver the whole way back and making him reply nonsensically too, so that *none* of us could fall asleep in the first place.

They were really something, those flights. I had a pretty young Mauritian woman off my very first, with her small son aged five or six, She said they were on a short visit to distant relatives here but it didn't hang together, and by the time I took them to Customs they were already half way to refusal although she still didn't have a clue. She was chatting and laughing, and her son was laughing too. But like a fool I took them up the escalator, and like the sub-continentals they'd never seen one before. Anyway I went first carrying the little boy, and it was only when his mother screamed shrilly that I turned, looked down and saw her just behind, half way up and starting to topple.

Her back was turned towards me as she began to fall away and I reached out my free arm despairingly, grabbed her bra strap through her shirt and hung on, for a second in real danger of going down myself, child and all. Then the situation stabilised, her brief adventure as the world's first short-fall tit-tied bungee jumper came to a flexing, juddering halt, and moments later we reached the top. There she stood back from me and looked down blushing in embarrassment, as did I *inter alia*. And then she thanked me profusely whilst her son looked on with shining eyes.

Much later though when my doubts had proved correct, when I'd left their already-arrived illegal husband/father standing on the Concourse in tearful despair and when then I formally refused her and her son entry and told her they were going back by the return flight, *she* burst into tears too. But her son looked at her and then turned towards me, and he *didn't* cry: instead his expression just changed, slowly so that I saw it happen, from joy and trust to a belated puzzled realisation that I wasn't Mummy's new friend after all but somehow her enemy, and that I'd hurt her, badly. And it didn't take long before his face had fully closed up, the way I'd seen so many other third world faces go but until then only those of adults; and yet again I felt guilty and ashamed. At times, it was a *rotten* job.

CHRISTMAS BOX

December 25th, rejoice, rejoice – except that it was my turn on duty. Still at least it was double pay, and only one dirty flight to come but not till the early afternoon – someone always tried it on on Christmas Day, thinking we'd all be as pissed as newts and would just let 'em in regardless, and they were always half-right. Thus there Mark sat, newt-like and bent over the gleaming new EXTEL with pre-tape facility, state-of-the-art so that you could prepare and amend at your leisure a draft of what you wanted to say and get it exactly right in advance, and only then press the button and send it in a flash to any Brit post in the world. "Draft finished," he sighed finally, cheerfully – but out loud, the prize prat – and sat back in satisfaction. Which was when someone *else* said, "What case needs an overseas message?" and leant over to see.

But it was internal UK instead, admirably succinct and addressed to Box, and it said, '*Personal to Snuffbox from Browning M., IO, IS Gatwick. I have had enough, no, more than enough of this crap and I am defecting directly to Mother Russia with my SIs and stamps. So fuck you.*' Yeah, somehow you've guessed it, a spoof, because young Browning had neither any claim nor desire to be the Fourth Man[19]. And he grinned proudly at his perverse creation but only momentarily, then looked on in incredulous, frozen horror as an anonymous hand appeared over his shoulder and pressed 'Send' and the machine whirred into instant remorseless life, its missive on the desk of a bored Box Duty Officer long before the frantic, remorse-filled originator had stopped running madly round our office – and he *could* run, remember – shouting, *"How the hell d'you turn the bloody thing off?"*

Then the long silence as we looked at each other and at the white-faced, sprawled and still-panting Browning, and speculated, loudly, on the likely response. A knock on the door, which opened to reveal an apologetic, equally-pissed but non-smiling Branch officer with cuffs and a job to do? Or perhaps a phone call from above – *"Browning? In God's name, man, what-have-you-done? Clear your desk, hand in your equipment and take unpaid leave pending the Enquiry! Now!"* Or even – blithest vision – the sudden, practised, irresistible choking hand over the mouth, the whispered, *"Just relax, mate. I'm sorry, but orders are orders. Still, I'll make it easy, forget that pint you owe me and you won't feel a thing,"* and which of his erstwhile 'friends' would it be? He looked at us all uneasily and we looked back, agog with expectation – all it lacked was Noddy and Slade[20].

Then, finally, a reaction as The EXTEL burst into life again but this time we were *receiving* a message, so everyone rushed to see. And it was from Box all right, but just the usual annual Season's Greetings – a concoction of letter 'X's into an appropriate shape, this year a large upright Christmas Tree adorned with a brief label – 'Merry Xmas' – so we all relaxed. Well, all but one.

Then the machine whirred once more, briefly, not much

more than an apologetic burp, and someone said, "There's a postscript," and there was. *'Personal, to Browning from D.O. Box. Message received. Bon Voyage,'* and beside it another Christmas Tree, this one also made of 'X's but smaller, the only other difference that it was superimposed at an acute angle, as if for appropriate conifer-barbed insertion, though precisely where it didn't say. At times, it was a *cracking* job.

THE BRANCH BUNCH

From Box then logically onward to SB, the Branch itself, and an event which even now, or *ever* for that matter, I can't relate in detailed, glorious Technicolor save to say that it involved copious alcohol, three close friends, two parties in two counties, bilateral fog, one night, one small car and a uniform or two (no sex, though, nor even a solitary partridge in a pair tree).

But I *can* recount my first brief solo excursion, as it happens that very same busy evening but much earlier in the proceedings, into the dubious and necessarily frustrating world of the voyeur as I stared transfixed from the foot of the stairs at the slow-motion play enacted in eerie, erotic silence outside, back-lit by a streetlamp and barely visible through the frosted front-door glass – doubly frosted you might say because it was snowing hard, but that didn't stop them or increase their speed and I thought, *You'd better get a move on or it'll drop off.* But when I saw Geoff alone later (himself a Branch man, *what* a surprise), he was still smiling, so I assumed he had and it hadn't.

And now I recall another individual excursion – once started (or rather, once past the point of no return), as inevitable as it was involuntary (like the last, I suppose, from both our standpoints), but with no other similarity that I can think of and potentially life-changing if not downright life-ending to boot – when the fucking, *fucking* Russian SU, the Aeroflot (on which I was doing a *solo* crew check in total and insane defiance of Standing Instructions, with my priorities all wrong and only because the bloody, *bloody* Branch had failed to show up in prescribed support) suddenly shut its doors with me still aboard, and with a shriek of jet engines began to lumber purposefully down the taxi-way, an action calculated to give almost anyone similarly placed the bubble-shits.

But not *me* naturally, *I didn't* panic at the off and remained quite calm for some short time, but only because I couldn't believe it, not *here*, not *in England* and *at Gatwick*, not *now*, and above all not to *me* – a blatant ground/air kidnap, a Gary Powers in reverse (and what a prize cock-up *that* was), with a stupid, *moronic* IO (me again) the Lubyanka-bound victim and my SIs the real prize. And in any case I began to get the message all right when the crew, who had earlier been speaking in reasonable, respectful, English, seemed gradually to lose both their knowledge of the language and their erstwhile respect in direct and inverse proportion to the aircraft's rising speed, so that by the time we began to turn left off the taxi-way to prepare for the main event I was almost a gibbering wreck and more than pleased when, just as I looked despairingly outside to catch possibly my last-ever glimpse of Blighty, the engine-shriek died, the aircraft suddenly began to slow and I saw that wonderful, *wonderful* Branch car drawing alongside, festooned with white-faced bodies like something straight out of the Keystones but in plain clothes, some as I recall even with weapons drawn (though I could be wrong and they'd deny it anyway), and all of them waving furiously at the cockpit as they hung off and out of it (the car I mean). Happy daze.

In general, the Branch – the sole possessor of that title by then, since on 1/1/03 we'd become the Service – didn't throw too many dos of their own (or if they did, the tight fuckers didn't invite *me*) but more than compensated by their constant willingness, indeed their positive enthusiasm, to act whenever necessary at parties of *ours* as intermediaries, interceding verbally on the nod with their neighbour-summoned uniformed colleagues or, better still, just as often and with the smallest excuse, as super-efficient bouncers – pro bono alcoholico, of course.

And now I do remember going one early year to their official Christmas do at the Met's sports ground which also then housed the horses of the Mounted Division, and how at the end a number of impeccably be-suited though wholly-pissed officers burgled the stables and thundered off bareback, whooping, into the again-frosty night. It took a while to catch them all and bring them back under unofficial arrest but we never heard another word, despite some genuine arse-ache. Need to Know, see?

BRIEF ENCOUNTER

Hmm. I remember vividly a short attendance at an IS party in Shoreham – short for *me*, anyway. A few of us had turned up together so we must have had a pint or six, but I was stone cold sober and dead nervous because, for the second time, *This was it.* The place was packed out and we were barely through the front door when I glanced up. And there, slowly descending the stairs, long slim stockinged legs in the highest of heels, was a colleague though not yet a particular friend, and one of the early hand-picked women in the job. (Well, you didn't think it was a *bloke*, did you?)

She it was who I'd come to see though she didn't know it, she was slender and beautiful and there-to-be-won and the only problem was that it looked like she already had been (won I mean, the bitch), because she was hand in hand with one of my mates. Then our eyes met, I nodded, she might have done, neither of us smiled and after a moment she vanished in the crowd. Perhaps she hadn't even seen me – she said she couldn't remember anything about it later (though she's said that about a lot of other things too), and I'd thought at the time that her thoughts were far away.

I'd asked her out months before and she'd refused outright which wasn't surprising, seeing that she was beautiful and years younger and that I came with two children. Now I knew for sure that I really *was* too late, and I left soon afterwards to drive home alone up the A23, OK, fast, but studying the road with great care – after all, I was all the children had. We married two years later. We still are. Give or take.

GOODNIGHT, VIETNAM

Early 1975, and American graffiti on the wall for the residual Yank civilians in Vietnam, their last regular combat troops having withdrawn months ago. At Gatwick we saw occasional South Viet families, all of them refugees now, their tickets one-way to the US; and their numbers had grown suddenly, desperately, once the NVA[21] had broken through and headed rapidly south.

So: it was a Friday, we were very busy as by then we almost always were (so the daily duty drinking was a perceived pest of the pissed past – well, mostly) and the whole Hall was full. I was on 'Others' and had just committed the cardinal sin of omission: intent on writing up the landing card of the last passenger, I hadn't observed the next one and was only aware of his presence when his shadow loomed – and I mean *loomed* – over my desk. Then I looked up sharply, like greased lightning in fact but still far too late, to see the second largest[22] man I've *ever* seen, anywhere, and I recognised him instantly, albeit only in silhouette. That same big frame, that same craggy jaw: it was, it *had* to be, Ethan Edwards from *'The Searchers'* minus his pistol (gun, I mean) but plus two inches and thirty pounds of muscle, the Duke but King-sized, and even before he handed me his US passport I thought *Yank,* and when I looked inside, he came from the only United State that further befitted both him and the film: Texas.

"Good morning," I said. I did that sometimes when I felt particularly polite, or when I thought I might otherwise be pulverised by a huge fist, and whichever the reason I did it now.

"Hi theyere, suyyun," he said – well, I suppose he was just old enough – as he bowed slightly to share the same atmosphere, and now I was *totally* confused. Because he'd given 'there' and 'son' a clear extra syllable, so he had to be Charlie McCorry and *couldn't* be Ethan; but *that* didn't work either because he (Charlie) was pint-sized by comparison with

Ethan himself let alone this *super-hombre*, even in a ten-gallon hat.

So, "How long will you be staying?" I asked him, whoever he was, to change the subject and definitely in the Queen's English, and then he gave me five other passports, all Vietnamese, and I looked down and sideways – déjà vu, but with a multiple sex and colour change – and saw how much I'd missed already through not looking *ahead*. Because there deep in his shadow stood a diminutive, a *tiny*, woman, small even by Vietnamese standards let alone African Witchdoctors' and positively dwarfed by *him*; and next to *her* were four young children, tinier still and arranged neatly in order of height, the largest (or rather the least small) at the furthest end, all holding hands and the tiniest (or least large) firmly clutching hers.

All of them, the woman included, looked back at me without speaking and as I picked up the six passports the man said deeply, "S'all in thar, suyyun," which left it finely balanced – the words as surely Charlie's as the pitch was Ethan's – and he was right, for each contained a current Saigon-issued UK 'Settlement' visa with appropriate additions for his wife and children, which was what the visas, themselves clearly genuine, revealed them to be. And so, finally, the ambiguity was nailed. He *was* Ethan after all because now one thing he surely *couldn't* have, for Charlie to ask Martin Pawley to *un-hayand*, was a *fy-an-cee*.

"Ah," I said cunningly to gain time, instantly dismissing for my own protection the first inevitable thought that had passed through my head when I saw the pair of them together, *How the hell do they ever manage to* – and resorting to a less provocative approach instead, "So you're all coming to the UK to live?" and he nodded and smiled, tightly. "*Rite*, suyyun," he said.

"I see," I said. But I didn't. I could readily understand why, the way things were, *any* Yank, especially one with a native family, would be desperate to leave 'Nam; but not why one with money – and he must have a *lot* of it, or he wouldn't have got the UK visas – should choose to come here rather than simply go home, and I couldn't resist it. As I began to endorse the passports – no, tell a lie, in fact I had to send them all to Port Health first so I was writing out the IS81[23] – he leant forward over the desk to watch and I said, "Look, I don't have to know, but d'you mind telling me why you and your family have chosen to settle *here*, and not in the US?"

And that's when he stood up straight and seemed to grow, to tower over me, and I waited trembling inside for *"The hell I will,"* and for whatever came next, which to my fevered brain seemed likely to be a grab for my balls so that my heart and mind would surely follow – Christ, I was confused, and nearly as scared of him as I'd been of the witchdoctor. (There now, I've finally admitted it to myself, about the shaman I mean. And they're right, too: when the chips are down, size *doesn't* matter, *either* way.)

Then, *"Listen*, suyyun," he said instead, just words after all, and I did, earnestly – he had my *full* attention. "Thiyiss li'll ole country o' *yorne* weren't ma *firyirst* choyoice, *nossir.* Ma fam'ly," – he waved a protective hand over them as they stood there, looking around, and I didn't know whether they could understand one woyord of what he was saying – "ma fam'ly ain't *never* been outta 'Nam before, and ah figured the *Stayates*," – I thought he uttered the word with a degree of contempt, and recalled that he was a Texan – "the *Stayates* wuz the *only* playace fer us. So ah took them aloyong to our Embassy, rite thar in Saigon."

He paused and his gaze grew suddenly distant. And then bugger me, he seemed to grow *again* so that now his shape blocked out the sky and I was looking round for a squad of the Branch and trying to identify escape routes when he exploded and banged his fist down hard on the heavy desk which shook and I thought, *I'm stuffed, he'll breyake my neyeck before I can take a steyep,* and suddenly he yelled out, "Thoyose *lousy suyyuns of bitches!* Thoyose *lilly-livered sayacks of shit!*" He really said 'shee-it' but I'm not sure how to spell it, and the only two crumbs of comfort I could find – and believe me, I tried – were that presumably he wasn't talking about *us*, not yet at least, and that his fam'ly didn't seem at all concerned, and continued to look arouyound with interest.

"Thoyose *stinking yeller bass-turds*," he continued, seemingly warming to his theme. "Charlie[24] wuz rite thar in the City and the whole goddayam NVA jist teyen miyiles awayay, and those Harvard-edicated Es-O-Beyees didn't giyive a *shee-it*" – what the hell, I'll just go for it – "'bouyout *us, or* 'bouyout the other fam'lies ah saw thar – they wuz too busy savin' their *oyown skee-ins.* So we jist stooyood arouyound and no-one diyid a goddayam thiying, and theyen two 'Cong rockets feyell, OK rite outsiyide but not *too* dayam cloyose, and those chicken-shee-it mother-fuckers, sorry darlin'," – so she did understand *some* English – "left us stayandin' thar while they stuyuck their own goddayam heyeds under their own goddayam deyesks and *ah* thought, <u>*Fuck you*</u>, – sorry agin, darlin' – and theyen ah tooyook ma fam'ly *hoyome.*"

He paused at that and took a deep breath, and ah – sorry, I – began to relax a little. Then I noticed that not surprisingly the IOs on either side of me were half-listening in now (and perhaps planning their *own* escapes too, so I had to go on, if only to give them time).

"And?" I prompted. It seemed fully adequate in the circumstances, and I didn't want to draw his personal attention any more than I could help.

"And *theyen*," he said, "ah remembered ah'd heayerd good thiyings 'bout *some* of yew Briyits from *some* of ma own foyolks," – I assumed he specifically meant Teyexans – "and ah figured it wuz woyorth a shoyot so ah tooyook my fam'ly to *yore* embassy, and we weyent to seyee the Visa Mayan and as we wayalked in he wuz jist havin' some tea – a *cuyup* o' tea, I mean – and *ah* tell *you* no *lie*, as he raiyaised that *itty-bitty cuyup* to his liyips *two more* goddayam 'Cong rockets landed outsiyide, in *yore* compouyound, *jist as* he tooyook a *li'l siyip!* And *he* didn't hiyide under *his* deyesk, *nossir*, but his fayace chayanged and his hayands shooyook and then he sayaid *'Jesus Christ,'* and *ah* thouyought *shee-it, another wuyyun,* and tuyurned to leave, but *he* jist looyooked round at us and saiyaid, woyord fer woyord," – at this point he tried to imitate a plummy English accent, but if you thiyink I'm going to try to imitate a Texan trying to imitate a plummy Briyit, you've got *another* thiyink coming – "*'Oh, please don't go, I won't keep you a moment,'* and he rayang his li'l old beyell and a boy cayame and *then* he jist saiyaid, *'Look here, Minh old son, this is just not on! The fucking tea is cold so get it sorted, there's a sport, and bring some more for my guests too,'* and *that's* wheyen *ah* just *nooyoo* the UK wuz *rite* fer us."

I have to say that I felt proud as well as relieved once I'd worked it all out, and when I looked sideways the other IOs were pursing their lips and nodding their heads too, in silent, studied, British approval. I also thought that the account no less than the accent merited a proper positive response, a gesture of national welcome of some sort, and so I looked at The Giant carefully. He was beaming at me now, kiyindly, and his wife and children were following his lead and beaming kiyindly too. So, *Whayat the heyell*, I thought and stood on tiptoe, reached up and shook his hand. It hurt a lot, but I said "We're *very* glad to have you," anyway, and took the pluyunge.

"Look, you're going to have to wait a bit to see the doctor, anyway. So can you spare me a minute – I want to tell *you* a story."

He looked sideways – no, downways – at his wife, considering; then, "Sure *thiying*, suyyun. Go *rite* aheyed." So I diyid.

"You see that officer up there at the end?" I asked, pointing to Bernie, busy on the British desk.

He looked. "*Yessir.* Ah see *hiyim*," he said.

"Well," I said, "in 1968, seven years back, he was a sailor in the RFA, the Royal Fleet Auxiliary – the supply arm of the British Royal Navy – and his ship had just birthed in Hong Kong."

"*Yeah?*" he said, eagerly now, but he'd looked grim for a moment when I'd mentioned the year of the Tet offensive. God knows what memories he had of *that*. Still, onwards.

"Well, once the crew got ashore they all headed for a Kowloon bar – The Seven Seas, I think he said it was."

"Yeah?" he said, still polite but beginning to fidget a little, and I thought, *O-oh old mate, your attention span is as short as your temper,* and hurried on.

"And they were in there with the boys off a couple of British destroyers when half the crew of a US carrier walked in, fresh from the South China Sea."

"*Yeah?*" he said, but eagerly again this time. He thought he knew what was coming, and at the mention of the Stayates he'd once more become all attention.

"So there was a sudden silence in the bar, you know the way it is, but the Yanks –" (I gulped) "sorry, the – " but he raised a giant, re-assuring hand.

"Suyyun, s'all OK. Go *rite aheyed*," he said, his eyes gleaming.

"But *your people* stayed at the bar and *we*, the Brits I mean, stayed at the tables at the back, so for a while everything was fine."

"Oh," he said, clearly disappointed.

"But then, a diminutive Liverpudlian – that's a very small Englishman from a big city up north here called Liverpool – a stoker from one of the destroyers, went up to the bar for another round and a giant black *American* stoker turned to him and said loudly, 'And when are you goddamn yellow limeys gonna enter this war?' and there was *another* sudden silence."

"Yeah?" he said, all ears now. "And *theyen?"*

"Well, for a second the little Liverpudlian just looked up at him, craning his neck. And then *he* said, '*I* don't know, mate. *Ho Chi Fuckin' Minh* hasn't *axed* us yet,' and for a moment the huge Yank just looked down at *him* as he thought it through, and then it started." (The bar, Bernie said, had been well and truly wrecked, even by naval standards.)

I sensed the IOs on either side falling about and heard the laughter rippling along the control as the story was repeated – obviously, they hadn't heard it before directly from Bernie. But I kept my gaze fixed on the Texan, and my heart sank to my boots. He was glaring back at me with narrowed eyes, another huge Yank thinking it through himself, and his fam'ly had stood clear a trifle and was looking at him expectantly.

Shee-it, I thought, *I've done it now.* And then his great laugh boomed out, *"Haw*, Haw," so it was back to '*The Searchers'* again and bloody Charlie for sure this time, *that* laugh but louder and deeper, oh hell, just like Ethan's. And then *he (super-hombre* I mean*)* reached out and enclosed my puny fist in his. It huyurt a loyot moyore thayan befoyore, believe me.

"Yew Briyits," he said. "Yew Briyits *slay* me. Ah *noo* I wuz rite. This *is* the playace fer us," and he led his fam'ly off to see the doctor, still laughing.

If they're still here, I hope he still thinks so, because since then a hell of a lot of water has gone under the bridge. But you never knoyow, maybe they went to Liverpool.

EGG AND DOUBLE CHIPS

There we were, Andy, Phil and me, meeting up that summer evening in The Parrot just for a couple, truly impromptu and I can't even remember who'd suggested it. Andy was a colleague and friend – he'd been one of my several past lodgers (Christ, how I needed the money) until his own recent marriage – and Phil was one of the few outsiders admitted, big deal, to the IS circle: it must have been his odd way of thinking. Anyway, we didn't get there till nine and only had four then called it a day – we didn't even stay till closing time.

Afterwards, we stood outside in the close warm night for a moment – *companionably*, you know, close-bonding and all that psycho-bollocks – then Phil pushed off and I was all set to follow when Andy said, "Fancy some nosh? Hazel will fix up something." Well, the children would have been safely tucked up in bed hours ago – Jeannie the latest nanny had proved invaluable, as reliable as they come – and it didn't take long to make up my mind; milli-seconds, in fact.

"OK," I said. "Thanks." Decisive, see?

And it was good to see Hazel again; the first time since their wedding, six months before. She looked blooming, marriage suited her and she proudly showed me round the house and then got busy in the kitchen: nothing fancy, just double egg and chips, but that was fine by me. She joined us too, and we were all sitting round the card table chatting about nothing as we ate when there was a brief lull. And I remember that I was head down, intent on my food, when Andy spoke into the friendly silence. "Hazel," he said and I looked up sharply, because one of the job's curses is that it makes you constantly aware of such things, and suddenly his voice had sounded a little odd.

"Yes, darling," she said as she smiled at him, and there was a short pregnant pause. Then he said, "Hazel, I'm sorry. I'm leaving you," and then, "I love somebody else," and as my mouth dropped open I thought, *You selfish bastard,* for *two* good reasons because it had ruined *my meal* as well, and I wanted to fall through the floor. But then there was another short silence, less friendly now, as Hazel just looked at him with *her* mouth open too, and for a second I thought absurdly, *She's going to say, "That's perfectly all right darling, just finish your food while it's hot, there's a good boy, and we can talk about it later, when Mike's gone."*

But she didn't. Finally she managed *"What?"* instead, just that. And then she screamed and cried but it was Andy who ran out, leaving us two sitting there. Then we both stood up and my still-new chair caught in the still-new carpet and overturned and whilst I was trying to think of something, *anything*, to say, *she* said "Oh, *Mike*," and half-choked and came round the table and I put my arms round her while she sobbed and I held her for a while, muttering helpless soothing platitudes into her ear. Then I left because really there was fuck-all *I* could do, and oddly enough the divorce went through pretty much on the nod.

And the worst thing from my point of view was that it turned out that the selfish bastard had fallen in love with Jeannie, *my nanny*, so *she* left *me* as well, and there were *two* of us picking up the bloody pieces.

STRETCHER PARTY

And to change the subject completely: parties, in general. In the early years they came in endless succession, my very first starting damply as we staggered in a body into Ken the ex-rocker's front hall well past closing time after the standard eight preparatory pints and looked up to see Kirsten his wife majestically backlit on the balcony like the blond Nordic goddess that she was, then shrank back like violets as we glimpsed the large loaded silver bucket in her hand: all of us that is except Ken himself, the only one who somehow, like the proverbial copper in the miners' strike who didn't look up either, *hadn't* seen her. And then the cold, cold water (iced as I recall, still with solids, and beautifully aimed), shooting out and down in slow, slow motion to drench him and him alone (Ken I mean, not the copper: *he* got a lump of clay slap bang on his helmet) so that he stood there dripping philosophically in an admiring circle, feeling his bruises and quietly cursing – his wife or his luck or both, we couldn't tell – as she screamed, 'You bloody, *bloody* bastard!' because she'd done hot food after he'd promised, *promised* her we'd be back at the latest by nine.

And another early one, ours this time – my first wife and I's, I mean – with the four of us carrying the lifeless ground girl at a desperate stumbling run through the warm smoking rain to the Cottage Hospital across the rise, running maybe to save her life as drugs were involved but we didn't know which, and *she* couldn't tell us because she was right out of it. Then the outrage of the Matron who finally opened the door to our frantic knocking, but only to say, 'You should be *ashamed*, do you know what *time* it is?' as she turned us away without a glance at the patient, and our stumbling run back so that we could put her – the ground girl that is, we'd already told the Matron where we'd like to put *her* – to bed and sit by her all night, so that when she woke up the following morning with a sleepy smile and a cheerful 'Good morning, boys, what's up?" at least she wasn't alone.

I remember a third too, later, and gently removing the spectacles from some prat's face to keep them from harm whilst I punched his lights out – scotch again, and the now-certain state of our marriage – because he'd insulted the Bottler who was now nowhere to be found, and the sudden commotion in the back garden which pre-empted my violence and made us all run out and there he was, the Bottler himself, morris-dancing with pegs but no bells in a frenzied fixed circle on obligatory tipsytoe, clutching vainly at his throat and slowly choking to death because he'd fallen down then stood up within the welcoming embrace of a rotary clothes line, and somehow got his wires crossed.

And for a change a party without any incident at all until the last couple to leave jumped into their mini and reversed briskly up the drive in a line admirably straight but so alcoholicly misconceived as to mow down Graham's's entire row of prized young conifers as he ran bellowing beside them. The driver's error was, however, understandable: he'd been momentarily but wholly distracted when in the act of putting on her seatbelt his wife had slumped sideways into his lap with a brief deceptive moan, face-downwards and open-mouthed yippee, but also instantly unconscious.

And finally – years out of synch, but what the hell – I remember an honour guard of IOs standing in my own back garden – *mine*, not *ours* any longer, because the first marriage was by then quite dead – on another hot mid-summer's night during a shed-moving party (it took about twenty of us and a *lot* of beer because it was a big, *big* bugger, but then it lifted a treat). We were firing off volleys of .22 mini-flares which exploded high in the air above the hostile tree-line and the house next door, and when the police turned up to ask suspiciously if we'd heard or seen anyone acting suspiciously because the locals had reported multiple gun-shots, the dubious credibility of our bland blank denial despite the hanging reek of cordite was immeasurably, nay, invincibly, strengthened by the firm assurances of several attendant Branch officers, the flare guns themselves having long since been returned safely to the attic, where I forgot them when I moved so that they probably remain there to this day. Yeah.

But in the end the party of parties wasn't one of ours at all, although an elite (?) IS squad – five of us – went by specific invitation: Pat, Mark, Bernie, Bugsy and me. Bugsy said as usual that he'd better travel alone, "just in case", so Bernie drove me and Pat drove Mark as we headed for a country estate somewhere near Ascot, the owner of which threw an annual do, the way one does, for all his staff, domestic and polo, and to which we had been invited because Maria, the lady who was by then *his* housekeeper, had for a while been mine (and a bloody good one) soon after the divorce.

So. Bugsy first. Now Bugsy was a *real* case. He'd joined the job a year after me and we'd heard in advance that he'd last been a Ship's Steward which we hadn't had before, thus prompting lively if not wild speculation about his likely sexuality which reached its hysterical apogee when his first appearance was only minutes away. Would he arrive in leather bell-bottoms, in drag, in *irons*?

No, no, wrong again, we saw instead a short-haired soft-shoe shuffler of medium height in a shabby suit, and his first closely-observed encounter with the ground girls was enough to dispel all our foolish fears – or maybe one or two hopes, if the cap fits. But it wasn't so much the girls' effect on *him*, though his immediate, if casual, interest was apparent enough: it was his on *them*, and if they could have bedded him three at a time they would have done, and for all I know they did, later, but I don't and I didn't (know, I mean).

Bloody Bugsy: he would regularly appear after an occasional long weekend off looking a pale, pastel blue in the face, truly exhausted, and we admiringly put that down wholly to his sexual activities, to the fact that he was literally shagged out, until we learned that in another of his many past lives he'd been an RN clearance diver, that he was still in the Wavy Navy and that he'd spent the days away doing shadowy semi-official things in the then-troubled waters of Northern Ireland. How he filled his nights there God knows but one way and another he was a *very* busy man, and our awe increased correspondingly. He was 007 to the life except that they'd clearly had to excise half of what *Bugsy really* did, not least the sex, to make the character credible.

But enough Bugsy background: I never like to think about him for too long because I always finish up with those old male feelings of comparative inadequacy – yes, they're just starting now – no, yes, no… Anyway on the evening in question what's-his-name was having his standard trouble of girl-juggling and, he said, would probably come later, as by all accounts he usually did – oh shit, back to the inadequacies – so we took two cars in case he turned up on foot, which proved of some importance at the end.

And on to Bernie, he of Hong Kong fame and by contrast a mercurial six foot four Welsh rugby fullback with hollow legs who'd moved in with me when his own marriage had recently gone tits up through the demon drink – him of course, not his wife. With Bernie it was always chicken and egg, always debatable whether he or the alcohol were the root cause of the scrapes in which he consistently found himself, and from which he mainly escaped. Take just one as an example – one which as it happened hadn't happened *yet* and indeed *wouldn't* happen for a few more years to come, but where the tale's clear anachronism is secondary to its value as a demonstration of how whenever things *did* happen, they *always* happened to *him*.

I'm thinking about how he met his second wife, a lady almost as Viet-tiny as he was almost Texas-tall so that when they were together (which, the way it turned out, overall wasn't itself very long) they made a memorable couple, provided you had good peripheral vision. Anyway their first encounter was neither enchanted nor across a crowded room but did occur with equal and dramatic suddenness because there he was, the Prince of her Dreams, appearing from nowhere to wrest her from an icy grave at Virginia Water – no, not from the Lake but from a chest freezer instead, because he was looking straight at her as she bent over to pluck out a packet of fish fingers from the bottom, lost her balance (top-heavy, perhaps) and fell in with a swish of silk, a faint cry and a clatter of heels, the lid promptly shutting with the shock.

Well, you can laugh about it now, especially as they're

long since divorced, but it could have been bloody serious at the time, and think about the effect on the next poor devil who innocently opened it up again to select his own bit of frozen cod and uncovered the Catch of the Day instead? Still, hindsight's a wonderful thing (take the first prophetic, if swiftly vanishing, view of her that Bernie had), and I suppose with a start like that, their relationship was first bound to warm up considerably, but later inexorably to cool.

And the rest of us, Pat the Geordie, Mark the speed king and me? By *their* standards boringly conventional I'm afraid, but you can't have everything.

Anyway, the night was another as black as pitch and we arrived late, having had some trouble finding the place. But we finally turned in by a wooden sign-post set on a grassy (but sniper-free) knoll in the middle of a leafy lane, and drove up a long and winding drive before emerging from a final copse. And there we were, we had to be, because the warm thick darkness was suddenly lit as bright as day by a number (four) of large open fires over which crouched numerous (twenty) figures – clearly Argentinian grooms to a trained eye – intently roasting whole sheep. There was a large open bar overseen by a large open gent with magnificent whiskers who proved to be an ex-Guards RSM; and a blaring disco in the form of a massive pantechnicon, one side of which opened largely onto what seemed to be a ploughed, albeit half-grassed, field in comparative darkness, which served as the dance floor.

At first we couldn't find Maria herself so we wandered over and chatted to the be-whiskered Mac whilst pouring free drink down our practised necks. Then we joined the queue for roast mutton, each piece pampas-sized and ripped from the carcase before your very eyes, manually and abruptly though by then by no means untimely and if you wanted more there was plenty – not that any of us did, Eddie's training notwithstanding.

Thus greasily replete we decided to look further for Maria, again starting at the bar; but now Bernie had disappeared, a phenomenon wholly without precedent when there was not just any old bar about but a free one at that. Still, there was nothing *we* could do except worry which didn't take long, and we were minding our own business and shouting above the disco when it stopped without warning, and long enough for all to hear a largely one-sided exchange from within a milling group nearby. And I would have recognised that strident Welsh lilt anywhere, as distinctive as the fervour which only booze and rugby conjoined could produce – in a Welshman anyway.

"Polo," Bernie cried out in the sudden lull, his voice booming out eerily as the crowd parted and I saw them, *"Polo – is – a – cissy's – game,"* and between words he pushed his listener in the chest to add emphasis, propelling him slowly backwards whilst the latter remained admirably calm, his arms firmly at his sides and his responses limited to a mild, "Oh, *I say*, surely not." The only problem was that he was the bloody host – we didn't know *who* he was at the time but we all recognised *what*, the rest of us that is – and I glanced nervously at Mac, who thankfully showed no sign of intervening. *"Bernie,"* I shouted, and he turned round at once, saw me, detached himself abruptly with a final baleful glare and came shambling over as the music restarted and the crowd closed up again.

"For Christ's sake," I said, "d'you know who that was?"

"Him? I haven't got a *bloody clue,"* he said. He was visibly furious, shaking with rage. "All I know is that he *insulted rugby, and -"*

"That," I interjected, "was our *host."*

"So bloody what," he said, still furiously, then as it sunk

in, "*Oh hell*, Mike," and he turned back again to apologise, but I said "Just leave it," and he did. I wondered years later how things would have gone if he'd realised at the time that the bloke he'd just been pushing about bore a striking resemblance to the Father of the Woman who would become the Wife of the Brother of his Prince (until they Divorced). But he wasn't a Clairvoyant was he, and perhaps it wouldn't have made the slightest difference because one way or another, beer is a great leveller. At any event I reckon that we got off lightly because whatever else polo players might be, they are on the whole emphatically *not* what Bernie said they were, although some must be very forgiving.

Then above the renewed blasts of sound I heard another voice which too I recognised instantly, because both substance and accent were so distinctive.

"Sorry, Julia love, but can I just lean on you for a moment? *Aaah,* that's *much* better. I'm not often like this but I've had a long day at Hereford and besides, the escape took a hell of a lot out of me…"

"Escape?" young, posh, already half-interested, and I resigned myself, *Here we go again*, but didn't look round, I didn't need to because I'd seen Mac's face as he listened in, expressionless save for a single raised and equally magnificent eyebrow. Bugsy, did I say? Alfie, more like, and *fuck* 007.

"Yeah – not from the Hereford boys of course," – she tittered convulsively and I saw a momentary appreciative gleam in Mac's eye – "no, no, from the, um, er, the *Sultan of Borneo's dungeons*. I can't say much, natch, but I was doing a spot of work out there for HMG – "

"HMG?" Well, no-one said she had to be bright too.

"Yes love, the government – well, the SIS, MI6 actually, *you* know." (Bond to the life like I said a while back, except that *he*, Bugsy, had already hung *his* hat, first throw, on a hell of a lot more hat-stands – every one of them, once he'd left, *deeply* and *irrevocably* notched.)

"Oh, Bugsy," Julia sighed, already wriggling deliciously both on his arm and on the hook – metaphorically, anyway. "Tell me more."

"Sure love, I'll give you everything I possibly can," he said, as I thought viciously, *He's got that right, at least,* but that must have been when he saw me, and he paused for a second – as if he hadn't known I was there all along. "But look darlin', here's Mike, *my boss, he* knows *all* about it and *perhaps he* can speak more freely. Mike, Julia, Julia, Mike. Look mate, can *you* tell her – Borneo, the dungeons and the rest, *you* know." He was always like that the bastard, a born-again chancer, and if there wasn't a real problem to deal with already he'd create one, *especially* for his so-called fucking mates.

And Julia was just as blonde and fit to bust as I'd known she'd be, and I spent the next five minutes sweating as I ad-libbed madly whilst he stood silent by her side holding her hand, nodding and grinning at me and letting me do all the talking with a poker-faced Mac leaning on the bar behind the pair of them and listening in as well, and I was digging myself deeper with every word and didn't know how to get out of it when Bernie's second foray of the night came to my timely rescue.

"*Look at me, Boyo,*" came the familiar voice again, *over* the music this time but still barely audible despite the strength of his self-astonished shout, "I'm bloody *dancing,*" and he was, capering about with his too-short trousers half-masting round his too-skinny ankles which gleamed palely in the too-white strobes, his companion starkly silhouetted as they flashed – the strobes, I mean. But they were both really enjoying themselves, so it couldn't last. And it didn't. *"Look at me,"* he yelled again, and then, rhetorically – his yell continuing into a second silence as the music once more magically stopped – "Can *anybody* tell me why I *always* end up with the *ugliest* bird in the place – oh, now where's *she* gone?" as his partner smartly exited stage right, sobbing bitterly into the welcoming darkness.

Well OK, so Bernie could be a bit insensitive at times. But he wasn't naturally cruel, and I'd rather believe that this was simply one of those several occasions when his own chat-up line was a tad less smooth and efficacious than, say, Bugsy's. Anyway, you didn't have to be hyper-sensitive or even sober to recognise the instant sexual polarisation of the crowd, all the men, especially those with partners, frowning – to the casual observer, in deep silent disapproval of Bernie's words, but more probably in a real and contrary effort to keep the fellow-smiles off their faces or is that just me – and all the women favouring him with a collective and contemptuous glare whilst each basked securely in the eternal secret superior knowledge, now vicariously confirmed, that *she* at least was one of the *more* attractive ones there. And then, as Bernie took one last regretful Fred-like look in the direction of the disappearing Ginger then turned as ever to the cosy, familiar and far safer consolation of the bar, Mac spoke – his first words for some time. "Interesting people, your friends," he said to me, his voice as flat as his face, and that was all.

Three hours later things were winding down, and our situation was pretty much par for the course. Bugsy had vanished with Julia: Mark and Pat, having failed in their own amorous attempts, had rejoined Bernie and me at the bar, from which I at least had never – well, hardly ever – strayed;

and the long and short of it was that the four of us were now well, *well*-pissed.

"Oh," Mark mumbled, "I bumped into Maria eventually," – *Maria: Oh, shit*, I thought in vivid self-disgust – "and she invited us back. All we have to do is find out where the hell she lives. But it can't be that hard. Can it?"

"Then you three carry on and I'll join you shortly," said Bernie shortly. We'd expected nothing less, and he was calling loudly for Mac as we walked away.

"Well, these are the bunk-houses," Pat said a little later. "It must be up here somewhere," and we wandered up a row of outbuildings straight out of Stalag 14 but without the wire, some in total darkness, some ablaze with light. We saw a variety of talking heads, and faces, and soon enough we saw *her*, Maria, peering out through a window. She saw us too, and waved furiously, and pointed.

"Follow me," said Mark, but when I looked I couldn't see any way in and by the time I'd opened my mouth to say so, he and Pat had somehow disappeared. So I wandered on alone, and soon came to a small house which seemed to me to lead into the end of Maria's block. It was one of those in total darkness and I remember distinctly that it was in fact detached too but at the time so was I pretty well, and neither fact seemed that real *or* relevant as I knocked on the door. But the house remained dark and silent, and detached, and I knocked again, and again, louder and louder without effect and was on the point of heading round the end of the quay to the *Copa* again[25] when, finally, a light appeared within, and the door opened.

"*Yes*, mate?" He was young, muscular, clearly non-Argentinian (*and* non-Australian), dishevelled, and in a dressing gown, I'd obviously just woken him up and he was not best pleased. But at least it couldn't be the Mission[26] because he was a man and he didn't say, *"Oui?"* and so he wasn't French either.

"I just need to come in to see Maria," I said, clearly and politely, in English – that's what I *meant* to say anyway but I can't have said it clearly or politely or maybe even intelligibly *enough*, because his reply was brief and to the point.

"*Fuck off*, mate," he said, just like that, and as he started to close the door the red mist came down, or perhaps I should call it red sludge this time because I saw it descending, thickly and sluggishly from my forehead, and when I tried to enter and he barred my way I took his arm in an unbreakable judo hold that I'd seen once in a book.

But I was well, *well*-pissed like I said, and the small print had probably said that you had to be sober in the first place and perhaps he was the author anyway or at least some kind of athletic magician, because he just waved his hands, like this, and the next moment I found myself flying lightly through the air, alone and with no trouble at all, to land heavily nearby in an open stable where I skidded briefly along on my back through inch-deep horse-shit until I hit a large motorbike, which I knocked clean off its stand so that it fell on top of me.

So: I lay there for a few seconds in no pain whatever, quite comfortable but wholly immobilised, smelling strongly and reflecting sagely on the stunning current aptness of the maker's name writ large on the petrol tank snug against my chest, gently dripping fuel and pinning me to the ground. 'TRIUMPH' it said. But I soon forgot about that as I peered half-hypnotised through the still-spinning spokes. For as my assailant turned to go back inside without another word – so it can't have been *his* bike – I heard more footsteps and another voice, awfully familiar. "*Thish*," it intoned, "has got to *shtop*," and into my blurred vision came Bernie, wet and grass-stained trousers still clinging closely to his spindly legs, fag in mouth, feet flat and fists raised as he advanced, again angry, on the man still in the doorway.

He just sighed, muttered, *"Fuck. Another one,"* philosophically, and turned again to confront Bernie too, who would surely soon have wound up stretched out neatly beside me, which, what with the fuel and the fag, would have *really* warmed things up; but at that moment a third voice, again familiar, rapped out, *" As you were,"* and then, "Both of you – *Stand still!"* so I figured he wasn't talking to me, and as Mac took easy charge it was all sorted. I and the doorman apologised to each other – in the circumstances it was very generous of him, Christ, in his own way he must have been as forgiving as our host and Maria – and soon Bernie and I were re-united in her (Maria's) room with the others, not least Bugsy who had re-appeared alone but with a limp smile on his face and who now sat recovering and drinking her coffee like the rest of us, except for Bernie who now sat drinking her brandy.

Dawn was breaking as we finally left, but only four of us because Bugsy, it seemed fully himself again although already a very *light* blue, had decided to stay the rest of the night with one of Maria's girls to learn all about crochet; and by now Bernie was utterly, madly, *colossally* pissed. Nonetheless he insisted on driving and wasn't safe to be on his own so I went with him as once again we set off down the long and winding drive, with us in front and Pat and Mark close behind.

Now I know I said that Bernie was beyond well-Brahms, and so he was. But you have to understand that we only knew that because we all knew him so well, and everything would have seemed fine to an independent observer's eye as we smoothly negotiated the curves and bends of the estate at a reasonable speed. True, he wasn't saying much but then he never did when he was concentrating, and the crisis didn't come until we reached the country lane and were confronted by the little grassy knoll. There we slowed, then stopped, because although it was small it was quite high and we both had to peer up at the signpost which necessarily gave us a simple directional choice, left or right. The only trouble was that neither of the places specified thereon meant jack-shit to either of us, and after a moment Bernie spoke, posing a question of such astute penetration as wholly to belie his condition.

"Which fucking way then?" he asked, but I hadn't got a bloody clue. So I said, "I haven't got a bloody clue," at which Bernie just nodded in empathy, considered sagely, swore again gently and continued to stare up at the sign, his head back-lit by Pat's headlights as he waited patiently behind. *Perhaps they know,* I thought, and I wound my window down to listen. But there was no sound, helpful or abusive, coming from the rear so it was reasonable to assume that they hadn't got a bloody clue either.

Still, taking decisions was our stock in trade, so when Bernie made his move it was decisive, not to say irrevocable, and based no doubt on the premise that if you couldn't solve a problem, you changed it. Because with an elaborate sigh and an admirably fluid motion of his left hand worthy of a racing driver or even *in extremis* (perhaps in the Sultan's cells) of a lonely and frustrated Bugsy, he eased the car into gear, accelerated hard and purposefully charged the knoll which he duly mounted head-on, ramming amidships the offending signpost which promptly broke clean off and fell across the windscreen. He then braked sharply and as the vehicle came to an abrupt halt astride the post-stump, he engaged neutral, applied the handbrake, switched off the engine, opened his door and fell out, almost John-Newhaven-style[27], except that whilst his upper body disappeared completely into the pool of darkness alongside, his long legs remained visible, fully at ease, aslant and still within the car. And whilst it would be untrue to say that he was truly flat, his feet being raised up inside the car and his trunk invisibly extended down the sharp side-slope of the grassy knoll, he was as near-horizontal as, in the circumstances, you could reasonably expect: a great leveller, like I said.

And I remember clearly – strange enough in itself – that I sat there for a while, breathing in the still-warm night air through my still-open window and Bernie's gaping door, and that I stayed calm if no longer detached, though all I could now see beyond the shattered signpost were our headlights pointing steeply up at the sky (I knew I'd been *there* before, too) and, when I glanced sideways, Bernie's feet and damp spindly legs – legs which I found singularly unappetising, his trousers having now ridden right up. I may also have sworn at him for a short while without response but that is where my memory ends, and for an accurate description of the next few events, or hours, it is better to rely on the testimony of Mark and Pat, who were still behind in their unmoved car.

They both maintain that they too had been frozen into immobility – apart from a joint muttered *'shit'* – when Bernie first killed the signpost, then parked up on top of it and fell out. In a way, they support my contention that I stayed calm because according to them I just sat there in my seat looking straight ahead – *they* say that I didn't turn my head at all, even to look at Bernie's remains beside me, but what do *they* know – until after some time had passed I alighted, swore loudly, went round the back, pulled him *right* out, and tried but failed to lift him up.

This, it seems, galvanised them (at long fucking last) into helping, and between us, manoeuvring with difficulty in the restricted space on top of the now less-grassy and somewhat greasy knoll, we eventually put him, still lifeless but unmarked and breathing normally, back into the car but this time on the passenger side. I then removed the signpost from the bonnet, got into the driver's seat, reversed off the stump with a cracking of wood and a creaking of metal and drove smartly away in what *they* had by now decided was the wrong direction. They then thus opted to drive to my house the other way, to await us there – a journey which took them about an hour and a quarter.

Meantime I was in difficulty on two counts – firstly we had like fools put Bernie in the front and although he was now wearing one of the then new-fangled belts he slipped down in his seat whenever I braked and fell against me on every left turn so that I spent a lot of time driving one-handed and propping him up; and secondly it was only when we were crossing the Thames at Shepperton for the third time that I realised that my sign-reading was deeply amiss, and not just at the greasy knoll.

So we finally reached home after an otherwise uneventful journey of some three hours, to find the rest still sitting anxiously outside. Between us we got the Boyo upstairs and still-dressed into his bed and it seemed only moments later when I awoke in my own, still smelling sweetly of horse manure, to hear the sound of Annie the then Nanny hoovering the house, the children having long since gone to school. I lay there for a while then finally forced myself to go downstairs and have the obligatory breakfast on these occasions (mandarin yogurt and two paracetomol), and thanked my lucky stars that I wasn't on duty for the next two days.

Sometime later and feeling more myself, I was chatting to Annie when we heard slow and hesitant footsteps on the stairs, and Bernie appeared round the corner. We looked at him in studied silence for a moment and then Annie gave a gasp and stifled giggle, and ran from the room; and I must say in her defence that there were times when he'd looked better. Many, even most, times in fact, because at present his eyes were red, his hair dishevelled and the pipe in his mouth empty – it had to be because it was upside down, but at least it had a bowl – and at some point he must have changed because he was now sporting a red silk dressing gown, dark blue drainpipe-legged pyjamas and matching socks and slippers.

It was an ensemble which I'd never seen before and still almost elegant, although on his tall skinny frame and with his legs protruding by the inevitable three inches below the pyjama bottoms, it would have turned heads anywhere. But then I looked again, more closely, and saw the likely precise source of Annie's mirth. For Bernie was in fact sockless, and what I had taken to *be* socks were in fact his ankles and lower shins, each effectively one massive bruise, the colour of which exactly matched his pyjamas – a true Oxford blue which would have gone beautifully with Bugsy's facial Cambridge; and his pyjama legs weren't drainpipes at all but just seemed to be because the legs within were already so swollen as to put immense pressure on the stitching – indeed they seemed to be swelling further before my very eyes, so that I waited tensely for a seam to rip.

So Bernie stood there, speechless and gently swaying, for a moment. Then his red eyes followed my gaze and he looked down. "*Christ*," he said, "no wonder they hurt. What the *hell* was I *doing* last night?" and his eyes clouded, then cleared (whilst remaining red throughout) and he said in wonder, "The party. I remember now. I was *dancing*. I *never* dance." Then they clouded again as he continued, "dancing in a bloody *ploughed field*, and Jesus Christ, *what else?*" And as soon as I could speak, I told him.

LIGHT RELIEF

Newhaven. A seaport. Another place, another world. But I can't ignore it or pretend that it didn't happen; nor if I'm honest do I want to. It's just that if I don't, you might get the wrong impression – or the right one instead, but what the hell, you probably won't believe it in the first place. Out of my seven and a half years at Gatwick I only spent four months down by the seaside, by the beautiful sea, on summer relief, but if my memories thereof remain disproportionately graphic, the real wonder is that I can remember anything at all. Because whilst at the airport you'd been regularly sustained by a steady but now much-diminished and generally gentle and soothing stream of alcohol, at Newhaven, especially on relief, you were elevated every time, borne up upon a veritable flood of it – except that as with any swimmer (especially an occasional and ungifted amateur) undertaking a tricky channel crossing, particularly by a longer route than Dover-Calais, you were liable from time to time suddenly, abruptly, to sink.

Newhaven, then. Every designated port of entry, large or small, had its own permanent staff; but seaports' complements were set at their predicted *winter* traffic levels, so those where passenger numbers rose sharply every year in the late spring and summer were provided with seasonal assistance, i.e. relief, from airports to help them out during the busy months. Newhaven was just such a place and Gatwick, by some distance the major airport closest to it, was its main relief provider. Each Gatwick IO went there for about a month at a time about every other year, each spell allocated on a strictly rotating basis and highly prized because it afforded a change from the relentless and ever-growing (and increasingly arid) airport grind.

And it had a double value. From the job's point of view it widened your experience, because your average foreign seaport passenger was often very different from those you saw at the airport – or at least a very different kind of *refusal*, because those we encountered on the Newhaven-Dieppe route formed by and large the really poor end of the market. And from ours, the sea air refreshed and reinvigorated you, especially on the crossings, so that you returned to Gatwick bronzed, fit and better able to cope with the daily skyborne pressure.

Refreshed? Reinvigorated? *Fit?* Well, that was the theory, but *'Bollocks'* is the word which again springs instantly to mind. You returned *changed,* certainly, or even *transformed* – especially your liver – and in a few cases never the same again, though most recovered (their livers did, anyway).. But it wasn't the *sea air* that caused it, it was the fucking *ship's liquid*. Before we went there for the first time, we were all made aware of the port's fearsome alcoholic reputation, of the effects it could and often *did* have on relief officers, and we were told all the stories. Unfortunately, because they were told faithfully and in full, they also included an account of the reliably restorative intervention, job-wise and in the most *cordiale* of *ententes,* of the ships' crews – especially the French – whenever real disaster threatened, so that their overall deterrent effect was minimal in most cases (not least, the way it turned out, in my own).

There was, for example, the story of the CIO back in Blighty who received a frantic cross-channel telephone message from the two (both newly arrived and on relief) Crossing Officers.

"Alan? I'm very sorry. We've – we've missed the boat back and we're still in Dieppe." The voice was subdued, shamefaced, and rightly so. Missing the Boat was the Cardinal if not quite the Papal Sin.

"*What? Missed the boat?*" Pause. "*Missed* the bloody *boat?*" Incredulous, or seeming to be. "*Both* of you?" Rage. Real. "*Right*: and *where, may* I *ask,* are your *official cases?*"

"Oh. That's another thing. Still on board. Alan, I'm so – "

"*Save it.* That's the last crossing you'll be doing *this* visit – *if* you *ever* come again. *I'll* pick up the cases, and *you'll* both be back at your home ports tomorrow. "

"All right. But how are we going to – "

"That's *your* bloody problem, and now you've got plenty of time to sort it out," and Alan slammed down the phone and began to organise a Shore Control, i.e. to call in IOs on other duties or other shifts or even on days off, to clear the boat at Newhaven when it arrived.

And by the time it did, the port was all ready to go with the extra staff poised like tense hungry tethered tigers at their desks and smiling happy hungry tigers' toothy expectant smiles, their annoyance at any personal disruption mollified by the consequential overtime to a greater or lesser degree, depending on their domestic circumstances. (Though it must be said that more rarely the first reaction of an individual thus summoned would be one of deep and instant despair, the unexpected call for help having already revealed by default to the hitherto-unsuspecting wife – or on occasion by 1973 husband too, naturally – who picked up the phone that her – or his – partner *wasn't* hard at work *already*, and was thus surely, metaphorically, *right* over the side.)

Anyway, when the boat duly docked, the CIO sped up the gangway to instruct the purser to keep everyone on board, pending the commencement of their clearance on shore.

"But why, *pourquoi,* monsieur?" Jean the purser spread his hands gallantly, gallicly – it was indeed one of the French boats. "Tout le travail, ce'st fini, *all done,*" he said. And it was. Somehow – don't ask – he'd known the combination to the IOs' safe, and somehow he'd broken undetectably into one of their secure cases – the ones with detector locks so you would know instantly if someone *had* broken in, but not this time – and *he* had sat at the IO's desks with a landing stamp and a set of SIs, and had seen and dealt with all the passengers himself. And when then naturally they checked, thoroughly, he had, *vraiment,* done an *excellent* job, indeed a true *tour de force.* The right passports had the right stamps and more than that, he had sat down three doubtfuls for further interview, all in due course refused, *and,* solo, he had cleared the whole boat.

And we were told the other story too, of the CIO who sat in his office blithely untroubled by any such call from afar, and watched the boat dock before he boarded himself at his leisure and strolled through to the IOs' office as the cars and foot passengers, all cleared, streamed off; and there, sitting demurely outside the Passport Office, were the average two hold-ups and inside on the two official desks were the two official cases, safely locked and ready for their two official owners' own disembarkation. But where the fuck were the IOs (inevitably both relief officers) themselves? *'Quis custodes ipsos custodiet?'* Or rather this time, *'Quo?',* for their seats were empty. *Maybe they've both gone to the loo,* the CIO thought nervously, perhaps already knowingly self-deceptive, and so he waited a while. But when he checked they weren't there, and now he *had* to face it.

Christ, he thought, *criminals, terrorists, poor sods, they're both over the side,* (except this time he meant *bodily*, of course), and he was about to make the urgent, irrevocable call to SB (who routinely *didn't* cross), when the purser – as it happened, Jean again – stopped him and took him back to the Passport Office and pointed silently down *behind* the desks. And *voila*, there, at ground level, horizontal, sleeping peacefully and carefully concealed from public view, were the two IOs, neatly laid out side by side, and to be fair, they *had* made a start. But then, when one after the other they had become heavily and finally fatally disguised in liquor and slid gracefully from sight, he, Jean, had taken over and finished the job.

So we listened, and *we* thought *Bollocks* too (but of an ignorant, uninformed, kind) and *Impossible,* (but in French, you know, to get in the mood). And even if the stories were true, which they *couldn't* be – after all, the detector locks were the best you could buy, they were made in *Leipzig*, in *East Germany*, for Christ's sake – *we* were made of sterner stuff. And so we went. (And in case you're afraid that such things could happen now, don't worry. The SIs are computerised so they *couldn't*, possibly, now could they? And the crossings have stopped, anyway.)

So skip to the summer of 1976, my third spell of relief and during the last two I'd seen it and done it, done it *all*, and as I looked back I *knew* I knew the score. For example, on the first day of my first spell in 1971, I'd driven into the staff car park and parked beside John's old camper which I recognised instantly because he was in it, behind the wheel and although it was half past seven in the morning, apparently fast asleep.

So I went and knocked on his window and when there was no response I opened the driver's door and he fell out at once like a log, quite like Bernie[28] later in fact but this time all of him, collapsing hard onto the gravel but pretty neatly for a big man. He lay there for a moment or two, face down and breathing heavily then quite *un*like Bernie, opened his eyes, grunted and staggered swearing to his feet.

"Are you all right?" I asked him, as one does. But his reply was inconclusive.

"Mike? What time is it?" he asked, then corrected himself – he was always a stickler for detail. "What fucking *day* is it?"

I looked at my watch. "Seven thirty, and it's Tuesday," I said. I reckoned that covered it, but added, "I'm Early Shore," to be sure. (Early Shore *Duty*, I meant.)

"*Shit*," he said, "I must've been here all night." So overall, it was probably a 'no'.

Then he got back in the van, shook his head violently, held it for a moment in both hands, shivered, groaned, swore again, then wound down his window and started the engine. "I promised Jill I'd be home before eight last night," he said. "That was my first double (he meant double *crossing*), and the bastards sent me over with – " he named a local officer, as it happened ex-Gatwick himself and infamous for his capacity to drink red wine, something for which you were bound to develop a high tolerance if you liked it and worked there full time and wanted to survive (in the job I mean, or do I). "Watch your step, mate," he said as a parting shot. "Because everything they said is *true*. It's fucking *lethal* down here." And then he accelerated hard away, in a flying shower of gravel.

Well, I didn't have to wait long to find out exactly what he meant because as I entered the office that first morning, I glanced out of the window and saw the 5/6 boat[29] coming in, well behind time, and half an hour later as I was being issued with my Newhaven stamps I glanced out again. By now all of the cleared passengers, both car and foot, were off the boat and long gone, and walking down the gangway was one of the two crossing IOs. He was chatting cheerfully to the CIO who had boarded in the usual way, and they were followed by three obvious hold-ups with a security escort. *Where's the second Crossing Officer?* I thought idly. *Perhaps he's left already.*

But he hadn't. For some distance behind the first group of IS and associated personnel a small, slow and solemn procession appeared, also descending the gangway onto the dock but with less apparent confidence. It consisted of three men in suits whom I knew I *didn't* know, fully occupied with the safe transport of a fourth whom I thought I *did*, because I recognised his (suit, I mean). It was brown and well-cut – the flares flapping in the breeze were particularly wide and fashionable, but then Ken had been a rock-star – and I thought it was his but I couldn't be sure because its wearer was horizontal and immobile and being borne carefully, bodily, by two of his minders, preceded by the third, facing backwards, who with one hand steadied the chest of the forward body-bearer, very much in the manner of a ramp ceremony except for the absence of a coffin, whilst with the other he held what was quite clearly an IO's case. And I couldn't see his (brown suit's) head either, because it was covered by some kind of presumably-protective container, which glinted from time to time in the early morning sun. Then the group disappeared beneath me into my building and soon afterwards I heard steps on the stairs and the office door opened to reveal the CIO and the first crossing IO, still chatting happily.

I was relieved. *Well, if that was Ken, he can't be too badly hurt*, I thought (unless he really was already *dead* of course, which seemed unlikely). Then I heard further, more laboured, footsteps, and gasping voices: "*Slowly* for Christ's sake, mind his *head, Jesus* he's heavy, watch it, *not too fast, I'm losing my fucking grip*," and the door opened again to reveal the case-holder closely followed by the rest of the familiar procession, but the two upright were perspiring freely now and visibly more flustered than on the gangway. The CIO who was discussing one of the hold-ups glanced back casually as they came in, then resumed his conversation.

"Put him down there – no, on the floor," someone said. "Is the bin OK? Still empty?" and someone else checked and confirmed that it was, and that it was.

"Right," someone else said. It was the first crossing IO. "Who's Early Shore?"

"I am," I said, and stepped forward smartly to introduce myself.

"Oh. Hello there," he said, "I'm Martin, a local," and as we shook hands he gestured towards the motionless shape on the floor. "Can you look after *him*? He'll be all right in a while."

"Oh. OK." I said helpfully. "Is it – "

"Yep, Ken, last crossing this spell and he overdid it a trifle. So just make sure the bucket stays in place, will you? It helps with the carpet and amplifies the sound, which can be useful if you're busy. Well, I'm off. Cheers," and he was gone, just like that. I gazed at his disappearing back, then down at Ken, and I remembered John and thought, *And we thought we could drink!*

Then I examined him (Ken) objectively. Facially, he resembled no-one so much as The Man In The Iron Mask as you'd expect, except that even that false little shit Louis had left his poor sod of a bro a few essential holes – though of course those would now have been counter-productive. So I lifted him up gently by his head or rather by his bin – a waste paper bin, which I now recognised for what it was, only shiny tin and not armour-plate after all – and then I raised it up a little further (the bin I mean, not his head, and by 'up' I mean away from his chin, to reveal the lower part of his face). And it was Ken all right, I recognised the zappa instantly, but pure white (his face generally of course, not his moustache) and truly comatose. *Well, I can at least do something useful,* I thought, and as I loosened his kipper he opened his eyes and looked up at me. It came as something of a shock when he did that, I can tell you. I'd half-thought he'd already been embalmed.

"Mike? Is that you?" he asked faintly. "Where am I?" It was just like the old horror films, but more *Carry On* than *Hammer.*

"Hello, mate," I said. "You're back in the office. Just lie there for a bit – you're looking a little pail," and we all fell about – apart from him of course, he missed it completely. OK, a cheap shot but someone had to say it, and I thought we might as well get it out of the way. Besides, it was a start to making my local number. Whilst I still could.

"Oh," he said. Then, "Can I have a pillow?"

"'Course you can," I said, "but I don't think there's much point, *or* much room. It wouldn't be very hygienic either, and you might even suffocate," and I tapped the bin with a significant look. It clanged, hollowly.

He tried to look upwards at the sound, but gave up because it obviously hurt. "Oh, he said again. "No, I suppose not," and as he shut his eyes I lowered them both again (not his eyes but the bin first, to his chin, then the bin and his head together). Then he went back to sleep, and after a while the bin indeed usefully self-amplified. But Martin had been quite right because only a little made it out onto the carpet and fair dos, we left that and the rest for Ken to clear up when he woke, and when he did he did, and that was just my introduction to the place.

Well, I've never learned that I've never learned by others' mistakes, but I had to wait another three weeks for my own comeuppance. By then an experienced campaigner or so I thought, I'd gone out on my third 5/6 with a brand-new first-time relief officer as my oppo. The theory was that *I* held *his* hand but it didn't work out that way, firstly because he was a hardened ex-matelot and secondly because our exit from Newhaven was delayed by four hours due to engine failure, so that by the time we were approaching Dieppe we'd already had over eight hours on pernod, a drink with which I was until then (*and* ever since have been, thank God) wholly unfamiliar.

So as we neared the hostile shore, I excused myself to use the toilet – "I'll only be a moment" – my very words, I felt on top of the world – and when I suddenly regained consciousness after no more than the blink of an eye, Jolly Jack was at his own official desk by my side, I was asking passengers the usual questions and we were, it seemed, about half-way home. Still, I concealed my surprise reasonably well, and basked for some time in the unusual and unexpected level of politeness, deference even, shown to me by every passenger I saw. *Cracked it at last*, I thought, yet again, and it was only when I glanced *en passant* in the toilet mirror after my first (or next) pee and stood transfixed at what I saw that the true explanation was revealed. And it was a lot more prosaic and primitive and painful to my self-esteem than that.

Because as soon as I'd stood up in the bar it had hit me (the pernod I mean), but I didn't just collapse on the spot, *that* would have been far too easy. Instead, I waited thirty seconds until I could fall down the bloody iron stairs – all the way down, two decks' worth and somehow turning corners en route like a true stunt man – and split my skull open and knock myself clean out (*Cracked it* was right), to be found shortly thereafter by members of the French crew who helpfully held my bloody head under the tap then put me to bed and, doubtless respecting my privacy, told nobody about it, including my said oppo. And in bed I remained until discovered therein and pulled thence by Jack himself, still as sober as one or two judges I know but in a right sweat because by then we were well on our way back and between us had so far cleared sweet FA.

Once woken, he said later, I had risen, followed him without a word, sat meekly down at my desk, opened my case and so far as he knew had since then operated perfectly normally. And the only trouble was that whilst my deep and exposed scalp-wound was still wide open though no longer pulsing, the initial blood-flow had now fully dried in four long, straight and rather fetching red rivulets extending down to my eyebrows and equidistant across my forehead, so that to an unsuspecting eye the overall effect must have been even more distinctly *Hammer*-like and generally quite startling – at least it quite startled *me*.

So it hadn't been public respect after all, just plain terror. Hey, ho. Still, by the time the CIO boarded I'd cleaned myself up and kept turning constantly to face him with my head tilted back, so he didn't notice a thing. And like I said, I've never touched pernod since.

Anyway, back or forward again to 1976, my third spell, and a phenomenon that hadn't happened to *me* before, though I'd heard about it from others often enough. There I was, ashore in Dieppe, and I couldn't even enter the PAF's outer steel cage, let alone reach our own *Anglais* security locker within. I'd tried and tried but the keys I'd picked up at Newhaven simply didn't work, so there I stood like a lemon with the bloody thing (my case, I mean) clutched hotly in my hand and the long, long night ahead.

Well, it was embarrassing all right, but in itself no big deal. True, you had to hang on tight to your case until you reached the Mission, but then you could fall softly sleep with a smile on your face as it nestled snugly under the bed, safely protected by *you*; and on top of that, when I'd read the standing instructions on the 9/10 crossing, part of me had remembered Jean's past efforts and thought, *You call that secure, depositing the stuff in a Frog lock-up where their own people <u>must</u> have duplicate keys and can look at the SIs or copy the stamps in the small hours on any damn night they choose?* So I was a bit miffed but not greatly upset as I rejoined the others in the *Copa* before they worked the night-crossing back.

And so far you won't have a bloody clue what I'm talking about, so I'll explain. This was my first-ever 9/10, the one on the sole Brit boat which went out in the small hours and arrived back in Newhaven at c.1200 the same day, the only solo crossing because it was routinely so clean, the passengers themselves mainly Brits too, and although you *could* go out *on* it to sleep aboard and then to work it straight back, the norm was to ship out the previous evening with the two 5/6 officers on one of the two French boats and go round to kip in the aforementioned French Seamen's Mission before going aboard fully refreshed next morning, for the trip home.

I don't know why it was standard practice to do it that way, but whatever the reason it had stood the test of time. Maybe it was because then you didn't miss a good free French dinner on the way out, and on the way back you'd still get your free *real* full English breakfast, which beat the watery free French effort (De Gaulle would have smiled vengefully to see it, hot or cold) into a cocked *chapeau* any *jour* of the *semaine*. Oh, and the PAF? The *Police de L'air et des Frontiers*, our French equivalent. I think that almost covers it.

So anyway, as I entered the *Copa*, the dockyard bar currently in favour, I endured the brief derision of my two colleagues and then settled down to the standard round each before we went our respective ways, they to re-board the 5/6 and I to stroll round the end of the harbour to sleep. I watched the clock carefully though, because it was drummed into you: *be at the Mission door by 0100 and not a minute later,* because take it or leave it, *that is when it shuts.* But I'd given myself plenty of time as I left the others still sitting there and set off, case in hand, at a brisk precautionary trot which accelerated into a headlong rush as I realised belatedly that I'd marginally misjudged the distance and, after all, might be somewhat pushing it.

In the end I reached the door at 0058 or at worst 0059 hours by the hairs on my Everite watch, and I could still see the friendly welcoming light in the doorway only twenty yards away. But as I puffed to a timely halt the glow was abruptly extinguished, and I heard the key turn in the lock. *Pas de problème*, I thought blithely, *she* (the concierge) *must be having a petit joke and will still be right there on the autre side, waiting.* And so I knocked. And then knocked and shouted. And then knocked and shouted and swore, fluently, in several languages, most generally-known and especially in French, all to no avail. The place remained as still and dark and silent as the grave, and that's when I remembered her rumoured passion against *Les Anglais* – probably something to do with the war, because then that was still the explanation for everything – so that even if she had stayed to listen to my fluent multi-lingual *mal mots*, they were no more than *musique* to her ears.

Anyway, there I was: so far it had been the Night of the

Locks, and the only right quay I'd found so far was the one I *couldn't* miss. *Still*, I thought as I stood and watched the lights of the French boat sailing away and bearing my mates safely home, *at least they can't see me*. By now a chilly mist was forming, so I donned my raincoat – good thinking at least to have brought *that* – and began to trudge back slowly towards the bright lights of town.

It's only France, after all, I thought sagely. *The night is still young and I could easily find a local auberge and put my head down. My boat isn't due to dock until 0600, so there's bags of time for a few hours' good, restorative sleep.*

But *then* I thought, *On the other hand this is also La Belle France, and I could simply return to the Copa to while the night away because I'm young too, like the night, and I feel fine and can kip later and my boat will be arriving any minute so there's no point in getting my head down. Now is there?*

So I chose the second of the two extremes, *quelle surprise*, and whilst I can't pretend that booze had nothing to do with it, there was another reason, a general lightness of heart – or even, as some say these days, of being. Because I was still basking in the knowledge that for the second time in my life the home fire was not just lit but burning brightly, ardently, *fiercely* even, or at least it was about to in reality and already was inside my head, because the beautiful, wonderful woman I had been pursuing assiduously for the last two years – yes, that very same bitch who'd historically, albeit allegedly unknowingly, given me two metaphorical fingers at Shoreham – had finally been won over or perhaps just worn down[30] by my dogged persistence, but either way we were now *engaged* and I simply *could not* get over it.

So back to the *Copa* I went, to be received with minimal surprise by the barman. Hmm. Was the concierge perhaps on a percentage? That's how you get when your job engenders a suspicious mind. Anyway, soon I neither knew nor cared what time it was, nor whose fault, nor how much brandy I'd drunk, though Emile gave me a distinct clue on the latter when I signalled manually (because I found I could no longer speak) for another, by returning with a brim-full balloon on the house. But even as I raised it to my lips the air was rent by shouts, the thudding of feet and the squeal of whistles as the fucking police raided the place.

One moment the café was heaving and the next nigh-on empty, with bodies jammed in the doorway yelling 'cops' and yelling cops and fleeing figures everywhere. *Nigh-on* I say, for one person, only one, *was* left, displaying typical appropriate British sangfroid, yeah, *me* – well, I was just pissed really, so it took me longer than anyone else to register what the hell was going on and also affected my judgement when I did, because there is a strong argument that I should've done exactly what I've just described and continued to sit there on my stool, calmly sipping my brimming sauce as like Roger Moore I held up a languid warning *Saintly* hand at the onrushing officers, who in their turn would have ground to a jostling foreign halt before me, stunned to humble silence by my insouciance until I deigned to address them – *"Alors messieurs, ça va?"* – and slowly produced my warrant – *"Commisair Anglais,"* – to the infinite and delightful frustration of the French Forces of Justice.

But on the other hand they might have just beaten the crap out of me before I could say a word – just two minutes previously remember, I'd found I *couldn't* speak anyway – and besides, what I *did* do was rather different. Have *you* ever tried to keep a level head when all around you others are losing theirs? It's what I was supposed to do for a living after all, but it's not so bloody easy when the *frites* are *right* down, especially in the land of the looming (and then still thirsty) guillotine and when you've got no-one to think about except yourself. So whatever the reason, there were no Ifs and Buts about it, that night I was *not* a Man my Son because when *les autres* legged it, I ran *aussi* but behind, and later, pausing only to thrust my now-trembling *jambs* into my raincoat and to snatch up my *petit valise.*

And thus the movie continued, but definitely a *Hammer* now – or perhaps still a *Carry On,* because as we all erupted through the door with me firmly in the rear, two spare *flics* challenged me. But they were still yards away and everyone else had turned sharp right so I turned sharp left and left again to rub it in because I was British, or just pissed, and ran like hell away from the quay with the pair of them after me. My raincoat billowed round my legs, the mist was much thicker now and any chance Brit spectator would have thought it a strange sight, perhaps worthy of a Del' Boy Christmas Spectacular, Fools if not Horses too. Because pounding ponderously out of the mirk, breath pluming, teeth bared, raincoat flapping and flourishing his black doctor's bag came a balding bespectacled Dracula, hotly pursued by two mini-Caped Crusaders. And then they, *we*, were all gone again, swallowed up and vanishing wraith-like, in the blink of an eye.

But despite disappearances I was still going at top speed and no mere Trotter when I suddenly sobered up and realised what I should have done, five minutes and five hundred paces too bloody late. *Shit! But I can't stop now*, I thought between gasps. *If I do, the locals are sure to give me a swift passage à tabac* (a good official French thumping) *before I can say a bon mot, and God knows what will happen when, if, I get home. But if I don't, they'll catch or maybe even shoot me – oh, this fucking, fucking bag!* I couldn't drop it, but it was starting to weigh a ton: heroin or swag to them, evidence anyway, and well worth taking their own pot at me if they had to.

Another hundred yards, and I was still going fairly strong when I came to a T-junction and saw at last why everyone else had turned right. Because I had reached the fucking *plage* not the town centre, and the sea-front road, traffic-and people-free, lay dead ahead, brightly, incandescently lit until it too vanished abruptly and silently into the thick and dripping mist. It ran as straight as a *flèche* to the left and bent away seawards to the right, heading towards the invisible harbour. On its far side was a waist-high wall, beyond that nothing but fog and total darkness, and as I slowed in an agony of indecision, *gauche* or *droit,* above my panting I could hear the steady hiss and suck of the cruel and hungry sea.

So I looked over my shoulder and saw nothing, although I could hear their footsteps pounding up behind me. Then there they were, at first just vague dark moving forms in the mist, then rapidly taking shape as real men with real guns, now really drawn. They saw me too and came on, dropping to walking pace. It was their *ville* after all, and they knew I had nowhere to go.

But suddenly I had other ideas. It wasn't a conscious decision, simply that the consequence of my capture didn't bear contemplation. Or it could just have been the heady cocktail of alcohol, adrenalin and panic, or maybe even too many re-runs of *The Great Escape*, who knows? Anyway, I took a firmer, no, a convulsive grip on my bag, yelled out "Fuck it!" aloud, which seemed good enough as a potential epitaph, especially when given in evidence at the Post Mortem, and sprinted directly across the road at my highest speed yet. My own *passage* generated twin startled shouts of *'Arrêtez!'* and *'Merde!'*, perhaps because it was strictly <u>non</u>-*tabac or* perhaps as a simple reflection on the different personal or job philosophies of the two *flics* as they saw me vault high and fast over the sea wall and again vanish abruptly, legs flailing, into the black and mist-filled void beyond, straight through the sci-fi looking glass of the next decade.

Well, so far, so good etc., and it wasn't until I was airborne that it struck me that the tide might be in. But it was out, right out instead, so I was spared the immediate prospect of a watery grave and the spectacular exit that *that* would have enjoined, the Lad in the Lake, one arm upraised in ultimate defiance as it disappeared slowly beneath the waves for the third and last time, hand still clutching his Excalibur-case; and instead I just landed heavily, loudly and prosaically enough in deep shale, by some miracle not only feet first but without breaking or even spraining an ankle. Behind me the wall, much higher on this side, loomed large through the darkness, silhouetted black against the haze beneath the street lights as I scrambled swiftly and noisily back up the slope just for somewhere to go, and cowered gasping under its defensive concavity.

I heard the two of them run up – *So at least I've made you run encore, mes petits braves,* I thought with perverse and resigned satisfaction, as they stopped, looked about them and began to chatter to each other, '*Disparu*', etc. Then they shone their torches out to sea and along the beach but it was real fog down there and reflected the beams straight back at them. Still, all they had to do to find me was to lean out and look straight down, and I waited hopelessly for my discovery.

And they didn't do it. Maybe they never thought that anyone could be so *stupide* as not again to leg it – maybe it wasn't a Gallic thing not to do, and of course they didn't know I was an Anglais. Perhaps my sudden disappearance had unnerved them, or they were over-tired, or just plain disinterested – they really should at least have clocked the *silence*, the total absence of my *pieds* on the *pierres*. Anyway, I wondered later how they wrote it up and whether they conducted a sea search in the morning, but I would've had to have been an Olympic long jumper to get even my toes wet.

After a while they went away, and as soon as I could hear nothing but the waves I walked a few yards away down into the fog, wrapped my now-sodden raincoat closely around me and lay down awkwardly on the sloping, soaking, shingle, *tête* on *valise*. The sounds of the continuing general search continued inshore for some time – shouts and whistles, and was there an occasional shot? But *personne* came back.

I awoke shivering violently to the blast of a foghorn right in my ear, and as I raised my head into the lightening day the first thing I saw was the superstructure of my very own 9/10 boat, floating high above the layered fog as it passed by, no more than fifty yards out on its way in, and it was only when I staggered to my feet that I found that I had chosen to relax in a pool of tar which, liberally sprinkled with shale, now not only covered a large part of my coat but was deep in my hair and beard. *'I look how I feel,'* I thought, in a sublime flash of self-discovery. And I felt like death.

I peered at my watch in the swift-growing light: it was a little past six, and I started to trudge along the beach after the boat, still invisible from the sea wall because of the fog (me, I mean). But things generally were improving. After a while I didn't feel like death any more, just like shit, and shallow shit at that. Then, as my mood like the day began to lighten still further, I rallied a little. *I'm on the beach, at a low ebb and all washed up,* I mused cleverly, *and my hopes for the future have been litorally pebble-dashed*, a real smart-arse. But I was alive, it wasn't far to the docks and I was closing unobserved on my floating sanctuary which I could see again now, moored up just ahead and promising a hot shower and even breakfast too, if I could stomach it. *I might still just get out of this,* I thought – but alas prematurely, because that was when a new *flic* appeared round the corner, young, keen and worst of all, crème-fresh on duty.

And so I finally surrendered to fate and accepted that the Night of the Long Locks hadn't nearly finished with me yet. *I'll go quietly, doucement,* I thought in something like relief as he approached. *God, he's young, he must be the dock's own green Dixon,* but I didn't say any of *that* out loud either, of course. Then, *"Tu,"* – peremptory, the way French police speak to lesser mortals if they speak at all, and accompanied by the beckoning paramilitary finger that brooks no argument – *"Tu, que fais-tu ici? Papiers!"* and he was already relishing his triumph when, several hours too late but in the current nick of *temps* my brain leapt into some semblance of pond-life and I produced my warrant, albeit with a severely shaking hand: "Bonjour, monsieur. *Ça va?* Commisair Anglais!"

Well, give him his due, he crumpled instantly and *sans demur*. Perhaps he clocked the royal crest on the bag or perhaps he simply recognised that the contradiction between my appearance and my documentation meant that my claimed status *had* to be true – who but Les Anglais? In any event, he didn't even take a closer look: a second's frank incredulity, then a gallic shrug of resigned disbelief, a muttered *"Merci, monsieur,"* and even a grudging salute: at least he had a good story for his *amis*, and if later in the day anyone put *deux and deux* together, linked the missing/presumed drowned *cochon* of a drug dealer with the later appearance of a foreign official madman and made it *cinq*, it would get even better.

Thus to the deck guard, Brit of course, and another one who'd seen it all before. *He* just gave me a silent appraising grin (doubtless another fucking ex-matelot) and waved me aboard with a mock flourish, and once in the cabin I managed to clean off the most prominent facial encrustations before the first passengers began to embark. By then there was no time for breakfast anyway so I couldn't bring it up, and the crossing was as quiet and unremarkable as had been predicted until – no hold-ups, most people seen and no-one else in sight – I slipped out (again) to the loo next door, leaving my equipment unsecured – another cardinal sin, but I was only going to be two shakes and wholly forgot *déjà vue*.

So: I probably *had* only been out for a few seconds when I came to, lying face up on the deserted toilet floor. But either way when I got back to the office it was still empty and nothing had been touched as far as I could tell, and there was only one more passenger to see, a young attractive Czech who would have been fine too if she hadn't been in the bloody SI, a security case but nothing to shout about – on the contrary indeed, one to keep quiet – and I had it all sorted before we docked. When we did, the boss came on board as usual and I told him of the Czech and made the obligatory call, and that was the end of it. I didn't tell him about my busy night, though. Well, there was no point in stirring up extra trouble for myself, was there?

Well, I did one more 9/10, on my next and final spell of Newhaven relief. And the only thing that went wrong *then* was that I grossly (and I *mean* gross) misjudged a young broke Yank whom I allowed secretly to share my room in the Mission. I've wondered since whether I wasn't as much unconsciously cocking a vengeful Anglo-Saxon snook at *madame* as showing genuine charity to *him*, but either way he repaid my trans-ocean fellowship by departing early and leaving a truly monumental turd in the wash basin. Still, at least *I* found and removed it, as I hope he intended, and thank God for that because otherwise it would have provided further solid grounds for the concierge's hatred of the British.

So the only problematic legacy from my various times at Newhaven is a relatively new one. Because my wife has always known about my night on the beach, of course; but it was only after I'd shown her the first draft of this epistle that she reminded me that I'd always told *her* that the only thing that the chasing coppers drew, apart from deep breaths, was their batons. I'd never mentioned their guns you see, and if they'd clocked her first reaction when she read the truth, they might have felt that *they* had won our duel, albeit once removed, after all.

LORDS OF THE RING

Gatwick still, that same long hot summer of '76 and in front of me the entire National Wrestling Squad from – I was going to name a continent at least, but on second thoughts let's just say 'afar,' and in transit to Canada for that year's Olympics. Ordinarily you made each individual in any apparent group see a separate IO to compare their stories, but this time the seven in immaculate and identical blazers and flannels stood out. *Aha. A team,* I thought, because I'm quick like that. So I waved to the presenter, "It's all right, let 'em all come together," and they did, proving to be six wrestlers and their manager plus an eighth in mufti, aptly enough tagging along, whose relevance, if any, to the proceedings was yet to be determined.

Without a word the six lined up as if I'd ordered them to

dress by the right, the smallest, a diminutive fly-weight, at one end and the largest, the super-heavy – and he *was large,* not *tall* like Ethan, but *wide* – at the other. Three – the small ones or at least shorter than I was, who for some reason put me in mind of enlarged Vietnamese – grinned hugely up at me. But the other three didn't, *they* glowered grimly down instead whilst I, outnumbered and potentially outflanked, smiled back obligingly at all six as the manager produced all their passports.

"Good morning, sir," he said in fair English. A standard opening, without significance, so "Hello there," I replied, conscious still of the temperature range between the warmth of the smiles and the chill of the glares as I tried to concentrate on my task. "How long will you be staying?" (Technically, by then the question should have been, 'How long do you *intend* to stay,' to satisfy the clever-clever appeal lawyers. But none of us knew that, or at least *I* didn't, and anyway the way things turned out, it didn't matter.)

"Just overnight, sir," the manager said. Then, proudly indicating his charges stood there silently at semi-attention, their expressions still neatly and dramatically split down the middle, "We are the ------- Olympic Wrestling Team, as you see; I am the manager, and we leave from Heathrow for the Games in Canada tomorrow."

"I see," I said, and this time I really did. All eight of them had dated onward tickets and seven of them had UK 'Transit' visas too, although they weren't compulsory.

"And who exactly is *this* gentleman?" I asked shrewdly, indicating the eighth, the one without visa or uniform and a physical reed by comparison, who was standing off a little to one side.

"Oh, that is my son and assistant," the manager replied,

and then he too grinned, almost apologetically. "He is – how d'you say – a late starter."

"OK, thanks. I hope you have a successful time," I said insincerely as I stamped them up. I meant it to apply to all of them but found that I was addressing the three large glowerers in particular, and arguably with more insincerity. And then, half-expectantly, I watched them disappear in a body towards the escalator and the Customs Hall. But no commotion ensued so I reckoned they'd encountered escalators before, and had made it.

By this time I'd been in the job for over 6 years and I was good at it, I knew I was – no, I really *was*. So I hadn't bothered to check them in the SI because it was all clearly above-board and I was a sound, seasoned judge of men. And I turned happily enough for a word with the Duty CIO, yet another Scotsman new to the port, as he loomed, on tiptoe, by my shoulder.

"Hello, Mike," he said, "who were that lot?" and I told him.

"Oh," he said, and paused; then, "Did you look them up?" Smart-arse: he always had to have the last word.

"No, Brian," I said, a little testily. "I'll do it now," and I started on their landing cards. I'd done three and was beginning to chose the words to let him know gently but firmly that *I* wasn't the new boy round here, when there it was in black and white. Number Four, the manager's son, was *In the Bloody Book*, he'd been *refused* a UK visa for Christ's sake. The only one visa-less and in mufti and so the readily identifiable odd man out and I'd damn-well missed him! And more than that, somehow I must have missed the visa refusal signal[31] too!

By then the CIO had moved away, and I went after him. "Brian," I said hastily, my cutting phrase long forgotten, "one of them *is* in the book – he's been refused a visa. Sorry." Well, Brian didn't turn a hair, but just nodded and twisted the dirk. "Only one?" he asked, a *real* smart-arse, and I squirmed internally.

"Well," I said, "I've only checked four, but – "

"Leave the cards for the others, *we'll* check them," he said. "Now, *go and get him back.*"

I stared at him for a second – the prevailing view then was still that once a passenger had left our vicinity duly stamped, and certainly if he had passed through Customs, he was home and dry so far as the On Entry control was concerned[32], always providing he wasn't sprinting, or hurdling, or 20 going on 65: then, "*Right,*" I said, and ran up the stairs and into the Customs Hall. *Bugger,* there was no sign of them, and I sped – no, by then staggered – out onto the concourse, still zilch, and on again out into the blinding sun of the pick-up area. And there they were, just getting into two taxis.

"*Oi!*" I shouted – no, by then gasped – "*You!*" And the manager turned, saw me and went pale. He knew what was coming of course but tried to act the innocent for a moment longer; and I couldn't blame him. After all, it would be stupid if you'd fooled a total tosser once, not to try again. "Yes, sir," he said. "Is something wrong?"

I was pretty angry, with myself mostly, but he'd done his bit too. So, "Yes," I said, between gasps, "and you bloody well know what it is." And that was when he nodded, and gave up.

"Yes," he said. "It is my son – he really *is* my son," and he beckoned him from the cab, where he had been sitting peering nervously out at the pair of us.

"All right," I said. "The others can get out and wait inside, but I need you two. Come with me," and they followed me like lambs back through Customs and down into the Arrivals

Hall. "Got him," I reported to Brian, "and the other one's.his father and the team's manager," and he nodded his head in satisfaction, though whether that was purely at a job belatedly well done I don't know: he was a Scot and I was English, remember. Then I took a deep breath. "And the others?"

"No," he said, and I heaved a sigh of relief. It could have been worse, and I couldn't have run another yard.

In due course and despite his father's half-hearted protestations, I refused the son. He soon admitted that he had fuck-all to do with the Team, and for a while I pretended that I was seriously thinking of sending Dad back with him too for aiding and abetting. But we'd already decided that to muck up the whole outfit could result in a diplomatic incident which for good reasons – the CIO's more readily officially acceptable than mine – we both wanted to avoid. So I contented myself with binning the son pending removal, breathed a further heartfelt sigh and got back to work. OK, so I wasn't *that* good, after all.

The next day, as soon as I'd confirmed that removal had been effected, I settled down to write my report. No doubt it was largely the relief and a touch of residual rebound bravado, but I decided that I would write a humdinger – you couldn't do it now, or at least, nobody *would*. 'The passenger,' I wrote, 'tried to pass himself off as a member of The ----- National Wrestling Team, but I saw straight through *his* game.' *Hmm, bit of a truncation of events and time-frame there,* I thought, *but never mind,* and continued. 'In fact, he tried to run rings round me but I knew the ropes, so I wasn't thrown and soon had him cornered and pinned whereupon he rapidly submitted, and was removed as shown above.'

I put it up through Brian who read it, grinned himself this time because it was his turn and signed it off unchanged. He knew I'd learnt my lesson – I had – and it must have been eighteen months or more and I'd already moved to Heathrow when the first phone call came, asking for me by name.

"Hello?" I said, "Mike Clarke." I suppose if I'd known what was coming, I might have tried a complete alias but it would only have delayed things and anyway, in a crowded office? Probably not.

"Hello," said the voice. "Is that the Mike Clarke who was at Gatwick two years back?" (By then there were three of us in the job, at different ports, and very handy it proved to be from time to time for each of us. Eventually, the question became, 'Is that the *real* Mike Clarke,' and no doubt all three of us truthfully answered 'Yes' to that, too.)

"Yes," I said, "that's me." Well, it was, wasn't it?

"Mike," said the voice. "Hello. You don't know me, but I'm," – he gave his name, and I got to know him later – "and I'm at the IU (The Service's old Intelligence Unit at Harmondsworth). I'm just reading your refusal report on that geezer who pretended to be with the ------- Wrestling Team. D'you remember it?"

"Yes," I said proudly, how could I forget, and I'd never not looked anyone up in the Book after that, either.

"I haven't read one like it before," he said. "It's quite funny," and I preened myself again – metaphorically that is, because I was already well on the way to premature baldness.

"Yes," he said, and then he paused, and I felt the first slight flutter of concern. "It's just that -" he continued, then paused again. "Well, d'you remember the rest of the team, the other seven?"

"Er. Yes?" I said, and my concern grew.

"Well," he said, "I thought I'd better let you know that

we've just picked one up on the street, the first as far as I can tell. He never left."

"*What?* Oh," I said, and tried not to because things were already bad enough, but it had to be asked. "You said 'the first'?"

"Yes," he said. "Once we'd got him, we checked on the others as well, and *none* of the buggers left, *not one.* But don't worry, we'll find them all eventually."

"Right," I said, abashed – it was like a re-run of the whole bloody case. "Thanks. Thanks very much," and rang off. And the caller was true to his word because for several years after that, roughly once a year, the phone would ring to say that they *had* caught *another* one, and how funny the report was, but not in that order.

So: talk about setting yourself up for a fall. Sometimes, it's not just that you can't win 'em all: you can't even win *one round.*

SOUND OF FATE

In April 1977 I finally married my second wife. And after the sudden crumbling of all that earlier stout resistance (hers, I mean) it's worth a line – or even a page or two – to describe how it finally happened, the strange thing being that this time *she* started it – well, she had to (not that she knew what she was doing at the time) because that Shoreham business (even though it had only lasted a week) had put me *right* off, not that I'm complaining now. And (as miracles are wont to do) it came out of the blue; and it went like this.

"Oh, hello Mike," she said brightly one white winter's day, *suspiciously* brightly so far as I was concerned, although we were on standard cordial speaking terms. So I hid my surprise, my *double* surprise because she'd clearly sought *me* out specifically to boot, and played it cool (I did, I mean). So, "Hello, Beth," I replied, coolly – well, I couldn't go far wrong with *that*, could I – and waited.

"Um, Mike," she said, then paused. "I've been meaning to ask you something."

Oh–oh, I thought. "*Oh-yes?*" I said.

"Well, er, have you heard that we're giving a New Year's Eve party, us four girls in the flat?" Now she sounded far too *casual*, and yet oddly tentative.

Heard? *Heard?* Of *course* I'd bloody heard. "No," I said, "I must have missed it," as I felt the first faint spark of hope begin to flicker weakly in my heart, if not yet (or still no longer) in my groin.

But her? She seemed to be becoming more uneasy and embarrassed by the minute. "No? Oh. Well anyway, it's a general invitation to the whole office – fancy dress optional. Um, do you think you can come?"

Instant expiry of spark, wherever it was. *Thanks for making it so personal,* I thought limply. "Well, I don't know, but I doubt it – it depends on my housekeeper."

"Oh. Oh yes, of course, the children," followed by a brief pause; and then in a brisk rush, "well anyway, if you can, could we *possibly* borrow your sound system?" So, *You bloody bitch,* I thought viciously. Again. But she was only obeying the first law of female survival, *always* hit a man hard where it hurts whether he's up *or* down, and she *had* said it awkwardly which was the bloody least she could do, given that the date was already December 30th. But I managed a weak smile. Or a weak grimace, anyway.

"Beth, you *shall* have it whether I come or not," I said grandly, thinking only of the stereo and barely resisting the strong temptation to tell her precisely where to install it unless – vain and wondrous vision, because the truth was that I still fancied her like mad – she'd let me do it for her. And then I played my unlooked-for ace as I heard myself say, "So long as I can take you out to dinner afterwards," and OK, now it was *my* turn to rush, and she hesitated just long enough to demonstrate her extreme reluctance. But sound systems were clearly in critically short supply, and we both knew it. So, "All right," she said. OK, grudgingly, but it was still a real triumph. I bowled her over, just like that.

And I *did* go, of course. My housekeeper was already tied up but I spent a fortune I didn't have (six months' Angel Delights-worth, the poor kids) to get a baby sitter who could come early, so that having told the said bloody bitch that I would just drop the stuff in with no guarantee of a later personal return, I appeared at the flat in good time to set it up *and* stay on.

Things, however, did not start well. *"Mike,"* she said as she opened the door with every appearance of pleasure, which only shows how similar it must be to relief. "I'm *so* glad you could come (glancing quickly at the stereo) – and wow, that's *some* fancy dress. Panam, or USAF?" She was obviously making a real effort.

"What?" I said, momentarily mystified, then made a real effort myself. "Oh, that. Yes. Thanks." *For nothing,* I thought. Because I *never* wear fancy dress – well, not deliberately. But I hung around after I'd done my stuff, helping with other preparations until the thing actually kicked off – *No harm in seeing who she's here with,* though *Nothing like a spot of masochism* was nearer the truth. Then we were all ready and anxious in

the pre-party lull and she'd got me a drink at least and at last, when the door-bell rang and my hopes, and anything else that might have been half-raised, slowly sank.

"*Ronald!* Mike, Ronald. Ronald, Mike. Mike's someone I work with and he's been helping us set up." Hell's bells, a Man Mountain a full head taller, with a laser gaze and a handshake from a crushing machine. Then instant relief *and* pleasure, and not just when he released my hand, "Ronald's my older brother," and a miracle too because no-one else came to claim her, and barring the odd dance later, mostly with me – those *very* odd, you've never seen me dance – she was and remained alone.

She drank white wine sparingly from a steel goblet whilst I drank furiously of and from anything I could lay my hands on in the best Service tradition apart from the nerves, and soon developed a strong – nay, an irresistible – aversion towards a large, overstuffed and intolerably loud gorilla already well in its simian cups, whose speech and manner seemed to me to reveal ever more clearly that it was a particularly obnoxious member of that particular rude primate sub-species which, in zoos and humans apart, takes a particular pride in the wanton exhibition of its particularly-swollen and bright-red arse.

And since I couldn't see his (or its) already on display, I proposed equally loudly first to uncover and then to stuff it, with or without his (or its) consent. But she, *she,* stopped me, trying to be severe but giggling convulsively instead and it was the first time I'd ever seen her eyes truly lit up and smiling at *anyone* let alone *me*, and if I hadn't been madly in love with her before (which as you might already have guessed, I had), I was now.

As midnight chimed, we kissed perfunctorily the way you do but only each other, and then she let me take her fully in my arms but still held her head away and the world stopped as we danced on in the bubble – well, I did anyway – and that was when she turned and looked me in the eye for a long, long moment like Fran Kubelik does with C.C. Baxter at the very end of *'The Apartment',* and whatever she saw there it wasn't only lust although I was well-pissed and that must have been a part of it and besides we were still very close and she *must* have noticed that I wasn't just shaken but stirred.

Then we slow, slow-danced for a long, long time, to *my* speakers, and the party was still in full swing when we left together for the all-too-short short drive in for the all-too-early early shift and we didn't hold hands but sat shyly apart like a couple of teenagers and I thought in disbelief, *Something's happening to me all right.* Corny? You'd better believe it. But real, and sexy too, in an all-too-possibly-pending kind of way? Roger *that.*

And the promised dinner? That wasn't due for another week, and I didn't do myself any favours meantime because our shifts hadn't matched again since, and I hadn't seen or called her. I wasn't playing it cool now though, it was cowardice pure and simple and I'd known all along that the speakers were shot anyway. But when I knocked again to take her down to Brighton she was ready and waiting, on naval time and truly stunning as usual. And me? This time I wore my best Italian suit – well, my *only* suit as it happened, of any nationality, apart from my US fancy dress. So she took one look, sighed and fell into my arms without a word? Did she hell, but there you go.

We went to the *'Pirandello',* as Italian as the suit – tiny, 'intimate' and 'romantic', the bistro I mean – with four long refectory tables against each side-wall and another small short one in the front bay window (turn sharp left as you enter) perched on a raised railed balcony abreast of the door and overlooking the rest. And they took one look at *us* and gave us the balcony, the romantic devils – or sadistic swine, depending on your point of view.

The place was packed out but we were insulated by the height and rail, the candles lit and the food good, our waiters inevitably enchanted by Beth and enviously contemptuous of me – or vice versa with the adverbs – and despite my week-long juvenile fears we were deep, deep in animated conversation when it started, right there, in front of and beneath us. (No, *no*, the bloody *riot* is what I'm talking about, although I couldn't help noticing that her mini-skirt *had* ridden up, just a tad, and it wasn't my heart I was worried about, nor thank God was it on my sleeve either. Still, she showed no sign of having noticed which is a pretty good way of cooling a man down in its own right, and I consoled myself with the dubious thought that if she had, she must have been well-used to it by now.)

So, the riot. At first we hardly noticed, it was just a few words between the men on the tables below us, on the left – "*Oi. Mate.* Keep the noise down a bit *please,* d'you *mind*?" But then their women glowered and brooded and goaded them on, and it kicked straight off. Hair was pulled and punches thrown and suddenly it had spread to the whole of the main floor and nobody noticed us at all but we stopped talking all the same because it's hard to concentrate when cutlery is flying past your ears. And now we did hold hands, tight, to watch spellbound. It was straight out of the movies, Dodge City complete with the shattered plates and breaking chairs but real wood, not balsa, and which one of the mad stupid fuckers was Feral Flynn?

Not that the waiters helped. They'd run wailing into the

kitchen right at the start and now the cooks came spilling out, shouting and brandishing meat cleavers in a most *un*helpful way. And us? One of the first things you picked up in the job was an ability regularly to talk people down (as well as up every now and then, when the mood suited). But we agreed tacitly that this was not a suitable time and place for us to intervene – in other words, it would be both useless *and* bloody dangerous – so we just sat there as the battle raged.

Then finally the police arrived, a man and a boy, and we looked on freshly entranced as the older one, blissfully and you might say criminally unaware that we were there, idled and sidled just inside the door, generously letting his young mate calm things down single-handed whilst *he* sashayed to the left then began to flex his legs rhythmically like any decent pantomime constable (or be-frosted Branch officer) should, fumbling behind him on every down-stroke first to nick and then swiftly to consume yet another item from the sweet trolley. What *is* it with me and coppers? But we kept his secret, and he never even knew we were there.

When it was all over the manager picked his way through the mess to see us. *Ah, an apology,* I thought, *that's nice.* But No. "Hey, *you-a*. (He meant *me-a*.) We-a never 'adda no trouble befora. The firsta tima *you-a* comma, *this* 'appens!" The little Eyetie shit, so this was all *our* fault, and my mind raced as I speculated wildly about Italians whom I'd refused way back in the non-EC past – that's also what the job does to you – or who perhaps had been sworn at by Pat, and I grabbed the menu. But there was no mention of *'vendetta'* under the cold anti-pasta, even by proxy, so perhaps it was down to mere suit-envy or perhaps he just couldn't help it – after all, he was excited and Eyetie, an unfortunate if inevitable combo at the best of times – and his next sally proved it, "*Donna* you-a

comma *bakka*." And I said *nothinga* and we *lefta* and we never
did go *bakka, evva*. We hadn't *paida*.

In the car we looked at each other with the same question.
"Is this a normal evening for *you*?" Then we laughed and drove
back up the A23 to my house but slowly and happily this time,
and when we finally got there she sat close, my arm around
her, whilst I read her Shakespeare's Sonnets, those glorious
long legs (hers) stretched out before my disbelieving eyes (I'd
long since got used to my own legs, anyway).

She'd worn a mini-skirt (like I said), and high boots (I
hadn't mentioned them though), and it was now that a variety
of ideas irresistibly entered my head. But I contrived to ignore
them all, because a) I wasn't sure which to try first; b)) I was
pretty certain that whichever I chose, the result would be the
same – a swift and experienced elbow (or worse, knee) in the
groin, which prospect scared me shit- if not quite nut-less; c)
I was *already* scared shit-less (though *not* nut-less) anyway; and
d) (please forgive my numerical directness) much as I dearly
wanted to give her one then, on the spot, I *didn't* want it to be
a one-*off* because I already knew that what I really wanted was
to give her one, or perhaps two or maybe even *several, whenever*
I wanted, *indefinitely*, and one of the perverse (but not sexually)
reasons for *that* was that I knew that to achieve it, if ever I
could, would take time, and somehow I wanted that too.

Well, that's love I suppose, and I never said that sex wasn't
part of it, did I? But winning the mind-game hands-down
(not strength of will though, just plain fear) was one thing,
subduing the inevitable physical Battle of the Bulge quite
another, and it was only much later that she told me just
how much she had silently enjoyed my (as I'd thought, well-
hidden) discomfiture, which *she* said, *I* thought somewhat
sniffily, had been "all-too-readily apparent". (A real bitch, like

I've already said. Twice.) Still, when I dropped her off (from the car, I mean), we *did* share a *real* kiss, so I *had* achieved Stage One of Idea One, finally, and the others would surely follow, as in the fruitful fullness of time they all (though not simultaneously) did.

So that was the start of it, and things went rapidly downhill until there was only one thing left outstanding: marriage. And Beth had made it crystal clear well beforehand that there was only one condition attached to *that*, namely that she *would not* live – not for long, anyway – in any house previously inhabited by my ex-wife, which was fair enough – she was after all taking on my two young children.

And so, since I couldn't afford to move myself, the way forward was clear. To London Heathrow, LHR, I would go, where they always desperately needed staff, even by Gatwick standards; and so on a government-assisted transfer my application was granted in two weeks, a record at the time and perhaps a reflection on my worsening relationship with some of the local management, though I could be entirely wrong.

And what I was about to do, though not without precedent, was still extremely rare – you went to *The* Airport, then the largest in the world, *ab initio* or from a seaport, not from the second largest airport in the UK where you'd already done your porridge – but, I thought, it would give me a clear advantage compared to the other transferees: only half a new boy.

Anyway, they gave me a final night duty, like Sam's with another hand-picked crew, and at least *I* made it through to the small hours. But then I made the big mistake of taking a "little nap", and when they woke me up at 0530 for the early New York and Lagos flights I tried to decline on the basis of ill-health. OK, I truly felt like shit and it wasn't *my* twenty-first, but I can't deny that it was a disgraceful dereliction of duty which anyway cut no ice whatsoever with my colleagues who, as I cowered cravenly in my sleeping bag, simply dragged it out and deposited it on the Control with me naked within it.

Then it was birthday bonfire night all over again, with passengers simply stepping over me without a second glance as I lay there until eventually I cracked and did a perfect Effie, leaping high and two-footed back into the office in my private but all too public version of the sack race, my head on fire and feeling violently sick.

And where exactly, in June 1977, was I going? Well, it was inevitable: to Terminal *Three*, *The* Terminal of *The* Airport. As those already there described *themselves*, of course.

Chapter Three

THREE

Christ was it big, *and* busy, and although Gatwick had been a damned good preparation, I'd never seen anything like it. So big in fact that the IOs had to be split into three rooms, Red, Green and Blue, to give them any sense of group identity; and so busy that more often than not the pen, aptly named, where we put detainees when we first held them up, was pure bloody bedlam.

But let's start away from the control – with the staff car park in fact, the first shock after the gentle ten-minutes' walk (or even the occasional quarter-hour's bowl-less stagger) at Gatwick. Because Northside, the Heathrow park for all newcomers and for your next seven or eight years after that until you'd done your *local* porridge, was two miles off and you did those by staff bus, without *too* long a wait if you were lucky. And if coming into work that way was bad enough, waiting to go home knackered in a peevish pissed-off bus queue on a dark cold winter's evening was a lot, lot worse.

It had its compensations though. Because once in a while the return bus would just have reached its Northside goal when someone – man or woman, it happened to both, it could be any airport worker, BAA, us, customs, aircrew, ground-crew, handler, cleaner, *anyone*, and it always seemed to be someone who'd had to *stand* on the bus as well – would, out of nowhere and seemingly quite involuntarily, suddenly spring to jerky life and with real venom yell out *'Shit!'* or *'Fuck!'*, one or the other, but in my own observation never both.

Those really were the only words that I ever heard (though I suppose you can't wholly discount the likelihood of an occasional *'Bugger!'* from a workforce so large), or that, when it happened to me, twice, I used myself in the particular, peculiar circumstance which applied. And in a few short years those two alternative monosyllables had already achieved the status of a race memory for audience as well as speaker, because you knew the instant you heard either that some poor sod had just remembered far too late that that day, for whatever reason, he/she had parked in the bloody *Centre*; and it sent a familiar thrill of pleasure, a real *Schadenfreude*, through you – well, through me, anyway: *It could have been me*, you thought or perhaps, better and more satisfying still, *Last time, it was me*. And then the rest of us would look at each other under lowered lids whilst we all smiled in the same false sympathy oft displayed by other women towards the ugliest one in the room. (And by the way, both times when it *was* me, I favoured *'Shit!'*, don't ask me why.)

But the best sensation of all was when you were going *into* work early in the morning and boarding at Stop A – and A only, because when the bus reached there it was about to begin its way back into the Centre again right after dropping off at all stops, so logically it *had* to be empty. But if it *wasn't*, and if there was a single passenger already on board and sitting red-faced and embarrassed in a corner and trying to shrink through the floor – or even sometimes, delight of delights, *two* of them, and *together, and extra red,* which increased the speculative options wonderfully –you knew exactly why he/she/they was/were still there and it set you up, however rough you felt at that ungodly hour, for the rest of the day.

The other great benefit of Northside was that from a drink-driving point of view it afforded a much safer starting point than setting off directly under your own steam from the Centre. Because that meant driving through The Tunnel under the perimeter road and if the police happened, for any reason, to put a stop at one end, which now and then they did, then whoever else they *didn't* get, they *had* at least got *you*. But let me enlarge a little, alcoholically speaking.

Although at *The* Airport – and *I,* miserable turncoat, was calling it that too, within weeks of my arrival – there was overall much less regular drinking to our particular perceived level of excess or for that matter to any other point well over the legal limit than there had been at *Gay* (sorry, *Gat*wick, doubly disloyal bastard), for myself and many of my colleagues a couple at the end of an always-busy day was still the best if not the only way to unwind. But a couple would often stretch to three or perhaps four and if you were tired, and we always were, even two was enough potentially to do you right in.

So back now to the Terminal itself and I found myself in the Blue Room, clearly and indisputably the one with most of the real 'characters' though this was inevitably hotly disputed by the comparatively few real 'characters' in each of the other two. Be that as it may, even with the three-way split there were so many people on duty in any one room at any one time that it was still hard swiftly to acquire a sense of belonging, and the easiest answer was to spend a lot of time on the control, which had its own fascination. Three then, well before the advent of Four still less Five, was the *only* long haul Terminal, handling pretty much all of the major intercontinental carriers, BA included. And it followed that you were almost bound to meet people in the public eye, politicians, film stars, etc., *celebs* as they call them or they call themselves now, big bloody deal. But even at Three, you couldn't have *everything*, *all* the time. Not *quite*. Thank God.

FIRST IMPRESSIONS

My first day was memorable all right, but not for any predictable reason. I'd only just been given my new Three stamps, (a pair, if you remember: landing and embarkation) when the daily JAL (Japanese Airlines) flight came over the tannoy, and because the very few Japanese I'd ever seen at Gatwick had never spoken any English, I thought I'd just pop out onto the Control to see how they were dealt with by the experts, and in numbers. As usual the flight was mainly filled with elderly Jap tourists who also spoke no English, and I soon discovered that you could accept them on the nod, perhaps simply asking 'Dantai?' (Group?') from time to time, whilst pushing them through at a rate of knots, not unlike the two-day Yanks. After all, *they definitely* weren't going to work here either, were they?

But I didn't find that out that day – or at least, not immediately. Knowing no-one, I selected a desk with mature, experienced-looking colleagues on either side and stood back for a second, to follow their lead. So I was listening intently as the first passengers, a couple well into their sixties, reached the desk to my left and the male bowed slightly and smiled a toothy Jap smile as he handed over the passports. *This is it,* I thought expectantly. And then my colleague spoke, asking the first question of the first examination I was ever to hear at Heathrow.

"Right, Tojo," he said brightly in English. "And what, I wonder, were *you* doing between '41 and '45?" And without further ado he stamped the passports, stamped them *hard*, and without waiting for a response handed them back, scowled and jerked his thumb towards the rear. The old man smiled again, bowed again and walked through with his wife. He hadn't understood a word, of course, and I found out later that my new colleague had lost his father on the Death Railway, memories of which, like those who had worked on it, died slowly[33]; and I was reminded of Chris with his Germans. (Later still, I learned that for years after the war some officers with particular and personal fond martial reminiscences of their own or their family's would place signs in front of their desks, 'No Germans or Japanese served here.' And if passengers of those nationalities did present themselves despite the signs, they were duly directed elsewhere, doubtless with varying degrees of sincere politeness.)

But my first day wasn't over yet. The next flight I saw was the good old Biman – *Just like old times,* I thought in relief – and having used one of the regular interpreters (we'd only had them piecemeal at Gatwick) to deal swiftly with my first two passengers, I looked briefly in the passport of the third, an apparent returning UK resident, and to the surprise of both him and the interpreter, served him with an 81 and sat him down without a word.

"Er, why did you do that?" the interpreter asked. He didn't know me from a bar of soap of course, nor I him, though I got to later. He was a really good old boy but (unlike us) prone to hit the bottle, and once he got going (also unlike us) there would be no stopping him verbally either: for example

I remember how at a farewell do, pissed, he greeted the late-arriving Three ACI with a cheery "Hello, you four-eyed cunt", to his face of course, because he (the ACI) wore glasses and he (the interpreter) was never a back-stabber; and how the next day when he (the interpreter) appeared still groggy for a late shift it took the entire Blue Room speaking on oath to convince him that he *had really* said what we all *said* he'd said, so that he then went to see the ACI to apologise humbly for his epithet, however accurate in part or whole it might have been, and we all had views on that.

But back to my very first day. "Because his last Brit embarkation stamp is a forgery," I replied with absolute confidence, and the interpreter looked at me with surprise and new respect (although I suppose it could have been well-disguised contempt instead because he was stone-cold sober at the time and I wore glasses too, and especially if he thought I was a *real* new-boy).

"Wow. How d'you know?" he asked, and I realised with regret that his instant esteem for my apparent prescience, *if* that's what it was in the first place, wouldn't last.

"Because I know its shape *especially* well," I said, pushing it anyway. "The poor unlucky sod, that stamp they've used is a copy of my old one at Gatwick, number 47," – thus cunningly demonstrating also that I *wasn't* a new-boy – and he shook his head in disbelief.

"Wow," he said again. "What are the chances of *that*?"

"Fuck knows, mate. Anyway, let's keep this short. Tell him I know it's forged and so does he, and if he tells me the truth right off he can go straight back and save himself a couple of nights in detention."

So they spoke for a minute or so: question, pause and surprised hurt look, answer, long question and long sad answer as the passenger hung his head, then the interpreter turned again to me.

"All right," he said. "He's spilled the lot, he apologises and he wants to go back today," which consummate precis also revealed that the Heathrow interpreters sometimes interpreted a little loosely the official limitations on their role – and a good thing too, when done properly – and as I got up to take the passenger to the pen and to make my notes, I asked, "Did you tell him how I knew about the stamp?" and he nodded and smiled.

"Yes," he said, "I did. But he thinks you're lying to conceal a secret British detection device. He says he'll never come here again and will tell everyone else in his village not to, as well."

So I was pretty satisfied as I took Ali into the pen and as I've already said, it was its usual true bedlam. No small individual interview rooms as we'd had by then at the newly extended Gatwick, just one *big* one with a number of desks in it – eight, as I remember, but it could have been ten – all occupied with interviews going on in a number of languages and each IO shouting his head off to be heard, and beyond that the true pen, the mass detention area itself, containing everyone held up so far that day who wasn't being interviewed, with a small head-high monochrome window which was itself always full of small high monochrome heads, craning out wide-eyed in every direction to try to see what the *hell* was going on.

I was destined to spend a lot of time in the pen, more than most in fact, but I didn't know it then, and I'm certain that it was one of my interviews there that got me promoted; but I'll come to that later. And I was only at Three for two and a half years, far too short a time for me to speak with any authority about the place as a whole or as an expert; so by and large I remember comparatively fewer events there. But that doesn't make what I *do* recall any less indelible.

SIMPLY READ

I worked hard at Three, often staying behind to finish a part-done case which I could quite legitimately just have passed on, and it became routine to sprint out of the office at half-past ten after a shift that should have ended at nine, waste a few more futile fretful ravenous clock-watching minutes in the Centre awaiting the bus, then speed madly out of Northside left up the westbound A and M4s, swerve sharp left again down the A332 to roar at high revs. into new Windsor town and finally, if I was lucky, burst on foot through the closing doors of the chippie at one minute past eleven, to leave proudly five later bearing left-over-cooked cod and chips to eat in bed after another ten; OK, bad for the digestion, but I was still almost young enough to know I was immortal, and anyway the extra salt and vinegar made all the difference.

Then came the time for the disclosure of my first Heathrow Annual Staff Report. In the good old tight-lipped days of yore you never saw your ASR at all unless you'd done very badly which was always possible or so well as to be superhuman which by definition was not, and otherwise you'd get no more than a terse "OK for another year," from your CIO, who for all I know had in fact written fuck-all down in the first place. But by this time it was all done publicly – 'transparently,' they'd say now – for what it was worth, because all that did was to change the problem, with weak CIOs upping their marks when necessary to avoid personal confrontations. Anyway I knew that my caseload had been high and was pretty sure that I'd be 'OK'. So, this surmise having already been confirmed to me verbally, old-style, by Grant my CIO, I was surprised to be called down the corridor to see Guy, Grant's immediate boss and my Inspector, even before I'd seen the final written article.

Now Guy was a big, bluff, hearty man, an HMI of long-standing with nothing to prove. And although I hadn't seen him much in the nine months I'd been there, we'd got on all right as far as I knew so I wasn't too worried as I knocked on his door and went in.

""Mike lad, take a seat," he said. But then straight off and whilst I was still in pre-sedentary motion, "So what's all this about your late paper work?" and I knew I was in a *spot* of bother, and thought rapidly about an appropriate response. The trouble was that he was dead right, I *was* well behind with my own case reports, a natural and inevitable consequence of spending so much time on the Control where extra bodies were always welcome, and then picking up yet more new cases when I could and arguably *should* have stayed inside out of harm's way in the first place, writing up my old ones (though doing which, as it happened, always pissed me off).

And that rationale would I thought be perfectly acceptable, especially if I left out the last bit. But then it struck me that I'd kept my head down at Three long enough and that it might be time for some small projection of my individuality, some minor revision of my *public persona*. (Or put more simply, my entire actual thought process was *Fuck this*.) So I tried another, seemingly confident, quite different tack – though with my fingers crossed, of course.

"Well. Tell me, Guy," I said. "Have you read… 'My Silent War'?" I paused for a second or two before the actual book title, so that if he didn't recognise it he wouldn't think by default that it was something I'd written myself, and I watched carefully for his reaction. Well, what he did was to sit back in his chair with a look of surprise on his face and, years before the Tango advert, I thought with satisfaction, *He wasn't expecting that.*

"My Silent War?'" he replied. "Book, I presume. No, can't say I have. Who's it by?"

"Kim Philby," I said, and watched closely as he went white, catapulted forward in his seat, half-stood and gripped the edge of the table with both hands.

"What? Who? *Who* did you say? *Philby, Kim Philby*?" he asked in a faint, strangled voice, and I felt a moment's gleeful sympathy. Philby was the infamous Third Man, ex-MI6, notorious colleague of Burgess and McLean and now safe and comparatively sound in Moscow the bastard after sending God knows how many British and other western agents to their deaths during and after the hot war. Sympathetic but gleeful, because I could tell what Guy (the HMI I mean, not that other fucker Burgess) was thinking, or thought I could. This had been due to be a routine bollocking, necessary for the record but mild at most and probably not even that if I'd stuck to the script. But I hadn't, and now he was facing a major security breach, a rampant Red in the heart of the Blue Room for Chrissake and a self-proclaimed one at that so actually proud of it, the SIs fatally compromised and who knows what other damage done. Or maybe, just maybe and with a bit of luck, only your average attention-seeking IO lunatic instead.

"Yes, that's the one," I said easily as I stared Guy boldly in the face. But then my still-crossed fingers started to sweat a little as I noticed that suddenly *he* was red too, bright red in fact and still deepening. Well, it was much too late to stop now.

"Go on," he said hoarsely, skilled examiner that he was or perhaps playing for time, and I kept a close eye on his movements – manual, I mean – as Gatwick SB had taught me long ago. "*Listen.* If you're saying something indiscreet or actionable, or if in other words it's all about to go generally tits-up and chummy's hand strays to his pocket, *stop talking and shut yer gob, right there.* Because pound to a penny he's switching on his miniature Pearlcorder." Sound advice then (ha ha) and fucking *crucial* today, in the age of the universal mobile phone.

But Guy's hands stayed right where they were, still gripping the table, his knuckles as white as his face was now purple, his breathing stertorous, and I thought (again) *Shit, what have I done,* but then hastened hastily on. "Well," I said, "most of the book is crap, of course." – I got that in quickly for both our sakes, and his face did lose a touch of its lividity – "But somewhere he says that a man can't be a complete, rounded person without his own area of *ir*responsibility, and I admit that timely paperwork is mine. So you've got me, hands up, and I apologise."

Thank God, it's working, I thought. For Guy's grip visibly relaxed, and his breathing slowed. He sat down properly again in his chair, sighed, then looked at me from under lowered brows, as I peeped coyly back.

"Is that it?" he asked, after a pause.

"Yes, Guy," I said.

"*All* of it?"

"Yes, Guy."

"Nothing more? You're sure?"

"No. Yes," I said.

He paused again, and let the silence lengthen. Then, "Mike," he said.

"Yes, Guy?" I asked.

"*Fuck off,* there's a good lad," he said. Just like that.

"Yes, all right, Guy," I said. And I did.

Our next meeting a few days later was momentary, shits that passed in the night or the corridor, and as I grinned nervously at him he couldn't maintain his own nascent scowl. *"Bastard,"* he muttered under his breath but that was all, and after that we got on like a house on fire. Of course, that could have been because *he* really *was* a Russian agent, but somehow even these days it seemed unlikely. Still, perhaps I should have put him to the test more severely, and clocked his reaction when I called him *'Tovarich'* out loud. Or something like that.

RIOT

1978 to 1979 was the formal span of the Iranian Revolution, and we saw it in daily cameo on the arriving Iran Air. First came those refugees – both red (really red) and religious – who were fleeing the Main Man himself. Then later, when His, the Shah's, own beloved Immortals had learnt the hard hot final way that in truth they had precisely the same bodily limitations as you and I – and especially after Mr. Peacock had sensibly fled the country himself and left them to rot – we encountered the imperial refugees instead, themselves fleeing that same earlier level of persecution but in reverse, and swiftly joined by the really reds, who soon found they were no more acceptable to the now-victorious fundamentalists than they'd been to Savak[34] before.

It was a typical civil war. The physical evidence was identical throughout, the photographs no less sickening whoever produced them except that as ever you soon became used to it. So when you saw daily the images of dead men, women and children eviscerated or strangled or with axes embedded deep in their heads, it really didn't matter which fucker had wielded the knife or the garrotte or the axe, a Savak thug or a commie or a Revolutionary Guard.

But that, however unpleasant, is just scene-setting for a particular day in the middle of it all. The phenomenon which then occurred was not that surprising, as the airline's scheduled arrival time put it right in with the Arab flights – from Egypt, Syria, Jordan, Iraq and so on – and at the best of times Iranians and Arabs just don't get on (try calling an Iranian an Arab or vice versa, and see what you get). Anyway, on the day in question everything came together to achieve the inevitable eventual result, and the only wonder was that it didn't happen more often. Because this time, when the Iranair arrived in the Hall at much the same time as the Syrian Arab and the Iraq or was it the Egypt Air, it *all* went very wrong.

Someone must have said *something, you* know, like in the 'Pirandello', and it may not even have been between separate flights, because on the Iranair itself there was often a volatile mix of refugees from the two extremes, whether reds and fundamentalists or, later, imperialists and reds. But however it started, fighting – small, vicious separate fights, involving two or three or six people, lots of them – spread across the entire width of the Hall, also Eytie-restaurant-style, the police were called and sensibly arrived in numbers, and I remember vividly the bizarre sensation of sitting there in the line asking routine questions of routine passengers, mixed Arab and Iranian, who answered me and my colleagues politely albeit with voices necessarily raised, whilst other shouting figures crawled on the floor and struggled and fought all round us and a Northside Inspector formed up thick wedges of uniforms against our rear wall and then used his bull-horn to spearhead them into the crowd whilst SB rapidly stacked prisoners like sandbags, horizontally, vertically and in threes.

It can only have lasted an hour or so, the British nature if not scale of the violence reasonable for the time so no knives, and once peace and order were restored it was as if it had never been. But perhaps that was the very day when some smart London brief suddenly, finally, had a bright, bright thought. Because in my memory, at Three at least, '78 to '79 was when the asylum trickle started to become first a major river then a flood, when claimants began to turn up from *anywhere*, and when the UK as well as most of the happy aspirants (genuine or not) reached, and soon enough passed, the point of no return.

FINGERED

Spring 1979 now, and I sat in the Blue Room reading the file on a Bangladeshi whose passport described him as Abdur Hassan aged fourteen – his true real pukka age, he said. But all the other IOs who'd seen him so far, five of them over a period of some three weeks, had believed him to be in his late twenties (or in other words, if they were right, good old Shahnaz Begum's 'wronged' son Ali in reverse). Anyway we'd spent more than enough time on his case and now it was make or break day: either Abdur would make the promised land or, finally, *we'd* break *him*. I hadn't seen him myself in the flesh yet but the file, for all its careful objective phrasing, was redolent of the angry frustration felt by each successive IO as he or she wrote up the notes after another fruitless interview.

'Bone age', the process by which we would refer to the PMI any hold-up where age was an issue and in due course receive back an allegedly-reliable scientific assessment based on an X-ray, had only recently been discontinued – exactly why now I can't remember, it might have been medically discredited[35] or it might well have simply gone the way of the so-called 'virginity test', a PMI examination of young sub-continental women who claimed to be unmarried, eventually stopped when it became both politically and (therefore?) morally unsustainable.

At any event, we couldn't use it anymore, and as I finished my thorough reading of the file – which I'd begun with a degree of hope, because although I knew by now that I was nothing special I never ceased to be amazed at how many colleagues routinely just skipped through any existing notes, thus often perpetuating in ignorance an extant IS sin, whether of omission or commission – I'd found absolutely nothing that *had* been missed *or* got wrong. So what it boiled down to was that after a last symbolic chat *I* was going to be the one who actually threw in the notional national towel. *'Shit,'* I reflected, yet again, but this time only mildly because it was probably my turn and if even by then you couldn't be philosophical about it, especially at Three, you wouldn't stay sane very long.

So into the Pen I went with Hanif, one of the other regular interpreters, straight into the usual general shouting match and when the guards brought the 'boy' in it was blindingly obvious that all my colleagues had been right, spot on – no, at second glance they had if anything erred on the side of caution, because he must have been thirty plus if he was a day. And as we went through the usual pleasantries – it was readily apparent that

Hanif himself already knew the case and was resigned to the outcome – 'young' Abdur remained as cool as the proverbial spring cucumber which he had successfully imitated all along. There was just nowhere fresh for me to go, and simply to have repeated everything we'd done already could quite rightly have opened the door to a legal claim of oppression. So just for appearances' sake I leafed casually through the file again and finally dug out from the pouch at the rear all the papers that the passenger had volunteered or we'd found in the baggage search. And to cap it all – if not indeed to take the final piss – I saw that he'd brought his *own* X-rays.

They were his all right, Abdur Hassan's – or at least we couldn't prove they *weren't* – because there in the corner were the name and date of birth just as in the passport, *and* the date when they'd been taken. *He's probably brought them to show he hasn't got active TB,* I thought. A lot of Bangladeshis in particular did that (we routinely X-rayed all non-resident Banglas over 40 ourselves anyway for the same purpose), but there were several extra plates covering his entire upper body, which was unusual. Still, they meant sod-all to me and as I put them back in the medical envelope after no more than a glance I turned to Hanif and said something in English like, 'I'm sorry mate, you and I both know this is crap but there's nothing more I can do,' not for translation naturally, and as he sighed and inclined his head, Abdur must have sensed that he'd cracked it because he smiled and put both his hands on the desk, and I looked casually at them, then away then back again more carefully and then at the interpreter as I felt my pulse quicken, just a little.

"Hanif," I said, and tapped the envelope in front of me. "Can you ask him when these X-rays were taken?"

"Sure, Mike," he said. He looked a little surprised but

asked anyway, and Abdur looked at the X-rays then at me. I thought I could sense his brain working overtime but if so it was following the wrong line, perhaps because this was one question he hadn't been briefed on, and he hadn't made the right connection. We could have checked anyway – in fact we did, later – but his answer now made such confirmation redundant, *if* my memory of the plates was accurate.

"He was at the hospital the week before he came," Hanif said. "The X-rays were done then."

Well, that's not bad for a pure guess, old bean, I thought, *you're a little out but not enough to make a federal case, and anyway that's hardly the issue.* Then I sighed, somewhat theatrically I suppose because suddenly I was beginning to enjoy myself. But Abdur misinterpreted that too, and the small tell-tale furrows of anxiety which had formed on his brow cleared as if by magic. "Good," I said, and occupied myself in writing something banal on the file just to keep him happy for his own sake, and stewing for mine.

"OK then," I said, as I laid down my pen. "Now just ask him when he lost the little finger on his right hand," and as Hanif looked down at the table himself I sensed his own sudden interest. The hand was completely healed, in fact it looked like a very old injury to me, and the answer now confirmed it.

"He did it three years, ago," the interpreter said, and added, sourly, "when he was eleven."

"Did *he* actually *say* that last bit?" I asked, just in case.

"Yes, he said, surprised. "Of course."

"OK," I said, "fair enough." *Nail the lie,* especially if he's getting over-confident and surely now taking the piss. "Can you just ask him again?" He did, and received the same reply – not, I hoped, that now it was really going to matter.

"All right," I said and I re-opened the medical envelope with a silent prayer. I looked through the plates until I found the one I wanted, checked the name again then held it up to the light for a clearer view and this time heaved an entirely genuine sigh as I put down the plate in front of the passenger. "This plate is his?" I asked. *Nail this, too.*

"Yes," Hanif said, after asking him. Had I detected a slight reluctance in the reply? He was stuffed, either way.

"And it was taken only *a few weeks* ago?" I could afford a bit of latitude.

"Yes, that's right," said Hanif after asking him again. Well, what else could he say?

I dismissed the idea of a cheap shot about the hitherto unknown and miraculous advances, or perhaps retreats, in Bangladesh's medical science – it would have gone straight over his head and there was no reason to make him feel any smaller – and kept it simple.

"So. Look at the X-ray," I said, and Hanif translated. "That is a picture of your right hand. Now *hold up* your right hand," and Abdur did.

"In the picture, the hand has five fingers – one, two, three, four, five." *We won't get technical about the thumb,* I thought, and Abdur nodded reluctantly. He knew what was coming now, and tried to put his hand in his pocket.

"No, *keep it on the table and look at the picture.* But your hand has only *four*," and I went through the comparative time frames which he'd already given me himself. "Well, we can check with the hospital in Dacca and you'll stay locked up here while we do – it will take at least a week, and maybe longer – or you can save time and tell me now. This isn't your X-ray, is it?" and he looked at me and shook his head. "The *truth* now then, old son," – I couldn't resist it – "who are you, and what age?" and he told us, straight out, *and* that he was coming here to take a pre-arranged job as a cook, and was in his late twenties after all – so I'd got that a bit wrong, *perhaps,* but it didn't matter.

And then Hanif jumped to his feet and shouted with delight and waved his arms and did a spirited, joyful little jig on the floor of the pen, right there in front of everyone. *"Mike,"* he shouted, *"Mike, we've got him!"* and *that* was precisely when a be-suited man, a complete stranger to me, emerged from the inner door.

"Hello, Hanif," he said mildly, as the latter came to an abrupt halt and tried to stand to attention. "I didn't know you could dance. I still don't. Why the merriment?" and I just sat there as the interpreter explained it all to him and then he came over, shook hands and introduced himself and I realised who he was; an ACI lately himself in charge of Three (the one before Four-Eyes) and now national Head of IS Staffing, down on a one-day visit.

He asked who *I* was and I told him, and then he asked me to go through the case again, briefly, so I did. Then he said, "Well done," just like that, and we shook hands again and he left and I thought no more of it until later in the year when the invitations to the CIO board came through and they'd asked me to go although I was still only a comparative sprog with just over nine years in. And I went and that ACI was the chairman of the Board and bugger me, I got it at the first try, and nothing will ever persuade me that Abdur wasn't the one I really had to thank. And Hanif, of course, the Old Jigger.

TB OR NOT TB

And that reminds me of another case with a much greater medical element, even if without similar digital enhancement: Ahmad Younis was *his* name and he was off the Biman too, *and* over forty, so before I did anything else I referred him to the PMI. And when he came back he was in trouble up to his chest if not his neck (Ahmad I mean, not the doctor, though truth to tell I always had my doubts about one or two of *them*), because *he did* have active TB, and he (the doctor, not Ahmad) gave me a Port 30 – you remember, the form which made him (Ahmad) a mandatory refusal as the possessor of a proscribed disease, active TB being highly infectious. So I duly refused him entry, but that's when the case became the predictable farce we all knew by then that it would.

Because Ahmad, once refused, stood to be removed asap as a danger to public health – that, after all, was what it was all about. But you couldn't remove anyone with active TB on a regular flight with other passengers, precisely because he *was* a danger to public health and highly infectious, a medical version of Catch 22. So he was given Temporary Admission to a specified address, the usual one in such circumstances and this time *truly* compulsory with the NHS providing the transport, to wit the TB ward in Hillingdon Hospital where in a month or two they cured him or at least made the TB inactive provided he stayed on the drugs, so that he *was* then safely removable.

But now he could either appeal or an MP might make representations on his behalf, because now he no longer *had* active TB and so wasn't a mandatory refusal any more. And sometimes, such a passenger would be allowed entry, and sometimes not – I can't remember which way it went with Ahmad, it was always a bit of a lottery and the treatment had of course been emergency so it was all on the taxpayer, and even if he *did* go straight back it was still Joe Soap who'd financed his cure which wouldn't last anyway because he couldn't afford his drugs in Bangla-land, always assuming they were available there in the first place. *Now* d'you see what I mean about the need for wind-down pints?

Anyway, sufferers continued to arrive regularly (who can blame them?) and because for medical reasons we couldn't let them physically *see* any waiting relatives we let them use our office phones instead; and eventually it occurred to me, albeit selfishly, that it might not be the most sensible of practices for our *own* health – I can't recall the phones ever being cleaned at all when I first arrived at Three and if they were, it wasn't often. So I popped round to the PMI seeking expert advice and general reassurance which I suppose I got, after a fashion. "Well," the doctor said grudgingly after some thought, "if you haven't all gone down with it by now, you should be OK."

"Well, *thanks,* Doc," I said wryly, for some reason un-reassured and with, I thought, a palpably growing lump in my throat. "Thank you *very* much."

BARBARIANS

Late 1979 now, the height, or depth, of Apartheid, or the early beginning of its end depending on your point of view, and either way it was two years since the Gleneagles Agreement had left South Africa the international pariah of the sporting world. But the Lions had last gone out there in '74 and played the 'Boks into the ground, literally, the return series here was already overdue and if they couldn't come officially, there were other ways. *This* at least *was* still a democracy – just about, although sometimes I wondered if they weren't working on it – and there was more than enough cruelty in the world for South Africa to have it all, and I distrusted the motives of demonstrators in general and of political demonstrators in particular. Moreover, OK it wasn't Cricket but it was the Next Best Thing – and, finally, what the hell did *any* of it have to do with *me*?

So I knew the 'rebel' UK tour, by the South African 'Barbarians' as they now called themselves, was coming up soon and that there would be aggro all over the place. But it hadn't even registered that the team was due to arrive here that very day as I drove in to work. October 1st it was, and the first match, in Devon, was due on 3rd. I only know those dates because I looked them up, they're *not* what I remember, and I was minding my own business when I was called to the CIOs' office.

"Ah, Mike boyo, a special job. Can you meet the Jo'burg flight – it's due down shortly – wait for the rest to get off, then board and clear the 'Boks – sorry, I mean the 'Baa-baas'. And then the cops'll take them out by the back door, to miss the press and the demos." That's when I *did* remember that I'd had to push my way in that morning through a heaving crowd of shouters and placard wavers landside, though I hadn't bothered to see precisely what the protest was about because by then there was usually one about something.

"All right," I said, again like a prize prat but this time far more comfortably, and hurried off to get my kit. It should be an interesting change and the CIO had been Grant, my own team boss and Welsh (as again you've guessed) to boot so I could hardly refuse, could I – not that I had any strong feelings on the matter, as I've said already. So I watched the rest of the passengers get off and then boarded, turned right into first-class and stopped dead as I saw a compact still-seated mass – no, phalanx is a better word – of thirty-odd blazers – green and gold as I recall, but I could be wrong because of course those were the 'Boks' *official* colours.

"Gentlemen," I said as I advanced again, an innocent abroad and still partly in a world of my own, though rapidly emerging therefrom. "Good morning. Welcome to Britain." Well, just how *big* a prize prat can you get?

And the response? Silence. *Total, oppressive, group* silence. And utter, watchful, stillness. But the threat, the corporate universal hostility bordering on hatred was almost palpable. Now I *really* looked at them, swallowed hard and thought, *Christ, I know the Greeks had 300, but there's more than enough here for me.* And not only that: with very few exceptions they were *Boers*, the very ones who'd run us ragged at the turn of the century and never forgiven us for finally winning or for how disgracefully Kitchener had treated their women and children, or forgotten it either (and can you blame them). Hell, their current Prime Minister was one, and most of those in front of me now were man mountains – even the half-backs were huge, all of them thinking every Brit was their sworn enemy, and who was the first poor solitary Brit bugger they saw? It was one of those times when you can suddenly feel very, *very* alone, and I swallowed again and managed, just, to stifle my own small Welsh bit, in particular the idiotic – no, the wholly insane – impulse to yell out '99'[36] which would surely have broken the impasse all right, but my neck along with it.

"Right then," I said brightly, or as brightly as I could under the circumstances. "Passports, please," and the Manager handed them to me, still without a word. Well, he of all people wasn't going to break team unity was he, especially when he *didn't* have a son in mufti. So I stamped them all in double quick time in the tense and still-enduring silence, and handed them back to him – after all, unlike some other foreign wrestlers, they were hardly likely to become UK immigration problems. *Well,* I thought in relief at the end, *they haven't lynched me yet.*

But then I reflected that because I *was* the first Englishman they'd met here, I ought to make some kind of gesture of patriotic solidarity before I left, otherwise we'd already lost Round One. I dismissed instantly the gesture which came automatically but wholly unbidden to mind because the Churchillian salute could so easily be misconstrued, and I still wanted to keep my head on my shoulders. So I contented myself with casting a hard but sensibly wordless look over the lot of them one by one, effectively inspecting them, before nodding dismissively in a superior British fashion (a pretty effete fashion really too, I suppose, and very like Caine in *Zulu* now I come to think of it, so hardly calculated to lower the ante either) and then leaving the aircraft at a rate of knots. Not one of them had said a dicky-bird and in a way it wouldn't have been a bad preparation for my Board, if I hadn't had the bloody thing already.

And thus the 'Barbarians' entered the UK, officially at least and through the front door in a way, and within hours the lot of them were forced to make a sharp exit when their coach burst into flames on the M4. I'd like to think it was divine intervention for their rudeness but no doubt it was just something like a leaking fuel pipe. Shades of 1969, the last time the 'Boks had toured here under that name, when the team bus was hi-jacked on the way to the first international at Twickers and crashed with half of them aboard. There were to be no formal internationals now of course, *they* didn't resume for another thirteen years. But the general job apart, it's the nearest I've ever come to playing for England so it's no wonder I wasn't picked again, even as a reserve.

RESULT

The verdicts of the promotion board were due out any day, and I was already fully content – no, gobsmacked, really – just to have been called. Very few people got it first time anyway, and whenever I looked along the line of IOs on the Control I saw a fair number, some of whom hadn't even been given the chance, who I knew were both more experienced and better than me. There were also a few perennial attenders, any one of whom would make an excellent operational CIO – they all did it in an Acting capacity often enough, and I hadn't even done that once – but they just seemed unable to hack it at the board itself and my secret hope was that if I were called again and again, I wouldn't *fail* again and again too, but that was all.

And then they came (the results, I mean). The theory was that you could tell how you'd done by the size and thickness of the envelope – thin and small for failure, thick and large for success though it doesn't always work that way, ask any sex therapist – but like I said I *knew* mine in advance and it didn't register that *mine was* thick and large (the envelope, I mean) so I wasn't just surprised at the contents, I was again gobsmacked but painfully this time, and I phoned my wife as I accepted what I took as the equally astonished congratulations of my colleagues, some themselves personally disappointed. "I've got it!" I yelled down the phone, and I could hardly act too upset if *she* seemed gobsmacked too, now could I?

But the big question now was 'where?' No-one was promoted in situ, and they only told you your destination later. It was bound to be Heathrow of course as I'd only just got there, but I didn't mind that. Which terminal though, One or Two? I knew next to nothing about either, except that Two was bigger and allegedly busier, and it had all the short-haul non-British carriers, whereas One was short-haul also, but BA only.

Two, I bet, I thought. Dubiously. *Apprehensively.* And sure enough, Two it was.

Chapter Four

TWO

Where I began on Christmas Eve 1979, with bad stomach cramp and four-fold trepidation, firstly because the Two *IO*s would be out to see what kind of *CIO* I was going to be generically, and even *I* didn't have a clue about that yet. Then again, to have been promoted on a first board was Strike Two and dodgy enough, but to have done so with less than ten years in the job was Strike Three and much worse, because it led to an immediate suspicion that I was some kind of thrusting smart-arse whizz-kid, a phenomenon which emphatically I was *not* – well, not consciously, I knew *that* much. And finally, Strike Four and the real clincher, I was moving to *Two* from *Three*, only a couple of hundred yards but it might just as well have been double the distance from bloody Gatwick for all the affinity between the pair. Because in the eyes of its incumbents Two *was* Heathrow, the *original terminal* (hence its number) and don't you forget it, *especially* if you're some know-it-all come-lately upstart, *however* smart your arse, from that new place across the road and before that, for God's sake, from bloody *Gay*-wick (which was what, in a rare show of unity with Three, *they* called it too and which, now I think about it, was Strike Five and yet *another* thing).

So: trepidation? Shit-scared more like, *bubble*-shit too, and when I got there you couldn't see me for butterflies, let alone revolting mixed metaphors. Anyway I turned up early for a late duty, a standard 1400 start but I was on a familiarisation day with nothing fixed, and Sod's Law cut straight in as someone went sick and within half an hour I found myself up to my neck, operating as the regular scheduled third Late CIO who covered the meal-breaks of the two main men in the Watch House, one (Floor) in charge of the Controls, Inward and Embarks – oh yes, we still manned Embarks in those days, and for years to come – and the other (SEA, standing for Secondary Examination Area) dealing with all the new cases off the Floor who were put in the holding room, the smaller equivalent of Three's Pen, by the Watch House. And at that time, all the Two CIOs *were* still men, though the first high heels were soon on their way.

And so there was no time for brown trousers or insects of *any* colour anymore, because now I was off with the fairies instead, trying to adjust to entirely new systems of floor-running and case-handling with a dozen or so IOs (identifiable only by their initials, which were at the time wholly unintelligible) both to run the Control and to cope with the sizeable and slow-dwindling residue of the forty-two cases which had been piled on my SEA colleague's desk, the first sift of the recently-arrived TK (Turkish Airlines) flight with one or two others thrown in.

Which was the *up*side of coming straight from Three. Because if this was a standard bad day at Two (with perhaps a little bonus for Christmas), thus also had it been at Three, the pressure almost welcoming in its sweaty familiarity, and I felt a twinge of compassion for those poor sods of transferred-in sea port officers who arrived, especially on promotion, at *any* Heathrow terminal fresh from anywhere except maybe Dover East, to be engulfed by a sheer instant volume of work they'd never seen before, often involving nationals (e.g. Turks) with whom they had had minimal if any contact and with a constant potential for wholly unfamiliar complex multi-sector removals light years away from their last ports where, wherever the refusals had originated, the norm had been to bung them straight back on the first appropriate boat, whence they'd come.

At any event it went well enough so far as I could tell. OK, I was struggling, but I was trying hard and together somehow we survived the day, notwithstanding a visibly purpling and palpably panicking Two Inspector hitherto unknown to me who burst into the Watch-House early in the afternoon when I was covering the Floor, saw with manifest horror the piles of Turkish passports as yet untouched and peremptorily ordered my SEA colleague to get all their owners refused and out *on the return flight,* leaving within two hours.

It was an absurd instruction, totally impractical and wholly illegal as well as plain daft, and I had my first experience of how a Two CIO dealt with a superior interfering in his business when Jim, the colleague aforesaid whom too I'd never met before, listened with barely concealed impatience to the semi-hysterical orders of the now-puce HMI then glanced significantly at me, turned back to the boss and said calmly and as near verbatim as I can recall, "Jeff, you're involving yourself in *CIOs'* business and I have a lot on. Furthermore you're distracting Mike here. Now, you weren't *invited* into the Watch House, so please leave."

"*What?* But – " said the Inspector.

"Jeff. *Look. Listen.*" Jim said, succinctly. "We're *busy.* So *fuck off!*" (this last *definitely* verbatim), and the Inspector did, without another word – shades of Gatwick, nine years before, just one grade up.

Or so I thought until the following afternoon, when we sat, the same three, all in a row in Jeff's upstairs office, abruptly summoned there and acting briefly like the wise monkeys as he vented his anger at his previous day's embarrassment. But it didn't last long. It couldn't. For one thing he knew that had we done as he'd instructed, *he'd* be the one in it right up to his neck soon enough so really Jim had saved his bacon; and for another, he (Jim) was *still* busy with no time to spare, so after the obligatory momentary silence he stood up abruptly and strode from the room, loudly repeating his brief final imperative of the day before, word for word over the despairing blusterings of our boss, and with us others both close behind him.

Solidarity, see? And I soon found out that Two had a *lot* of staff, both IOs and CIOs, with a length and depth of experience which a newcomer would be extremely foolish to ignore or attempt to override. Well, I wasn't *that* stupid, and in fact I reckoned I was going to be all right within a week, after an incident which, however unfairly, both established my reputation with the IOs – the ones who *really* mattered – and revealed to all, including myself, my natural or perhaps rather my involuntary management style.

It occurred on my third Late Duty, adding a bizarre physicality to the marginally favourable mental impression of me that by fickle chance if not quite downright mistake at least some of the staff had, it seemed, formed already. I'd just come on shift and having checked the stamping-on book ambled – amiably, and already far less up-tight than on Day One – into the IOs' ready room, where a number of them were sitting chatting or watching the TV or reading papers whilst awaiting a summons to the Control.

By now I had fixed on the face and character that I meant to adopt for public presentation, and the trick was to ensure that you were consistent in your approach – which in my case was easy, because I had extant, albeit unwitting, outside help. I'd always liked Eastwood films and I'd always smoked cigars and had lately discovered Scott's Imperial Number Twos, tight black Burmese cheroots – lovingly rolled between the warm thighs, or was it sighs, of dusky eastern maidens with fuck-all else to do (so probably thighs, or maybe both) – which lasted for bloody hours anyway, especially if you didn't light them. Put the two together then, and *Clint* it had to be.

So as I entered the room I was half-aware of the sudden silence and appraising half-looks of those I hadn't yet half-met, which were many. But I didn't let it faze me, not a jot. "Hello," I said, instead – softly, laconically and yet drawn out, with my eyes narrowed against the non-existent sun under my non-existent hat, the way *he* did. And I consciously refrained from adding any short general reflection on Control life – say, like 'Lyin's not much of a living, boys,' or perhaps something more specific, like 'Are you gonna ply those stamps, guys, or hum the Anthem?' – or even from proving my identity by flourishing my warrant, lest it should be instantly and forcibly transformed into a several- if not specifically seven-point suppository.

No, me, I simply rolled the cheroot, a lit one this time, effortlessly from one side of my mouth to the other for full effect as I said to myself, 'Go for it, punk,' selected an actual *seat* in the *IOs' very own room* for the *very first time* and slumped down heavily in my, and *his*, usual relaxed and untidy fashion, against one of the cushioned benches round the wall. And don't forget that I had one actual advantage, because *I* didn't have to keep my gun-hand free, *or* ensure that I didn't shoot myself in the leg.

The only trouble was that my particular usual relaxed

fashion involved my head momentarily rolling back unhindered well beyond the vertical before I swiftly retrieved it, and so it did this time. Or tried to. But I hadn't spotted that the fucking bench was fucking tight against the fucking wall and my head hit the latter with a resounding fucking thud that attracted *everyone's* attention, in a manner which ordinarily would have done my chosen image, and me, no fucking good at all.

But then the miracle happened. Because as I rebounded from the impact and my mouth opened involuntarily, the cheroot shot out bullet-like at high velocity across the room. And to the awed astonishment of all who saw it, not least me, I reacted at the speed of light, reached out, caught it in mid-flight at gun arm's length and replaced it wordlessly, still smoking *and* the right way round, in my mouth. OK, I could never do it again in a thousand years, I *know* that, but somehow I'd done it *then*, when it mattered, and in the stunned silence that followed I managed to freeze the moment for ever as if I did the thing ten times a day by rising slowly to my feet, taking two deep reflective puffs whilst I stared with still-narrowed eyes into the high-planes distance and willed myself not to burst out into hysterical laughter Indio-style, and then strolling casually from the room, effecting an authentic still-wordless saddle-sore slouch as I left.

And there you go. In those few moments not only was my reputation but my nickname also established – firmly and irrevocably, but inevitably in the alternative. Because although for a substantial part of the office – *and* without even having had otherwise to *hint* that that was my preferred sobriquet – I understandably became and remained *'Clint'*, for an equal number and for reasons that I can't even guess at unless perhaps a slight over-emphasis in my slouch or the IOs' own finely-honed sense of the ridiculous, I became forever *'Groucho'.* (Oh, and I almost forgot: to a select few I was already *'Ernie Alzheimer'* but I can't remember why[37].) *At least,* I thought wryly, *all three seem vaguely affectionate.*

QUICK WORK

Tall, handsome, saturnine – no, the passenger I mean – he came not from outer space but a poor island in the Indian Ocean instead, where he was a waiter during the just-ended tourist season but now abruptly unemployed. So a classic of its kind even without the usual crap two-week-visit story, but he had that too. Or in other words, his refusal was one of my easier early management decisions, and the only problem was that he'd arrived by a complex four-stage multi-sector route, home island /mainland Africa/mainland Europe/UK, and there was no identical return combination for a week. So I took the by-then already usual national path of least resistance and gave him seven days' TA to fit. After all he was no worse a bet than most, there was no detention room at the inn anyway and had there been, to use up a week's worth on one case when we could have accommodated several *quick* removals for one or two nights each made no sense at all. (Yeah, overall *total* crap *itself* I know, quart into a pint pot etc., but that was how we thought at the time, and probably still do.)

So (again) so far so good, all done and dusted; but it took an extra hour to work out the details of the prospective removal as he sat there glumly on the Control, with one of the carrying company's ground-girls as his minder. (Unlike Three and even Gatwick by then, good old trad Two still had no daytime professional guards to cover the terminal itself, and we relied on the inbound carrier to provide someone ad hoc to fit the bill.)

And I still remember that particular ground-girl well, not least because she'd popped her pretty, anxious head round the watch-house door beforehand to say, pretty anxiously, that she'd never had to do such an iffy job before and was pretty anxious about it. I think she thought at first that she might be guarding the Fiend of the Third World, but I managed to re-assure her that the whole thing was a mere formality by pointing him out, showing her that they would both be in plain sight of the rest of us and finally introducing them. Then I left them together, feeling fully at ease with things (I was, I mean) and as I looked back they were exchanging a few halting words as they sat side by side on the same bench but with a yawning two-yard gap between them as modesty (hers, I presumed) demanded, and as air-pond life went on around them.

Then, the removal details duly sorted, another problem arose: the provision of an appropriate TA address, given his claim – true or false, and I knew which *I* believed – that he knew no-one here. At that time, at Two anyway, we were still at least going through the motions and resisting letting passengers trog off with nothing more specific on their IS 96 than a truly ridiculous 'address to be notified to the IS as soon as possible' – which was of course the same as kissing them a last fond goodbye without the foggiest of where even to *start* looking for them if/when they failed to show – and yep, later even *we* really did routinely sink that low. But like I said there was nowhere to bang him up in the first place, so it could have come to that.

But then the problem solved itself, because when the IO went to explain the reason for the further delay the ground-girl, having listened very carefully from afar to all that was being said including her charge's continued protestations that he really *did* know *no-one* here, intervened meekly to say that in the circumstances and although she would normally never even *consider* doing such a thing with a *perfect stranger*, *she* could put him up – strictly for a week only, and no longer – if that might help.

Too right it might, ma'am, I thought (*Clint*, see, but in the outback). But involving impromptu airline minders as semi-custodial landladies wasn't something you did every day, even before Health and Safety, and I went to have a chat with both parties to ensure that each was aware of the significance of the proposal (whoops, Freudian slip there – no, Freudian *suggestion*, I mean) which in this case existed more in the letter of the law than in any enforceable obligation, not that I told her *that*. Anyway each said he/she was, and not without a degree of reluctance I authorised the deal, noting as I left that though the modesty gap still existed, it had shrunk to a single yard.

Well, sometimes you just can't win; and exactly a week later I was in the Two Casework Office – the inner office which dealt with extant longer-term cases – when an IO answered the phone then swore loudly (which was not uncommon), and into my hot hand thrust a refusal file which rang another immediate bell as He from the Indian Ocean. There was it seemed, a further problem. The first leg of his removal flights had just gone tech[38] and would miss its connection. So the obvious next cop-out – sorry, *solution* – was to extend TA for a further seven days, ironically now giving him exactly what he had professed to want in the first place; and to issue identical RDs, but for a week later.

It was then about an hour before he was due back for his removal, of the cancellation of which he was still unaware. There were no mobile phones in those days of course, and when we rang the ground-girl's address there was no reply, which was consistent both with him – and her? – being en route but also with a no-show, and I knew which *I* favoured *there*, too. And it was thus no small surprise when they both appeared ready and complete with his bags, so that we could tell them face to face that they'd had a wasted journey.

And they both took it pretty well – indeed, took it well *jointly,* because the erstwhile modesty gap had clearly morphed into a close-contact mutual admiration society as they went off happily hand in hand, promising to return when and as required. Which they duly did a week later, not only with his bags but also with exchanged rings and fast-track Marriage Certificate barely dry, and this was still 1980 when things were different so that my Casework colleague that day took one look and threw in the towel when *then* he could have simply said, "So what?" and next, "On your bike," and what *I* would have done I don't know, except to say that the particular circumstances surrounding the happy event did not seem conducive to its likely longevity..

But what can you do? Looking back, I suppose the writing was on the wall from the moment the first IO had looked in his passport. What else could you expect, after all, from a man named *Casanova?*

REMEMBER, REMEMBER

0045 hours, late January and pissing it down, the last delayed passenger having just departed howling into that good night. Still I wasn't tired, no, not me – like the rest of the shift I was fucking exhausted. So now was the time to start paperwork, and the place *to* start was obvious and unavoidable: a new Minister's case – an MP's *complaint,* naturally – and smack on top of the steaming pile.

So I read the refusal's name and shook my head wearily; it meant nothing to me, but *that* meant nothing too. It was the particular elements of a case – its individual and unique kaleidoscope of chronology and invention and discovery and lies – that always brought it back to you, usually in spades. But this time, once I'd finished reading the file, I was still none the wiser and sat back and stared blindly at the ceiling. *Oh-oh,* I thought. Spades, did I say? On this occasion I'd have settled for Clubs or Diamonds or even bleeding Hearts, or *anything.* But I knew one thing, for certain. Which was that I was well and truly stuffed.

Because it had been my case all right. There was my name on the IS126[39] as refusing CIO, confirmed in the case-notes and cut and dried to boot – a bogus Portuguese visitor (pre-EU naturally) so pretty run-of-the-mill or so *I'd* thought, except that you didn't need to read much between the lines to see that I had directed refusal *against* the best advice of the IO involved, a senior man whose knowledge and judgement I had, until then, always respected.

Which – here we go again – was the first problem, and the second that it had indeed been taken up by an MP, which by now[40] again *meant something,* even in general; and besides I knew this one in particular, who didn't take up *any* case lightly and *never* just to make a point. And he would always phone through to speak to the CIO, genuinely off the record (so that rarity of rarities, a *politician you could really trust*), before taking matters further. Which was the *third* problem, because his letter to the Minister went into considerable and embarrassing detail about our (his and my) verbatim and truly vitriolic telephone exchange, which itself had lead directly *to* his written reps. in the first place.

But the biggest problem, say a good twelve on a scale of one to ten, was the fourth, which was that I couldn't remember a bloody single thing about *any* of it, about the phone call *or* the case, and all I'd put on the file about the former was a brief and succinct – no, a curt – note: 'Spoke at length to --- ------ MP, who argued with some warmth against the decision. But in the end declined to alter it,' which was about as helpful (and welcome, as the Big Yin had first said the year before)) as a fart in a spacesuit, and provided no ammo. for any kind of defence now, either.

So there was only one logical explanation. I must have flipped, and flipped big time. A swiftly creeping inability to cope with the pressure had clearly lead to a one-off (at least I fucking *hoped* a one-off), sudden and calamitous misjudgement – or to put it more simply, I'd just cracked wide open. Going bananas had, I suppose, been my secret fear – or one of them – of CIO-ship all along. It had already happened to others, and now there it was, the undeniable evidence that it had happened to *me*.

Anyway staring at the ceiling didn't help so I tried shutting my eyes instead, and praying to my newly-accustomed deity, *Clint, help me now.* But this time he just wouldn't play, not even *Mistyly*, and perhaps this wasn't an area where he could really assist – after all, I couldn't recall a film where *he'd* ever totally lost it – his cool, yes, regularly, but never his marbles – wait though, there *was* that one where he lost a leg and ate the mushrooms[41], but I didn't have even either half *that* excuse… Then, *I could always embroider things a little,* but I dismissed the thought at once. I never had, and I wasn't going to start now. Honesty, telling the truth and the whole of it etc., had been ingrained deeply in me by dear old Dad, long since dead, and besides, that was where *Clint* surely *would* have intervened and given me a good whipping – verbally – if nothing else.

So I sat, and brooded, and as I brooded the problem grew and became first *really serious* and then a total *fucking nightmare,* a standard exaggeration of reality which often happens at night when you're shagged out for the wrong (or even the right) reason. *Christ, what the hell came over me?* I thought. *OK, there's nothing wrong with the case itself* – so I was deep, deep into self-delusion now, too – *but telling the MP –* this *MP – he could shove it right up his… and no-one will believe me if I say I can't remember because who'd forget a thing like that, and I'd rather resign and spare them the pleasure.*

And it was with this in mind that I was reaching for my pen for a first draft – "Dear Chief Inspector, It is with great regret…" – when there was a knock on the door and Don walked in. Hell, I must have been in as bad a state tonight too because I'd forgotten he was on, the very man whose advice I'd always valued – except on the case in question. "Don," I said, shaking myself free from my sorrows – well, almost. "What's up?"

"Hello, mate. Oh, nothing, really. Someone said earlier that you didn't look too good, so I just thought I'd check. *Are* you all right?" And he peered at me, searchingly, just as a good senior IO should.

"Yeah, yeah," I said. "Just tired, I expect." And then I pushed the Minister's file across. No harm in someone else having a look, especially when he'd been there and fully involved and *I* could remember fuck-all in the first place. "Ring any bells?"

He opened the file and read for a minute, then frowned and looked up. "Ah. Hmm. *Oh, yes, I* remember, the Portuguese. Our first and only argument. And to tell the truth, we all thought you, er, went out on a bit of a limb."

"Yeah," I said again, but bitterly this time. After all, by then I'd been in the job for twelve years and had been beginning to think that at long last I really *did* know something about it. "And now the MP's cut it off." The limb, I meant – *In like Clint?*

"Oh," he said, and then, lightly as his face cleared, "well, you can't win 'em all," a standard line of my own but one which I thought was far *too* fucking light in the circumstances, in fact almost goddamn flippant. But I said nothing, as he glanced down the 126. "Hey," he said after a moment, "noticed his place of birth?" The passenger's he meant, and he'd said *that* lightly, too.

"No," I said. I was beginning to lose patience, so I continued, "Can *you* think of anything –" but he cut me right off, the rude shit.

"Hmm. *Casas Parliamentieras*," he mused, with heavy emphasis. "I know Portugal pretty well but I've never come across that place before. I wonder whereabouts it is," but I wasn't really listening.

"Listen," I said, but he cut me off again.

"Hmmm. Very odd. And the *date* of birth too," he said. "November 5th."

"Don. *Listen*," I said again, but this time with an emphasis of my own. Now I was getting angry, because what I needed was some helpful, *relevant,* advice, not amateur astrology. But he was having none of it.

"And his *name.* That's *bloody* strange. *Guido Fauques,*" and he paused, and then grinned, and as *I* began to say, "Now *look,* Don," the penny finally, suddenly, dropped.

So I yelled out, *"You cunts!"* instead, to my mind·not unreasonably and in the plural because that was the moment when the door flew open and the rest of the night shift spilled in and fell about. So what can you do with staff like that? I'd have hung, drawn and quartered them all if I could, with Don last, and at least blown them all up. But you had to admit they'd played a blinder, made up the whole thing, genuine Commons notepaper and my counterfeit handwritten minutes included (that *bloody* ace Forgery Team). And although in due course I was as happy as the others – well, relieved might be more accurate – it struck me later that they must've thought I was well on the way in the first place, or I'd never have fallen for it. *Paranoia;* when you've got it, that's what you see, see? Plots, plots everywhere.

SUFFER THE CHILDREN

Fascist bastards (*and* bitches, naturally) by definition, that's what we were all right, especially at annual Union Conference time when so described by the ranting rest of the Civil Service membership. And *compassion? Us?* Never heard of it. Another easy charge was that we only dealt in stereotypes, so you want stereotypes, immigration-style? Then try this. They were *all* female, *all* Western European, *all* young or *almost* all, and most came from Spain or Portugal or appeared to, because neither was in the EC yet so they couldn't just routinely walk through the control unexamined like the rest, whilst the Curtain was still largely rust-and wholly hole-free, so their equivalents in the East – and there must have been a few, some, many – still couldn't even get out.

Young? Most were between eighteen and their early twenties; a few sixteen or seventeen and a further few much older, well into their thirties, and *their* extra dimension was there all right if you looked, or if you'd seen one of that age before: a certain false bravado, a barely hidden defiance, a harder shell born out of a hard life's other remembered vicissitudes. So you're half-way there, half-way to a so-called *stereotype* already. But let me offend the purists, the experts, the *sociologists* of this world still further.

Because when they, any of this group, reached the Control, they *all* lied, *every fucking one,* because that then, in their circumstances, was what you did, and all you could do. And whenever I could I'd give such a case to a keen, fresh recruit, just *bursting* to catch a first *real live liar* out in the act and having done so, to send him – or her – straight back whence they'd come, quoting the standard accepted universal Service logic that *any* passenger caught telling you *any* lie stood to be refused entry because after that you couldn't believe anything else he – or she – said.

'One pork pie and back they go.' That was the rule we lived and routine refusals left by[42]. But these cases were different, because they provided salutary object lessons to new staff – both technically, in the fundamental *legal* requirement of fairness, i.e. of hearing both sides, of giving a person a chance to explain things before reaching a final decision; and more basically still, in *human* terms, in the proper British exercise not only of power but also, when you could (which wasn't always), of compassion. And there was a third lesson too, of equal value to anyone who wanted to try at least to understand a basic truth, not just about passengers, but about people – *all* people: that lies conceal a multitude of perceived sins, only one of which is a wholly understandable desire to enter the UK.

So. All and always. They would always be travelling alone. They would all say they'd come for a few days, for a short holiday, and they would all have a lot of money – a lot for them, anyway – and always cash, although they were often though not always poor and employed at best in menial jobs. And usually they would say they knew nobody here and that they would find a cheap hotel in London – always London – once they got there. Ring a bell? They were, in short, classic 'credibility' refusals, open and shut, with 'credibility' a complete misnomer since it was precisely what they lacked, and all the more so because even a novice, even a *bloody fool*, couldn't fail to spot the lies. And the routine suspicion would rightly be that any passenger who told you such a ridiculous story, as many others routinely did, was really coming here to work.

But with these cases two things were always different: firstly, they always had dated return tickets consistent with their claimed length of stay; and secondly, you could always see guilt and shame and sometimes sorrow etched deep into their faces, even though they tried to hide it and even before they began to lie. Always, if you knew how to look (and believe me, *I* did, because now and then I used a mirror). *Always.*

Most experienced IOs could spot them in advance, and work the queue to see or to avoid them, according to personal choice. Lost, embarrassed, uneasy or with eyes down or roving wildly (the passengers I mean), this was often their first and for many would be their only trip abroad and they'd never been coached on how to respond and behave when properly, professionally, examined – well, how could they be, when there was no-one at home whom they could ask?

And when they were first sat down, they would stick firmly to their story, the one constant – stick desperately, *religiously* even you might say, because they were all always Catholic. And then the baggage search would reveal a real pre-arranged address, or a date and time for the Clinic. Or they would suddenly realise that the consequence of maintaining the lie would be an immediate return, *intact*, to their starting point, and that was mostly when the truth would emerge (though sometimes, finally, you had to ask directly). And then they usually cried, sometimes bitterly, because this was their first moment of truly shared release, because until now they'd told no-one in the world of their situation, unless perhaps a friend and least of all their parents, and because they were *truly* desperate.

Abortion, then: readily accessible in the UK at a price; by then, here, no longer a dirty word, easily said by many others and perfectly – to some, laudably – legal; but illegal and abhorrent, a *mortal sin*, in the eyes of the Church in their homeland. And now was when their eyes would fill with tears of fear and shame, if they weren't full already.

And on occasion, having got to the truth, the less sensitive of the new IOs, of both sexes, would still happily refer the case as a simple refusal, treating the delayed weeping confession as no more than the final proof of the initial lie.

"So," I would say, sitting back and fully at home at Two by now. "What do *you* want to do?" It was what you always asked all new IOs anyway whatever the nature of the case if they didn't volunteer their own opinion, to make them make their own minds up and to appreciate the weight of *any* refusal decision. But now there was something extra.

"Send her back of course," said sometimes almost indignantly – with 'What the hell d'you *think* I want to do?' loudly *un*said – and if there were any more senior IOs about and they overheard, they might stop and listen in, '*Clint* (or *Groucho*, or *Ernie*) at it again,' you could see and hear them if you looked. I did. But by and large the recruit would rattle on, blissfully unaware.

"Why?" I would ask, always a better, deeper, question than 'Who?' or 'When?' or 'Where?' but only when asked at the right time, and now designed either to wind them up still more, or to give them food for thought, or sometimes both.

"*Why?* Because she lied about her reason for coming, *that's* why!" – 'Silly dithering old sod with your heart on your sleeve, at this rate you'll be the next one hiding in the loo to avoid making *any* decisions.'

"Yes, that's true, she did. At first. And now?"

"*Now? Now* she's admitted she's *really* here for an abortion." – 'As you *already* damn-well know.'

"Right. And *now* you *believe* her?" (I resisted the smart-arse route of then adding 'Why?' again, given that she'd already lied, because this was a human problem, not an exercise in pure logic.)

"Yes, but -"

Which was when I let them have it. "And is that an *acceptable* reason for entry here as a visitor, if she'd told the truth straight off, providing she can pay? Or are you making a *moral* judgement?"

"Yes. No. But -"

"And do you believe she means to go home afterwards?"

"Yes, but -"

"And have you thought what will happen to her if you send her back *now*?"

"Yeah, tough, but that's not our concern and -"

"OK, you're right, it *needn't* be. But *'tough'*? Is that *it*? Do you think she's made this decision *lightly*? And if you were a young Catholic girl, desperate, ashamed, alone and with no-one to turn to, who'd somehow kept her dread secret from the world, would *you* tell the truth straight off to a complete stranger? And what might you do *next, here and now* even, if you were told you were going straight back? Thought of *that too*, have you?" (And this was where I had to keep a tight rein on myself and descend swiftly from the soap box *and* the moral pulpit, because it was getting very close to becoming visibly personal.)

Remorseless see, self-righteous even (the IOs I mean, of course), and then most of them, of both sexes and some Catholic themselves for all I knew, might start to think, *What if it was me?* and another valuable lesson would've been learned. And if one or two persisted I'd send them off for a talk with a more experienced IO colleague, and if *that* failed they'd have a private talk with me when I wouldn't always be so calm (though I tried, if only for my own protection), and if *that* failed too I'd watch them very closely for a while in case they were in the wrong job and were really suited for a black uniform and jack boots. Or even a bullet in the neck.

But it wasn't that simple, nothing ever is, and on abortion no-one is neutral. So sometimes I'd turn up in the bar that same evening for the wind-down pints to find them still hard at it, men *and* women, and I was constantly surprised to see who was on which side of the argument. And me? I'd just sit back and drink and listen and play Devil's Advocate and throw in the odd inflammatory word and buy an extra round because it was good for them (the extra round apart) and because it told me more about them, as the end-of-day pints always did (especially if we all overcooked it).

And all the time I probably knew a damn sight more about it than the rest of them put together, about the *practical* side of it that is and of course only from the male point of view, but I never told them *that*. So, hypocrite. No, *fucking* hypocrite. *That's* better, *that's* more *dynamically accurate*. Or *bloody* fucking hypocrite. *That's* more comprehensive and dynamically accurate still.

OUT OF THE BLUE

The unexpected happened predictably often at Terminal Two, partly because it seemed that whenever anyone anywhere else in the world phoned Directory Enquiries to ask for a number for UK Immigration, it was Two's that they were given. Early April1982 now, and for months the UK's eyes had been fixed on Poland, on Walensa and *Solidarnosc* and the striking Gdansk miners and what the hell was going to happen next. And we at Two had a particular interest, because we had our daily LOT (National Polish Airline) flights and so prepared daily for the worst (another Czecho, or even another Hungary perhaps). And then, overnight, the Falklands changed all that.

I was sitting minding my own business in the Casework Office one morning, browsing through the already thick file of one of the already growing number of asylum cases – oh yes, *that's* right, it was *'Crawford's'* file, that being the sobriquet we'd given him upon arrival; well, at least it had nothing to do with cigars, or slouches, and had seemed much less religiously inappropriate somehow than *'Jacob's'*, the obvious alternative for a man whose real name was Karim Karakas – when my phone rang. I'm not sure of the precise date, but the Argies had attacked on the 2nd and it was only a day or two later.

As I picked up and said, "Terminal Two," on the dubious but mostly well-founded premise that anyone calling us would already know that they were calling Immigration somewhere at Heathrow but might have the wrong terminal, there was a brief pause in which I could hear a distant humming and a little static but no defensive gunfire from the marines of Naval Party 8901, which would have made the story much more dramatic but was long since over. Then a calm male British voice destroyed the basis of my initial brief response by saying, "*Hello*. Is that the UK Immigration Service?"

"Yes," I said. "It is."

"And who am I talking to, please?"

I told him, and I sensed that he was writing it down.

Then, "Are you a Senior Officer?"

I confirmed that, comparatively, I was.

"Good. My name is Rex Hunt and I'm the Governor of the Falkland Islands. You will be aware -"

"Yes, sir, I am," I said, snapping out of my semi-stupor. Sir? It had been a guiding principle of mine from Day One in the job and in fact for years before – Dad, again – never to call *anyone* 'sir' unless they were so entitled, but this seemed a good time to make an exception (and besides, the way it turned out, I was only ahead of the game).

"You are? Right. Well, it's possible in the current circumstances that some of my people may want to leave, for a while anyway, until things are sorted out. Can you guarantee that if they decide to come to the UK, they will be let in without any condition – treated as if they were British?"

Well maybe I wasn't the fastest thinker on the planet, but it struck me in the blink of an eye that this gent might just have a lot on his mind and that the last thing he needed was some pompous pedantic prick, of whatever rank, laying down the technicalities of a law that wasn't designed for this situation in the first place. I also reckoned that I could safely predict Maggie's response, which would mirror that of the man in the street; and in any case a negative answer was unthinkable.

So. "Yes, sir," I repeated – decisively, I hoped.

"So then. Let's be quite clear. You are *guaranteeing* them entry, without any difficulty or formality?"

"Yes, sir," I said, yet again. Then, "certainly, of course." And I wanted to say more, even to utter a few words of encouragement, but it seemed presumptuous somehow. So I didn't.

"Good. Thank you then, Mr. Clarke," he said, and rang off. We never spoke again.

I put the phone down and turned to Pete, the Casework IO, sitting beside me. "Did you hear *exactly* what *I* said?" I asked. "Can you remember it?"

"Yes, Mike," he replied – after all it wasn't complicated, and the only problem was getting the right number of 'yes's'. *My* only problem was that I couldn't decide whether *he* thought I'd just been *Clint,* or *Groucho.*

"OK," I said. "Then write it out for me, would you?" and, albeit with raised eyebrows – so perhaps he really thought I was *Ernie* – he did, and was spot-on (five of them, I mean).

"Guess who that was," I said then, and when of course he couldn't, I told him. And then I did a brief report and sent it off and yet again never heard another word. Perhaps no-one ever read it, but I like to think that if they had and if somehow the whole Falklands business had gone tits-up, I would still have had the support of my superiors because in those days even the ones at the very top had started at the very bottom, and doing what you thought was right was almost always acceptable if not quite laudable, even if it turned out badly. (It seems laughable now, when in general the trick is always to avoid responsibility for anything bad, however deeply you've been involved in it, always to pass blame downwards and always to grab the plaudits for anything good, however personally undeserved. But there you go.)

In the event as far as I can remember, no Islander did decide to come at that time (though I believe one or two did later) so it all meant nothing. And now Sir Rex too, like far too many on either side at the time, is dead. I just wish I'd had a chance to talk to him later, again by phone if necessary, to apologise for not having seemed more supportive – I was, fully; but I simply thought he d be too bloody busy.

TWO EXCURSIONS

But before I delve more deeply into life at the terminal itself, I'd better describe the two ventures from it that I made in my early years there, one brief and voluntary to the MCU and the other to Appeals, predictably much longer though also self-inflicted, and in the end much longer still than even *I* had ever thought.

So: the MCU first: let's get that *right* out of the way. The

initials stood for the Ministerial Casework Unit, an outfit
hastily set up on the old government site at Harmondsworth
on the A4 some considerable time before, to deal with the
then still-burgeoning case representations made by MPs. And
what more can I usefully and constructively tell you about it,
especially without the use of obscenities? Well, not fucking
much but I'll try, and in the event I wasn't there long, only
three months or so. But it seemed endless – not because of the
staff who were of regular IS stamp and with many of whom,
especially those from Two and Three (it being a multi-terminal
operation), I already had at least a nodding acquaintance; nor
because of the work itself, which was plentiful, interesting
though paper-driven and quite different from anything I'd
done before.

No, my problem was with what lay *behind* the work, with
what seemed to me, to pretty much everyone else there and to
the IS at large a blatant abuse of the so-called system not just
by the cases (mostly extant refusals) themselves – after all, you
could hardly blame *them* for trying anything on offer to pre-
empt removal – but by a small and vociferous de facto caucus
of MPs which generated a large majority of the reps against
refusal, every one of which required its own individual reply.

These (these particular MPs, I mean), in their consistently
strident if *not quite* hysterical representations on behalf of
those who by definition could not themselves possibly be *any*
Member's constituents – and who, had *that* somewhat dubious
general privilege been at least possible, could often not then
have been any more specifically *theirs* by any geographical
stretch, given that they dwelt well outside the constituency in
question and sometimes whole cities away – these few MPs,
I say, would with obvious and, it seemed to us, downright
malicious glee repeat as established, indisputable fact quite

outrageous fiction which, if they *really* believed *any* of it, would at least explain their clear deep hatred of all immigration legislation and indeed of the very Service , a hatred which I can only conclude made them see it as their bound duty to use (or abuse) their position to attack the whole principle of Control itself (although if pressed, I could doubtless also ascribe other, more general and perhaps less noble motives).

Even so, in three months there must, *must,* have been a funny story or two to recount if I could recall them. But I can't – or rather I *can* but only one, and *that*, like the other involving the Branch, can't be told for a long time yet, if at all. So let's leave it that if there was ever any one place within the Service where you just *had* to have a strong and wishfully-macabre sense of humour to keep even a tenuous grip on your jangling marbles, it was at the MCU. And sorry for the brief rant of quasi-Ciceronian prose: for a moment I quite forgot myself, and thought that I was actually *back* there (or perhaps still at Appeals).

(Oh, and I almost forgot. What exactly *was* the extra *practical* value of an MP making reps on your behalf? Well surely by now you've guessed it. Simply that by the time the MCU's reply, whatever its nature, was finally forthcoming under the Minister's signature, you would have had even longer, say an extra year or so or even more at the phenomenon's height, gratefully to vanish into the receptive, retentive British woodwork.)

I don't have much more to say on this subject, which fills me still with those familiar co-emotions of anger and shame, but I'll say this. Anger *at others* I mean, especially that same coterie of MPs. Their identities became as wholly predictable to us as their actions, and when at last their endless arguments were so severely checked as to put a long-overdue stop to *that* abuse, they recovered swiftly to recast their general venom at *what* we did for a living into the next best specific thing. They attacked *how* we did it instead so that *representations* morphed into *complaints,* mere vehicles for a strong and sometimes again almost-hysterical outrage as they accepted on the nod and as self-evident the most manifestly absurd allegations of the Service's perennial incompetence, regular malpractice and occasional downright physical brutality when the *real* truth, just as apparent, was that they were still simply out for IS blood as they always had been, with no interest whatsoever in the facts which they still often refused to believe even after in our responses we had recounted them to the satisfaction of any reasonable man, crowing instead in triumph at the final and now-irrefutable proof of what in their paranoia they'd of course *also* known all along, namely that we were *excellent at cover-ups,* too.

And Shame *for* my front-line colleagues, who had to put up with this repetitive and cumulative load of crap, the other unlooked-for result – ironically, a sad one – being that when a genuine complaint did arise, as they inevitably did albeit comparatively rarely but all the more significantly for that, it stood a real risk of being treated as yet another figment generated in necessarily-jaundiced minds.

Anyway, *enough.* So let's move on swiftly to Appeals, where I went for the standard initial six months with an option for the same again, and finished up staying for almost two years. The Appeals Unit was at Harmondsworth too, in Building GA, a shabby Second World War hut in the same row as the MCU and the IS Training Unit, with the IU (the aforementioned Intelligence Unit) also located on site and within easy walking distance across the green and mossy cracked concrete ways. The other main IS-related operation on site was in Building

DA whose initials will loom large in the memories, nostalgic or otherwise, of anyone in IS (and not just Heathrow) at the time. Because it was the IS's main national Detention Centre, and *our* only local one, long-term.

Every new Heathrow CIO of my generation had to do a single month at Appeals soon after promotion, and much as an unhappy few disliked their stay intensely it was still extremely valuable because there's no better way of teaching the real meaning and effect of the Laws you are required to obey and to enforce than to make you publicly defend – before an independent, articulate and when appropriate, truly scathing Adjudicator – the sometimes-debatable front-line decisions of colleagues employed to do the same.

But to anyone with eyes it was abundantly clear that in such a short one-month spell, the first half under close supervision, you merely touched the tip of the legal iceberg in establishing a sound and wide-based knowledge of the relevant legislation, in which – erstwhile, like me – you had perhaps foolishly considered yourself a comparative expert; and if you'd enjoyed that brief initiation, you could apply to go back later for *six* months, and most of those who did then opted to stay on still longer, for a year or even two, and *that* was when you *really* learned what the other side of the job was all about.

At any given time there would be up to six long-term CIOs and one HMI in GA, where we prepared our own cases and held the hands of the one-monthers during their first two weeks. The block in between us and the Detention Centre was logically enough Building FA, which housed the Adjudicators and our standard quasi-legal opposition, the UKIAS (UK Immigrants' Advisory Service). And lest any amongst you is waiting for some witticism about the significance, in terms of the inmates, of *those* initials (FA I mean), let me say right now that pretty much without exception the Adjudicators were well-respected and highly competent and so were the UKIAS – well, most of them – as for that matter were we, in GA – well, by and large.

One or two other major ports in the country – Dover, for example – had their own Appeals Centres, but generally IS appeals came to us, and we also represented the Home Office in other immigration-related cases such as refusals of extensions of stay and proposed deportations. When we lost a case – and my memory now is that at that time we lost overall about fifteen per cent – we had the option of seeking leave to take it to the next higher court, The Immigration Tribunal in Fleet Street, and if our application was granted the Appeals HMI or one of the CIOs – usually the Admin. CIO, the longest-serving and most appeals-experienced CIO there – would trog off to old London Town, opposite the Law Courts and just past the *Wig and Pen,* to present it.

And that more or less is what we did day in, day out, with one notable addition: we were also responsible for the oversight of the Detention Centre, DA, itself staffed by guards from Securicor or Group 4 or whoever had the contract at the time – it did change hands now and then, but generally the same crew remained in situ and just put on different uniforms. So on top of his appeals caseload, each CIO had a specific responsibility for some part of the DA operation and when I started, I copped Health and Safety, a comparative sinecure which however included Fire precautions (fire the ultimate nightmare, given the spread of non-English speaking nationalities likely to be housed there at any one time and thus the difficulty in achieving swift or even sometimes *any* understanding and compliance in an emergency, especially at night).

And now that I've begun to talk about DA, I may as well

carry on. A *Detention* Centre, did I say? Well, so it was, but in terms of its effectiveness it was something between a probation hostel and an open prison. Inmates didn't escape that often, just regularly which meant whenever they really wanted to, and we knew how and where they got out but there was no political will for change and so it went on and on. For example, just before my first Christmas there – on December 23rd to be precise – two West Africans disappeared, over the wire as usual, and as usual we did our standard absconder reports and thought, *That's the last we'll ever see of them*. But late the next day, on a foggy, festive Christmas Eve, the surprised guards flung open the main doors in response to a thunderous knocking from outside. And there they were.

They were truly exhausted as they staggered in, and *begging* for food. But not because they had been running full-speed non-stop from their non-existent eager pursuers, and had mistakenly come full circle in the fog. No, no, they were bowed down instead under the weight of their Christmas shopping, which their laden bags revealed they had done sensibly and frugally, mainly at Woolies and Marks and Sparks. And the food they begged for was the next day's, their Christmas Dinners – were they too late to request their particular preference? – but while they were at it, if perchance there *was* anything left of *that* day's evening meal…

And the following summer we encountered a determined attempt by a larger group of West Africans – I don't know why it always seemed to be *them*, but it did – to change the whole basis on which the menu was constructed. They didn't like *a thing* on it they said, and would go on a united hunger-strike until it was changed. They didn't actually say 'Until death,' but their meaning was clear. So we monitored them very carefully, daily, over the succeeding weeks and fair dos, although they came nowhere close to Bobby Sands who had died in the preceding May and who perhaps gave them the idea in the first place, they stuck stubbornly to their self-appointed task, and it was still almost a month before they gave up and began to eat again. Between meals, that is.

The menu, then: always a difficult proposition, given the variety of inmates' cultures, conscience and religions, let alone their actual appetites. Still, there was a standard choice of nine main courses covering the whole gamut, all pretty good – I know because we in GA had to try them, once a week, a chore we never shirked because they *were* pretty good and on the house – and panic regularly ensued whenever one of the ageing freezers packed up and a whole batch of a particular dish had to be thrown away and replaced at the latest by the next day.

The *menu*: ah yes, now I remember. Eventually I became the Admin. CIO myself and one morning, in the absence elsewhere of the Inspector, I was informed out of the blue that a respected (sic) journalist for one of the dailies had asked to be shown round DA, that the requisite central permission had been given a week before and that the visit would take place that very day, within a couple of hours in fact, and Sorry about the lack of notice. Nothing needed to be done anyway – I always thought it best to show things as they really were, and red carpets would only have been nicked – so I was ready and waiting when the newshound aforesaid arrived, shepherded along by a clearly-apprehensive Home Office Press Officer. We shook hands – well, some of us did, I had no trouble with the journalist but the Press Officer seemed never to have encountered the human gesture before, not, I thought, a good opening sign, especially for one in her profession – and without further ado, we set off.

And things went smoothly until we reached the kitchen, where I pointed helpfully to a menu on the wall.

"Ah," the journalist said, "the *menu*," with an unusual emphasis, then paused and looked closely at me, presumably for effect, though for precisely *what* effect I didn't have a bloody clue.

"Yes," I said. Cautiously. I didn't like journalists as a breed and I still don't. I'd seen what they could do to the true facts of an immigration story before, and I have since. Still, so far so good. And the next question, "How many alternatives do you provide for each main course?"

"Nine," I said – you could see them all there, if you looked – and I waited for the next. But it was a statement instead.

"You're lying," the journalist said, just like that, with an intonation which I assume was meant to be interpreted as the ultimate menace, and presumably waited for me to crack instantly, confess all and throw myself either on my own sword or failing that, on his (or her) mercy.

Well, it affected me all right, but not in the way presumably expected. Instead, it was simply that I couldn't believe my ears. "Pardon?" I asked, sharply.

"I said you're *lying* – I have my own sources, and I *know* you are," he/she said proudly, in what I presume he/she took to be his/her finest investigative, provocative style – God, *what* an amateur – and momentarily I debated whether to throw the clown out on the spot, or to let the tour proceed. In the event, with no intercession whatsoever from the Press Officer who stood there mouth agape like a prize lemon, I did the latter and the remainder passed off without incident, albeit with a certain residual and perhaps unsurprising mutual coolness.

I duly reported the exchange verbatim – there was never an HQ response to *that* one, either – and when the article came out in one of the broadsheets, I read it with due interest. In my view it was somewhat biased but only mildly so, and had it not been for that one extraordinary allegation of which oddly enough no written mention was made, I would have thought no more about it. But that memory has informed my view of the competence and character of that particular journalist ever since, and if this book sells and if one day we chance again to meet, I hope to make my view clear, in person and ideally with an equally quiescent Home Office Press Officer and/or other suitable independent witness present, though either is of course most unlikely, let alone both.

So back to Appeals, our *raison d'etre,* the third sharp end of the Immigration Suppository – sorry, Service – and fundamentally different from both border and enforcement work, but no less daunting in its way. Because paperwork apart, in either of those fields you generally had a semblance of protection, a barrier both moral and physical – at the port from your colleagues and SB and on the street, then, from uniformed police – but in court as a Presenting Officer, there were the appellant, your legal opponent who could be anything from a UKIAS representative to a sometimes well-known barrister, the Adjudicator and any interpreter and any witnesses. And *you*, you and you alone for the IS/Home Office, and if that wasn't your cup of tea you could suddenly feel *very* much alone.

But it suited the extrovert, the showman – sorry, show-person – to a T, and although you might think that anyone who had done the main job long enough to get promoted, say (then) for a minimum of ten years, would be so used to speaking to people as to regard this as a doddle, it didn't always work out that way. For a start you suddenly found yourself *performing* and *in public*, which didn't come easily to the occasional introvert or naturally shy and which could knock you off your balance completely – I saw it happen only once there, and it was not a pretty sight; and on top of that, even then the Service had a sprinkling – small still, but growing – of CIOs whose first recourse was always the Rule Book, and whilst that might have seemed the ideal approach to have when defending a decision already taken under a specific and precise Immigration Rule or an even more precise part of The Act, in real life it just didn't cut it.

Because this was *theatre*, at least in part, unforgiving and instant, and if a problem arose it was often your wits and not your technical knowledge, the spoken not the written word that you had to rely on to get you out of it. In the end, it all came down to self-confidence and if you ever let yourself get really destroyed in court, just that once, unless you were a remarkable character you were finished there forever.

So it was apparent that those of us who stayed on beyond the first six months were either determined masochists or had both done well enough to be asked to and also enjoyed the experience enough to agree; and that covered most of the people who came, because in general we were neither introverted nor shy. And apart from anything else it was a welcome break from shifts, in particular from the nights which, little by little and dark forests apart, ground you down anyway.

I was lucky in my time at GA because I already knew each of the two successive HMIs and most of the other CIOs with whom I served, the Adjudicators proved with rare exceptions to be men or women of the world, and most of the opposition, particularly the UKIAS, proved to be both worthy and pleasant opponents. When I began, there were three full-time Adjudicators, two of them, both male, senior ex-Colonials and a much younger woman who was herself ex-UKIAS. Each was fair, forthright, tolerant of our occasional inevitable legal aberrations and in short nobody's fool, and when the elder of the two gents retired and was replaced by an ex-barrister with a prior Forces background and impeccable manners (though one doesn't *always* follow from the other), there was no noticeable break in continuity.

But Appeals was a serious business and sometimes a sad one, because from time to time you were a witness, often helpless, to the human tragedies played out in the endless comedy, writ large *and* long, of Immigration Control. Here though, as often as not what you saw was the result of a sin of blind and selfish commission, of what to a westerner was bound to appear as wholly misdirected family loyalty not to say greed, and destined to end in a personal disaster, often confirmed as such by the time the predictable victim appeared in person before you.

So let me describe a typical case of the time, because although you may well know the general publicised score, there may be one or two add-ons which you don't. Such a scenario would involve a young UK-born girl, second generation sub-continent but naturally English-speaking (though in the home they would all speak Punjabi/Urdu/Bengali, you name it, because even if her father had some small command of English, her mother would have none) and already British in many ways. For the cast (no pun) to be complete, she would sometimes already have an English boyfriend too (again sub-continental in origin of course, she wasn't *that* independent) but often it was just her, rebelling against the marriage arranged by her loving family to the illiterate subsistence farmer, say from the Punjab, who just happened to be her second cousin too and who was now the very subject of the appeal..

Sometimes, in Act One, the marriage had not yet occurred,

at least not the 'court' (legal) marriage in the UK; well, it couldn't have could it, because her husband or husband-to-be depending on your point of view was still in India (and in my time and memory it usually *was* India) and seeking his entry clearance, his 'visa', to join his wife here – and arguably she *was* his wife already because they had already had the 'custom' marriage, maybe years before, when the family had ostensibly taken her back, just for her first holiday, and there he was, the man of her future dreams except that they'd never told her that that was what he was pre-destined to be and that they were to be wed. But then there was the ceremony and the festivities and perhaps the bed too if she really wasn't *that* young, say seven or eight, and so she *was*, she *had* to be, hadn't she? (Married, I mean).

That was the way it worked, of course; *from* there *to* here, always. Well, we wouldn't be having an appeal in the first place if *she* were going to join *him there,* would we? But that would be pointless wouldn't it, a backward step after the family had itself got a foothold – and *that* was what it was all about, getting more family members out. And in.

And the girl's interests? Well, her father and the family knew best – and sometimes I'm sure that he and they genuinely thought that they really did, especially if they didn't think too much of *us,* and that it *would* all work out all right for *her* too. But at the end of the day, what did her view matter – she was after all only a woman.

And sometimes, we were already at Act Two, or more strictly Act Three, because the visa had *already* been granted to her cousin the farmer, and he had *already* come to join her here, and for a short while, a year or even two – and by then no-one with any realistic perspective could describe that by current UK standards as a particularly *short* marriage – everything seemed all right. But by then – if it really was Act Three – she'd had their baby too, and suddenly he was out drinking all the time and when she tried to talk to him about it he just beat her and that was why she'd written to the Home Office, secretly, just like the blushing bride or bride-to-be still in Act One, to ask that her strangely-changed husband be forced to 'go home', by which she meant the sub-continent, where he belonged.

And that was why we were now in the hearing room, because once the Home Office had decided to act on what she'd told them, the decision was subject to appeal and then what she'd said, naively assuming it would remain in confidence, *couldn't* be, and she was going to have to appear and say it all over again, out loud and in public. And so sometimes if her man hadn't yet come here she'd have a sudden change of heart and write again to say that she wanted to support him after all because her family had talked to her and she knew, now, that everything was going to be all right after all; and so the visa would be issued – and if *she* had been right in the first place instead, we would move perhaps sharply to Act Three. And if he *had* come, to say that to her delight his attitude had changed again, suddenly, even overnight, in fact right after the refusal letter from the Home Office, when, as if by a miracle, he had instantly become the man she'd always wanted him to be (as indeed, given the circumstances and strictly in the short term, he might well have done).

But sometimes the really brave ones – they might just have been plain wilful, of course – *did* make it to the hearing, and maintained what they'd said in the first place; and sometimes there'd be a no-show – by, say, a UK-resident relative of the appellant (the husband) if he was not yet himself here; or by the main man if he was, but who now for some sound reason found it impossible to attend. And then the hearing would be adjourned to allow him to have his day in court because it was no more than natural British justice, though in view of the wife's evidence things were already stacked against him. But sometimes – all right, if you want the truth of it, quite often – *that* would be when the letter of retraction arrived from the wife, its wording dependant on whether we'd only reached Act One, or a baby-less Act Two, or the full cast in Act Three.

And why? Pressure of course, verbal and physical, the violence sometimes severe or perhaps just the threat of it, applied simply to the woman or, in Act Three, to the child instead or as well, especially if female, and as often as not as much from her (the wife's) own father as from her husband, or indeed from the pair of them. Oh, I couldn't prove it, none of us could because if we'd been able to, we would have involved the police ourselves like a shot and to hell with fumbling, bumbling Social Services.

But we saw it in the residual cases, the ones where despite *all* the pressure, despite the adjournment and whatever followed, the wife *would* appear again, still manifestly brave but now sporting a swollen face or a broken limb sustained somehow by accident, and sometimes *that* was when she would, finally, reluctantly, recant, watched in helpless, silent outrage by the Adjudicator and our side at least, and by the UKIAS too if they were representing, and overseen/orchestrated carefully by the various members of her loving family who sat stony-faced – and complete with their own murmuring unofficial interpreter, just to make doubly sure – during her humiliation, and afterwards escorted her, oh so protectively, away.

But just, just occasionally the *really* brave ones would *still* not give in, they simply *would not*, and *they* were the ones who told *us* quietly in advance not to worry, who assured us that they'd made all the necessary arrangements for themselves, and for their babies if it was Act Three. But sometimes there would still be family members there and then afterwards we would form our own unofficial escort and take them (the brave ones, I mean) out of the building and right through onto the A4 and into the waiting car or cab, and watch them drive swiftly away And God knows what happened to them after that, except that once or twice – and I think it was twice, in the time I was there – we'd later get a call from a Child Protection Unit asking for details of our past involvement, and we'd tell them what we could.

Once again it was enough to make you just a tad cynical, if you weren't already. But not all such cases reflected a family loyalty, however perverted – or not *that* family loyalty anyway. We had others which seemed at first glance to be identical – wife rejecting husband or husband-to-be – but *they* turned out to hinge on the non-payment by the groom's family of the *extra* dowry suddenly demanded by the wife's family *here*, to enable them to continue honestly to support the young man's application. Oh, they'd often be quite reasonable about it. It didn't have to be up front after all, but could be paid over the years after he'd got here and had begun to earn good money; and that, I thought, added a further dimension that any marriage could do without.

So wind back a little and let's all lighten up, for if all power corrupts in the first place, add in a spot of confusion and you're really in a mess. In the second week of my initial obligatory single month, by now myself presenting but still under supervision, I watched dumbly fascinated by a scene redolent of Wilde, or perhaps Rix, or even Feydeau as I said before. I was appearing for the first time in front of Sir D., one of the ex-Colonials, who had a fearsome reputation for his unwillingness or – let's be fair – his congenital inability to suffer fools gladly as, come to think of it, did his colleague Sir R. also, so perhaps it was a common feature amongst senior ex-Imperial civil servants well-used to the stowing of thrones, and why the hell not?

All I can remember about the case now is that it concerned a very attractive young woman necessarily from overseas, who had just finished giving her own evidence; that she'd travelled a fair but not wildly excessive distance to be there, from Westcliff-on-Sea to be precise; that she'd arrived by taxi, perhaps because although unmarried she was clearly pregnant – so clearly in fact as to make it inconceivable that she could hide still less bury *that* bun – and what, if any, relevance her condition had to the legal case itself, I have no precise idea (Alzheimer's, remember?) though it probably had *some,* as in Act Three; and finally that her cabbie, presumably bored with waiting outside – you could never tell how long these things were going to take – had come in and sat down at the back.

At this point I should explain that the hearings were almost always open to the public and anyone could come and watch but rarely did, unless they themselves were involved. After all the site, with a non-descript subfusc entrance directly off the east-bound carriageway and fronted uninvitingly by the forbidding if ineffective wire of the Detention Centre, was much more effectively in the middle of nowhere; and the hearings, to the ear of the average man in the street, were generally as dull as dishwater. So by and large, the only times outsiders turned up were on the rare occasions when there was press interest or when, as on the day in question, they had some peripheral involvement and had nothing else to do; At Harmondsworth, once you'd got there, there never *was* anything else to do, even on a dry day; and that day it was *pissing* down.

So, after finishing my cross-examination of the young woman without having incurred the immediate open wrath of the Adjudicator or the open derision of the opposition or even the muttered criticism of my full-time colleague beside me, I heaved a small sigh of relief and was actually sitting back in my chair when Sir D. spoke. At first he seemed to be speaking to himself, or perhaps to no-one specific and rather to the world at large. But either way he spoke clearly, and loudly.

"It's a disgrace," he said, "a *bloody disgrace*," and I began to sweat in case *this,* after all, was his true albeit delayed verdict on my cross-examination. But I slowly relaxed again as I looked round and saw that no-one else there had taken it that way, that indeed no-one there seemed able to work out who precisely Sir D. was talking *to,* or what *about,* and that accordingly no-one made any response – nor did he seem to expect any.

"A *bloody disgrace*," he then repeated, and as we all continued to sit there in a confused but respectful silence his eyes roamed the room until they lit upon the cab-driver, huddled in his jacket and half-asleep in a corner.

"*A-ha,*" intoned Sir D., apparently fulfilled. "*You,* sir," but without reply. "*You, sir,*" he repeated, with some vigour. As I said, he didn't suffer fools gladly, even – or perhaps especially – if they had nothing to be foolish about. And the cabbie stirred from his reverie, glanced around, then looked uneasily at the speaker.

"Who?" he asked. "*Who,* mate, *me?*"

"Yes, yes, *you,*" snarled Sir D. "Please be *so kind* as to *come down here,*" and he pointed directly in front of him, to the witness seat.

"*Me?*" queried the cabbie again, the tone of his voice rising in understandable and horrified disbelief, and we won't go through the series of brief exchanges which resulted, in short order, in his due arrival in the said seat – the *hot* seat as you might rightly call it, in all the circumstances.

"Now then, *sir*," said Sir D. heavily, "*what* is your *name?*" and as the cabbie gave it, not without a visible degree of reluctance, the Court Clerk duly entered it into the records. "And your occupation?"

"I'm a *taxi-driver*," replied the taxi-driver in what he clearly thought was a blinding statement of the bleeding obvious, as indeed it was to all of us except Sir D. because his licence badge was affixed to his lapel; and that too went into the records (the reply, not the badge).

"And you *know* this young woman?" said Sir D., with a heavy, almost biblical, emphasis on *know,* and indicating the appellant who for some reason then blushed hotly, which didn't help things at all.

"Well, yes, in a way like," said the cabbie, doubtfully. "I'm from Westcliff too, see, *I'm* the one who – ", and if he'd managed to get out just three more words, like " – drove her here," (though on second thoughts, even *that* was open to potential misconstruction), or if I hadn't been pulled back down instantly by my colleague, a warning finger to his lips when I'd tried instinctively to stand up to interrupt, it might have turned out differently. But he hadn't, and I had, and by now Sir D. was in full flow.

"*Yes*, that's quite enough, thank you. I'm sure that we are *all fully aware* of the extent, and indeed of the *plain result,* of your *particular* knowledge, of your very own, ah, *efforts,*" he pronounced icily as he peered over his glasses at the condition of the still-blushing mother-to-be. She was, as

I've already said, pretty pretty, so I thought 'plain' was a bit strong.

"*But -*" the cabbie managed weakly in his only attempt to take the initiative because he was totally out of his depth the poor sod and by now, not surprisingly, wholly intimidated by the looming presence on the raised dais before him.

"*Be silent sir*, other than to answer my questions," boomed Sir D., and the cabbie raised his arms briefly in a typical Souf' Essex shrug as he abandoned himself to his fate. He'd clearly already decided that being Earnest would be of no importance or assistance whatsoever.

"Tell me, then," his tormentor continued relentlessly, intent now on exposing him for what he was and cutting through the crap as usual, "*why haven't you married her?*" And the cabbie's reply, however apposite and truthful, could hardly have proved more unfortunate.

"Who, *me*, guv'nor?" he blurted out. "Why, *I'm* married already ain't I, *an* I've got free kids."

And Sir D. Exploded. "What? *Wha-a-t?* Are you *entirely* without *any* moral sense? *Leave my Court, sir.* Yes, that's it, *get ye hence, go,* and wait outside. I'm *damned* if I'll force the lady to endure your further presence; and rest assured that my determination will include clear reference to *your own sordid part* in this matter." *That must have been how he talked to the occasional recalcitrant native,* I thought as the cabbie, mystified and vanquished in equal parts, shuffled off shaking his head without another word, probably like the native, as I sat there, head down and countenance slightly suffused.

"Right, that's *that* little piece of unpleasantness over: pity I can't put the clock back as easily," said Sir D., anxious now to get on, and he turned first one way towards me and then the other towards my opposite number. "Gentlemen, it may be somewhat unusual but I shan't require *any* submissions from you on this one. *Now then.* My *dear* young woman, I shall reserve my determination, which you will receive through the post in due course. But the great thing," – and he smiled at her reassuringly as we all stood up, and she smiled back, in total bewilderment I thought at the strange turn of recent events, and who can blame her? – "the *great* thing is *not to worry*. You have my assurance that there is *no need*."

Well, I thought, *that's not a bad hint, is it?*

I noticed as we left the Court that the Clerk, a lady of considerable experience whom so far I barely knew, had exchanged a quick glance with my colleague and raised her eyes briefly to the sky; and when, two weeks later and just as I was finishing, the determination was promulgated, it came as no surprise to find both that Miss X had won her case and that there was no reference whatsoever within it to the cabbie's brief role as a witness.

Anyway we decided after a brief discussion that we wouldn't challenge the decision. It was probably the right one in the first place and it could have caused embarrassment all round, inappropriate embarrassment, because overall Sir D. was a bloody good Adjudicator and everyone was entitled to an off day – the very day incidentally on which I decided, just as I had about the job overall after my first refusal at Gatwick, that sooner or later, and for six months at least, Appeals would *have* to be the place for me.

And so again to parties – I don't know why. But we had them at Appeals too, mainly at Christmas but comparatively refined given the status of some attending – the Adjudicators, I mean. In fact, we reckoned they could put the booze away as well as any of us, but it would have been presumptuous and perhaps potentially prejudicial to put it publicly to the test. So we stayed relatively sober each time until they left, which they did consistently early to keep their side of the bargain, and *then* we could get right down to it.

In the week before Christmas the Appeals-related party venues would rotate. There would be two in FA – one in their own rooms given by the Adjudicators themselves, the other in their office laid on by the UKIAS – and finally ours, in GA; and in my mind, again one stands out clearly from the rest. An IS do of course, bound to be, and, because it *was* ours, attended as usual by a few extras whom it was politically appropriate for us to invite and whom we also genuinely wanted to see, especially the DA guards as a small thank-you – not all of them at once, naturally, or even the most timid of detainees would have trogged off to do their Christmas shopping – and Service personnel from the IU and the Training Unit (the MCU having been wound up recently, totally and finally without either ceremony *or* regret).

And it must have been my last Appeals Christmas, because by then I was the Admin. CIO and so responsible if things went wrong – which was fair enough, especially the way things turned out. The two dos we'd already attended in sweet FA had both as usual been comparatively sober affairs and we were determined that ours would as usual be *very* different – not that we had much option, as all we were doing was following a long tradition. But it so happened that the particular group of IS officers then in long term situ was an extrovert lot even by normal Service standards, and since both the Adjudicators and the UKIAS were well aware of the fact I think they too must have been quietly looking forward to something a little livelier. Well, they got that all right.

So: the first image hit you as soon as you walked in – you couldn't miss it visually and it was how you reacted *physically* that would have engrossed any passing sociologist. For Rick – a jazz drummer, now the owner of a Barcelona bar and beyond doubt the most outrageous of us all – had obtained a very early and particularly realistic example of an eight inch slab of plastic vomit – you know, full hot curry complete with spinach, sauce, saliva and gobs of carrots and peas, all swimming in still-frothy beer and with what looked like fragments of the vomiter's own liver thrown in – and had placed it artistically in the centre of the doorway so that it was intermittently illuminated through the growing gloom by the flashing lights on our Christmas tree within, and shone dully against a backdrop of highly-polished lino. As I said, you just couldn't miss it and you have to remember that although things like that are *passé* now, then it was almost ahead of its time, not to say prescient, and none of us, even the self-proclaimed artistic *avant-gardists,* had ever seen such plastic puke before.

But wait a mo. Thinking ahead, it may behove me to dissociate myself as much as I can from *this* episode, right from the start. Yeah, I know I've already said that if anything went tits-up it would quite properly be down to the Admin. Man. and so it transpired, but it has only just struck me, all these years later, that to a suspicious observer the events of that day might have an alarming symmetry and I need to assure you that it wasn't planned that way because ideally, lest this book should fail, I need to *keep* my pension. So, I didn't *know* that Dick had it (the *plastique,* I mean) until he actually produced it; and I certainly didn't anticipate, still less *plan*, my own later effort either. That latter at least, you'll *surely* believe. Won't you?

Anyway, where was I? Oh yes. Everything was ready within: food and drink laid out, the tree all a-sparkle, the resident IS brushed up and smiling brightly and the puke duly shining dully in the doorway, when the guests started to arrive in work-related groups. And if we *had* invited a sociologist, and if he or she *had* arrived early – and had we known how it would go, we would have ensured that we *had*, from somewhere, and that *he* or *she* had, too – I can guarantee that he/she would have taken one quick look at the varied reactions of the various groups as they entered, and seized his/her notebook and pen to record it all for posterity, as a 'fascinating and successful experiment on peer-group psyche,' or some such pseudo-bollocks. Because once it began, it went like this.

The UKIAS came first: glad, festive shouts rent the air and merry seasonal cries rang out as they advanced up the path – following some forty years late in the very steps of another active Sir, Barnes Wallis, who'd kept his explosives for the Op. Chastise (bouncing bomb) trials in a huge-and-heavy-doored strong room within GA, now reserved for the abandoned and ever-expanding baggage of real and successful absconders from DA (and thus including no less than two pairs of crutches).

"Merry Christmas to you all," they cried gladly and merrily from afar as their happy breath plumed through the mirk, "The Season's Greetings and Good Will to all men," which *we* thought was a tad two-faced, given that we were at loggerheads for a living – not that we ever seriously contemplated the other extreme of telling *them* directly to fuck off (although for the sake of completeness I have to add that part of the reason for that might have been that one of *us* lusted most fearfully after one of *them* (heterosexually, of course), and we never did work out whether it was reciprocated or not (the lust *in principle*, I mean).

Anyway nothing lasts forever, and the collective stated IAS goodwill towards us particular men was itself so fragile as to endure only until their first sight of what seemed to be a wet and noisome pool, all a-glisten and directly in their path. "*Oh my God,*" they exclaimed in stomach-felt disgust, and, "*You filthy bastards* – haven't you even got the *decency* to clear it up," as if any one of *us* could have done *that,* or perhaps *that much, and* so early in the day. And they negotiated it with great care, creeping round it as if it was a thick molten slice of a ticking Grand Slam[43], which might have brought a wan smile to old Barnes's face if he'd still been alive to see it. *If we'd only known it would be that effective, we could have cut right down on the mince pies,* I reflected – ever the cost-conscious Admin. Man.

Next, in a dignified body, came the Adjudicators accompanied by their Clerks with no overt merriment apparent, just talking quietly amongst themselves but fully prepared to have a good time. And as we turned to watch intently from within there was a momentary pause, a second's silence, in their concourse as one first noticed, and murmured inaudibly to the others; then with one accord, as if at a signal, they began to talk again, as softly and urbanely as before apart from a barely noticeable adjustment to group formation and individual stride lengths, so that they could step singly and directly over it as if it wasn't there. And they never mentioned it once – well, not until later, when *we* did.

And then came the DA guards, whose circumspect reaction neatly bestrode that of their twin predecessors. *They* couldn't quite believe their eyes – after all, it was still only 1230 – and they spent a fair part of their time looking furtively from one to another of us, clearly trying to work out which had done it and yet contrive so soon afterwards outwardly to look so well.

And finally, the out-station IS, probably fresh – or already half-curdled, more like – from someone *else's* do. And *they* approached the whole thing objectively, albeit with a quiet superior smirk on their collective face which we were happy, once they were within, swiftly to dissolve. "Hmm," they said at first, *"someone's* a bit premature – Clarke probably," – I needn't add there was no damn need nor any particular previous for them to conclude *that* – "looks like he simply couldn't handle the carrots – though what kind of a dump puts veg. *that* size in a fucking Vindaloo?"

Anyway things went well, and soon Rick had drunk enough to give the game irretrievably away by snatching up the molten slab and, probably in a woefully misguided effort to make the IAS girls – and boys – squeal again and thus gain a psychological march at least in the adjudicators' eyes, somehow attaching it briefly to his right nostril, whence it dangled heavily like a gigantic piece of multi-coloured snot enlivened by what now looked like enlarged blood vessels and sizeable fragments of his brain. But this time, after no more than a further moment's involuntary retching revulsion, even the women of their party saw through *that*, metaphorically anyway.

And in due course the Adjudicators left in good spirits together with their Clerks, having eaten judiciously of everything on show and drunk in comparative moderation. The rest of us went outside to see them off and once we were satisfied that they were all safely on their way home, some local idiot came up with the unprecedented and wholly absurd notion that we hold a mock hearing in one of the Courts. They were all locked of course and out of bounds to boot, but we soon found the keys and chose to use the Court of Sir R. – by then the Senior Adjudicator, Sir D. having retired a while before.

God knows why we picked the residual Sir's Court of the four available, because although a thoroughly decent chap he had a Templar temper on him just like his fellow-Knight and we knew it, and whoever suggested it was a bloody fool, the drink talking again just as when we'd thought up the whole idea in the first place. And I'm not *entirely* sure but it *might, again,* have been me…

And so we began, with Rick for the Home Office, Stuart and Paul, two other colleagues, playing the appellant and a witness, James from the IAS bravely appearing as himself and – in the then apparently fortuitous early departure of the HMI, without which we'd never even have started –me exercising my right as senior presenter present to sit in state as the Adjudicator, Sir Michael Clark CDM (no 'e' on the end, naturally, because it was a disguise). But I took the role very seriously, to the extent that I insisted that the Clerk, *my* Clerk – a second part for the IAS – bedeck me with a draped raincoat as a gown and two carefully-clipped toilet rolls as a wig. And thus accoutred, I entered the Hearing Room in some state, making small condescending hand-movements as I gazed in benign approval at the assembled multitude which with one accord rose to its feet with loud shouts of acclamation and joy. (Or if you prefer, took the piss unmercifully, but I contrived to misinterpret that.)

And let me be the first to admit that the power went straight to my head, or perhaps it was the drink, but one way or the other I was corrupted from the off, abso-fuckin-lutely, and commenced so much to revel in my authority for its own sake – *you* know – that within five minutes I began to detect a certain rebellion in the assembly, which I *knew* had to be dealt with instantly and severely, in fact *summarily put down* – if nothing else, my old school cadet force's imperial riot training had at least taught me *that.*

So I began to hand out punishments, mild enough at first but increasingly harsh when I found that *no-one* would *listen;*

and they gave me chance after chance, and it was only when I began uttering wild cries of "*Off with his head!*" that they conferred briefly, acknowledged with regret that my time had really, finally come and advanced physically to de-frock me, both of coat and of rolls.

Well, I remember that I put up something of a fight – Gordon would have been proud of me, although *he's* supposed to have just stood there proudly as they ran him through – but I was soon overwhelmed and borne struggling from the room, my last convulsive act of defiance being to kick over my (the Adjudicator's) full water glass, a not inappropriate epitaph. I remember vividly too that as they took me away I looked over my shoulder and saw Rick, the treacherous foresighted swine, swiftly donning my ceremonials and vigorously banging a gavel *I* hadn't had – God knows where he'd got *that* from, perhaps the same joke-shop as the honk – on the desk (*my* desk, as I still saw it then) to restore order, and worst of all, it worked! It just proves that drink shows what a man is really like; I'd never realised that he was so two-faced, or so ambitious.

Anyway, the bastards abandoned me at the far end of the corridor and told me I was pissed, a claim I could not deny, and that I was de-barred until I sobered up, or some other impossible condition like that. So I sat for a moment in disgraced defeat and then, head now suddenly reeling, stood up and took a few uncertain steps back towards the scene of my downfall but knew at once that I would never make it. So I turned the handle of the first door on my right, staggered into the empty, darkened room and without further delay projectile-vomited a litre's worth of vodka, quiche and chicken-legs into the silent interior. God knows I don't want to boast, but in less than three seconds I must have got rid of more than double the weight of the *plastique*.

Anyway, as often happens I felt better almost at once so I left, the sound of my puke drip-dripping down the wall my only lasting memory, and returned to my seat in the corridor with something to spare. After a while I crept back to peer through the door-glass of the Hearing Room but they were still hard at it, and I was beginning to feel rough again so I went back to GA and consoled myself by eating a lot more food – I was suddenly ravenously hungry – and drinking a lot of water. Vodka always gets me like that.

Which is where they found me later, and somebody drove me home to a less than rapturous reception from Beth. Luckily it was a Friday, I had the Saturday and Sunday off (though we did run a skeleton staff) and there were never any hearings at the weekend, so I reckoned that we'd all be back to normal by Monday. But on the Sunday the phone rang: "You'd better come in," they said, but wouldn't say why.

So in I went – by bus as the car was still there, another element that had not pleased my long-suffering wife – and when I arrived my colleague, silent and white-faced but shaking strangely, produced the Hearing Room keys, walked with me back to the scene of my recent legal disgrace, unlocked the door and pointed still silently at the Adjudicator's desk. It was Sir R.'s own, a tangible symbol of his authority and thus lovingly cared for by his Clerk. But now, right across the calf inlay was a broad irregular swathe of lighter colour, the direct result of my frantic kick at the water glass which I now realised in horror had indeed been brim-full but of vodka substituted therein by me, the residue of which still nestled accusingly in numerous small indentations in the desk-top itself, themselves caused by Rick's over-energetic use of the gavel (I reckon he must have splashed himself a fair bit, too).

So I bent forwards with a suicidal oath and tried scrubbing with my sleeve, but that just made things worse. Then I remembered that it was Sunday and all the shops were shut, and I wouldn't have known how to deal with the damage anyway – perhaps it *couldn't* be repaired, short of a new inlay if not a whole new top. So I thought for a while and finally pushed a brief note under the door of Sir R.'s upstairs room, asking for an early interview with him before the round of cases the next morning, if he would be so kind as to call me as soon as he arrived. Then I drove slowly, soberly home.

The snow came that night naturally, the first of the winter, by the morning deep and crisp, and as I drove slowly, soberly back in again through a blizzard on the M4 I prayed silently that to start with at least, Sir R.'s temper would be commensurately even. As I drove into the car park I saw his car in its usual spot so he'd still beaten me, and as I got out resignedly and trudged towards GA I saw two of my colleagues standing in the doorway.

"Morning, old boy," said one. It was Rick, the sod. "Don't bother to take your coat off," he said. "He'll see you now." He was grinning and so was Stuart and I knew that Paul would've been too if he hadn't gone sick, because this was the moment when I finally recognised them all for what they were, truly insensitive shits, and Rick had clearly already forgotten his own part in it – or perhaps he simply hadn't actually *seen* the damage.

"*Thanks*," I said. "Thanks *a lot*," and I headed over to FA, up the stairs and knocked on Sir R.'s door. "Come in," the voice said. And I did.

The interview, though not a happy one, was mercifully brief and to the point – even crisper in fact than the aforesaid snow. Sir R. did not ask me to sit nor would I have done if he had, so I was standing as I apologised under his icy stare on behalf of the Unit for our intrusion into his Court and for myself for the damage to his desk, for which I offered personally to pay. I made no direct mention of drink or gavels, and nor did he; given the nature of the damage and the residual smell that still infused the official leather, perhaps it seemed superfluous to both of us. And at the end he remained silent for a moment as I squirmed inwardly under his stern gaze.

Then he accepted the apology, refused to accept my offer of payment, said that he never expected to be in a position where he would need to listen *again* to a similar speech from a *responsible* – he emphasised the word – IS officer (in tandem, something of a small compliment I thought afterwards, briefly, when I was still clutching at wildly mistaken straws), and dismissed me.

Five minutes later I found myself standing in for Paul and unexpectedly presenting the first case of the day, and inevitably it was before Sir R., now sat at his still-sodden desk – I thought nervously that the whole *room* reeked of booze but if it did, no-one else showed any sign of having noticed – who listened courteously to all the evidence and both submissions, and finally reserved judgement.

It was as if the final scene of the party had never happened and when, later, I knocked on the door of Ed – my own Inspector, and just about recovered from his heart attack (and him as slim and as fit as a racing snake, which should have told *me* something) – to tell *him* all about it, well, most of it anyway, *he* listened courteously too, showing no surprise and exhibiting even more remarkable restraint, and said that so far as he was concerned it was for Sir R. to approach him if he wanted to take the matter further. In the event I heard no more about it, but I would be astonished if a few quiet words hadn't already been exchanged between them, over nothing stronger than coffee.

So the only dismissal I received was from Sir R.'s presence after my apology. And the matter, which had remained festering in my mind only in terms of events up to and including my courtroom ejection – I had, by accident or perhaps by devious self-deceptive design wholly forgotten my own involuntary *oral* ejection soon afterwards, and I hadn't known exactly *where* it had occurred in the first place – would, I suppose in due course have vanished from the agenda entirely, the occasional jibes of my three two-faced so-called friends notwithstanding, had not my four further appearances in court that day, each one like the first with the IAS against me, led by gradual but inexorable degrees to the shocking denouement.

In total I thus presented five cases, all Paul's, and it was clear that he had properly prepared them – there were his notes in the front of each file but I'd never been able to read his writing and it might just as well have been short-hand. So all I could manage was a quick read-through of each Explanatory Statement, followed by a quick sprint through the snow across to FA and a necessarily winging every time. As it happened, each case was relatively straightforward: the Statement was brief, there was a minimal number of potential witnesses – in the snowy event, none actually showed at all – and from my read-through I reckoned that at the end of the day it would all depend on the opposing final submissions with honours likely to be about even, say three-two either way, with the Adjudicator, Sir R. every time, reserving every determination for another day, as was routine.

But to my surprise *my* submissions, though undeniably models of brevity, were unusually pithy and pertinent (fuelled no doubt by my nervous awareness that I had at all costs to hide the fact that I really knew fuck-all of what each case was about); whilst those of the opposition, whichever of the three IAS representatives in attendance was making it (and they all had a go), were all disparate, rambling and inconclusive. And not only that: the IAS staff themselves matched their performances, not just verbally but physically lack-lustre and distinctly below par, and when I looked more closely they all had red eyes and sunken cheeks and I noticed in the lunch break that none of them appeared, as was their wont, in the excellent Post Office canteen.

The flu? The plague? Badly hung-over? The latter two seemed unlikely because they were a pretty abstemious bunch, compared to us at least, and any rats that appeared in Court – and as you know already, there were a few, two-legged, from time to time – would surely have infected us as well. But whatever it was, at the end of the day I wandered over to their office, to make superior sympathetic noises. *Besides,* I thought in a delicious little spurt of vengeful self-righteousness, *if they <u>are</u> hung over it will fucking well serve them right because they were all there on Vodka Tag too, and just as unsympathetic as my own crowd.*

But as I pushed through the big swing-doors and turned the corner to their office, I saw to my surprise that they were all sitting in a shivering row outside it, hunched presumably over their following day's cases in the dim corridor light.

"Hello folks," I said, brightly but a little mystified, and one of the girls – the particularly attractive one – lifted her head and saw that it was me. I waited momentarily for the conventional pleasantry in reply – you know, 'Hello, Mike,' or something like that – but it wasn't forthcoming, far from it.

"*You bastard,*" she yelled instead, straight off which I thought was a bit strong, however well I might have done in Court. And then she pointed at the IAS office door. "*Just go in there*," she said, almost hysterically, and emphasising her words with a vicious thrusting finger, enough to put your eye out, like *This*.

"All right," I said, still mystified, and I turned the door handle and entered. Well, if the atmosphere outside was distinctly chilly it was nothing to that within and in no longer than it took for my senses to register the change, the veil dropped from my eyes. For it should have been *hot, sauna*-hot, inside as all the radiators were full on, including the *massive* one that they rarely ever used, even when it was as cold *out*side as it was today: but it wasn't, because all the windows were open too – wide, ridiculously open – so that unless you stood *right by* a radiator it was bloody brass knobs. And the reason for the unusual hot-cold combination, metaphorically useful and usual enough in formal oral interview but rare indeed for dictating actual room temperature, hit you right between the eyes – well, right up the hooter instead, because the stench was indescribable. And I reeled, retching deeply, out again and hurriedly closed the door.

"What the *hell* – " I began. But I got no further.

"*You shit!*" they yelled at me, all three of them this time, clearly a description not a bodily imperative because things were noisome enough as it was. "*You did it on purpose, didn't you?*"

"Did *what*? No," I said at once instinctively, whatever *it* was, a conditioned response. Then suddenly it all flooded back, but luckily only insubstantially. "Oh God," I said, "I'm sorry, I didn't even realize it was your room." But I sensed that somehow even that wasn't the true heart of the issue. And I was right.

"*No*," yelled the pretty one, "not just *there*," and she waved an arm vaguely at the door as she leapt up, held a handkerchief to her nose, flung it open (the door, I mean), and dived in. "But *there,* you *bloody* swine, you did it *behind it, didn't* you, *on purpose,* and we *can't even clean it out!*" And as she pointed again with a feverish, shaking hand at the huge throbbing radiator and I searched wildly for my own handkerchief I saw for the first time the precise point of the vodka etc.'s impact on the wall directly above it, imprinted there indelibly (though without related gavel-marks) by a now-familiar lightening of the paint and edged unmistakably by a long, descending fringe of now-dry solid matter which traced its remorseless slide down, down, out of sight and out of reach – *a mot juste indeed,* I thought in a momentary glow. And I finally realised precisely what I had achieved.

So: the stench lasted for a fortnight, give or take, and during that time no-one from IAS would talk to me.. At first they tried disinfectants, which they squeezed out and let run down the wall puke-style, and then a variety of spray-on personal deodorants – they couldn't use *roll*-ons, of course – but nothing worked, and they stopped when the overall mixture seemed to be becoming explosive. They never reported me though for which I was grateful, and finally the weather made the difference: as soon as there was a mild spell, they turned the heating off and that did the trick – that and natural wastage, I suppose.

So, overall? One of the benefits of working at Appeals and dealing theoretically with the Law was that you acquired the ability, both morally and mentally, to cerebralise everything – it must be how lawyers live with themselves, but who am I of all people to criticise that? Anyway, one day soon afterwards I used the technique in an idle moment to sum up my achievements at that particular Christmas party, and these were my conclusions.

As the Admin. CIO, part of my role was to expand general awareness of the IS's all-round ability to get even obscure and challenging things done and of its excellence in so doing, and I considered that the first element of my performance of the day, in the Hearing Room, had achieved that but hardly in the way intended, so the result, effectively a professional suicide, was distinctly negative. But the second was another thing altogether. Because for the whole of the offending – or offensive – fortnight, the IAS continued perforce to study their cases in the corridor (I say 'perforce', although I'd generously offered them a room in GA as soon as I'd recovered enough from my own fleeting encounter with my past/their present problem, so to do. But perhaps understandably they refused, and thus continued to prepare them comparatively poorly), and so continued to lose ones they should normally have won.

That first day back, for example, had come out four-one to me and as soon as I'd read it I was resigned to losing the fifth, and indeed confirmed as much when the hearing began by stating that I would 'rest on the papers,' in other words say nothing else at all: an uncommon approach though far from unique, and entirely appropriate whenever you encountered a case which was patently un-winnable, in this instance because although the overall rationale for refusal was sound enough the CIO, a joyously idiosyncratic individual at a small port, had chosen to summarise it in a formal notice to the passenger which read, doubtless accurately but legally indefensibly, 'You have sought entry to the United Kingdom for the weekend, but you have no pyjamas'.

Anyway, if my main function was to ensure that as many determinations as possible went in favour of the Home Office, I had during that period by my action probably made a distinct difference. Which, as a passing semi-humorous thought, was fine. But the next day I stopped short and said to myself, 'Hang on, if that argument is still in your mind, you're beginning to take it *half-seriously.*' And that's when I knew I'd been at Appeals, with all its human tragedies and triumphs, long enough; and that it was time to return to my alternative world, another sharp-end, before one way or another I was myself, next time perhaps forcibly, spewed out.

THE RAC

Listen then, and I'll tell you – no, not of Noggin the Nog, but rather an equally strange tale from a land a mere short Steppe away, a winter's tale of an incident which occurred one evening when, not long back at Two and still demob-happy as you can probably tell, I was out on the control running the Floor – comparatively well-manned for a change, thanks to a rare recent influx of yet more new staff – and idly watching the passengers off the lately-arrived Moscow flight (AEROFLOT, SU, remember?) as they slowly shuffled, muffled, to and fro across our front via the cattle grid.

It was mid–winter in Russia too, so most of them were up to their eyeballs and above in furs, just in fact like Noggin, and none more than two burly figures, duly duffeled and clearly a tad ruffled to boot, pushing a standard airport trolley teetering on the point of collapse under the weight of the single item balanced precariously thereon and retained only by the combined anxious hands of its escorts. Well, I say 'burly' and they looked like a typical pair of thick KGB heavies to me – we did see *them* from time to time. But in view of what went down (though not *off,* thank God), I suppose that beneath all that fur the shorter one at least might have been a brainy racing snake, albeit with a disproportionately wide and cobra-like head. Or perhaps the taller one.

Anyway, my attention soon shifted from *them* to the object in their loving charge. It was open and uncovered and therefore fully exposed to my gaze, and I have never seen its like before or since, anywhere, nor wanted to again. It was a large black cube, *very* large, so that it overhung by some distance the base of the trolley, which for all its acolytes' agonised efforts had still barely managed to negotiate the first turn in the grid. And its exterior was of grained metal, or perhaps plastic, and bristled with switches. And dials. And levers. And sockets. And I *mean* 'bristled'.

To me it was instantly sinister, exuding evil like the brain-child of some perverse professor, and I wondered for a mad moment whether it – and *this* – was *it*, you know, an atomic, hydrogen or other nuclear bomb, a fucking *big* one it seemed from my limited knowledge, hidden in plain sight and destined to become the opening surprise shot, on UK soil, of World War Three – after all, it had travelled here on a Tupolev which like all others of its breed would, come the day, convert within hours to a bomber. (I'd seen the military equipment hooks on the cabin walls at close range myself at Gatwick during that aborted attempted aerial abduction, remember?)

But I dismissed the notion almost at once, if only because I didn't *want* to confront the possibility that my life was about to be snuffed out in an ultra-bright millisecond. Besides, even if I'd been right in the first place, the tender, almost reverent, care with which its guardians were handling the device – jeez, now they were even *stroking* and *caressing* it in what *I* can only describe as a kind of bizarre affection, though no doubt there's a better, simpler, shorter phrase – was surely a sign that it wasn't due to explode *yet*, not so far as *they* knew anyway. Because happy and fulfilled suicide bombers were generally still a few years off (and those less happy if they knew at all, because destined for remote detonation, a few years more).

So call it selfish if you like, or perhaps treason, or even plain cowardice, but my next impulse was to ensure that I got *them*, and *it*, through the Control as fast as possible, just in case, so that if the damn thing *was* going to atomise, it could do it somewhere else. But the first problem – this time, of only two – was that they were still only in the middle of the grid, shuffling awkwardly along – with a significant gap, I noticed, between them and those next aft, so perhaps they too secretly shared my own suspicions – and the second that the queue itself was slow, *bloody* slow as SU queues always were, and long before the polar boyos had reached the head of it I had decided not without considerable reluctance that my duty lay in the opposite direction, that I had to find out what the hell the thing really was *before* we landed them, and *it*, however long it took – though precisely what the refusal formula would be for a Russki found toting a nuclear bomb with malevolent intent, I didn't know. I supposed it would have to involve his presence being marginally non-conducive to the public good and a tad contrary to the public interest or something like that, but my new-found courage only stretched so far and I resolved that if any baggage search became necessary, it would be *straight* down to Customs and without the *slightest* need for an IO to attend (to pre-empt any potential contamination – of the evidence chain I mean, naturally).

Anyway, when after what seemed an eternity they reached an IO's desk up at the right-hand end, I walked over and hovered on his shoulder to listen. I heard the usual opening question – "How long d'you intend to stay?" – and the brief guttural answer, "One week," from the smaller of the two – let's call him Number One – and I saw that they did have UK visas in their passports. But the IO had been head-down as they approached, probably with fatigue, and I wasn't sure that he'd even noticed the monster in their charge, now largely hidden by the overhang of the desk. So I committed the normally unforgivable sin and *intervened, unasked*. But he didn't seem to mind and I *was ultra*-polite about it – after all, it could be the last thing the poor sod ever heard.

"Very sorry, Mal," I said, "forgive me, but I need to ask these two something," and pressed straight on. "Gentlemen," I said, "good evening," because for some reason I felt that an extra degree of formality was fitting on such a sombre and perhaps eternally unique occasion, as with shaking hand I pointed downwards (but only a trifle). "Gentlemen, please enlighten me," (which on reflection and in the circumstances was not perhaps the brightest thing to have said but still), "*what* exactly is *that*?"

"Good *evening*," the larger of the pair – let's call *him* Number Two – replied. He was not the one who'd spoken before as you know, his voice was deeper as (again) befitted someone of his size and I waited for the inevitable "..., *English,*" to end whatever he said, because his accent was very Stok-like and straight out of Len[44], which didn't make me feel any better at all. But it didn't materialise. Instead, "*This,*" – he looked proudly at the machine between them, and now as I forced myself to listen I could hear a distinct ticking, not unlike that of the A-bomb in *Goldfinger* – "*This* is the *Russian Atomic Clock*," and I paused, momentarily. So time clearly *was* of the essence and I'd been half-right at least, assuming of course that that wasn't just a cover story. And the next question was obvious.

"Oh. I see," I said. Though I didn't. "Right. And *what* exactly is it doing *here*?" Well, fucking *ticking* obviously, but you know what I mean. Anyway, the bigger man looked at his colleague: perhaps they could only speak in turn and perhaps One was the Commissar – well, one was bound to be, though so far I couldn't tell which.

"*So.* We bring it here, to England, every ten years," One replied, in a voice somewhat higher than but otherwise identical to Two's. "It is the Russian *Master* Clock, and we are taking it to Greenwich," – he called it 'Gren-witch' – "to be precisely, *pre-cise-ly,* re-timed." Then they looked at each other, nodded simultaneously – Stan and Ollie to the life, if only the small one had been smaller and they'd both had bowler hats (although it could already have been a winter scene from '*Way out West*') – and waited expectantly for my next sally. But there was no answer to that, and if it *was* a cover story it was a pretty good one and much too good for me. *Besides*, I reminded myself, *the clock is ticking.* So, "OK," I said. "Sorry to have bothered you. Carry on, Mal," and I breathed out and walked bravely back to the middle of the Control, to give myself an extra three milliseconds.

By the time they'd been processed I was back in the Watch House, and prepared to let out another deep involuntary sigh – but this time of relief – as they passed out of sight on the way to Customs. But I was wildly premature. Because they *didn't* pass, the buggers, they *stopped* instead, and the next moment they were *in* the bloody Watch House right next to *me* with the infernal machine blocking the door, and instead of sighing I swallowed hard – *Perhaps I'm pre-destined to be minutely, atomically, fucked,* I thought. And then, worse still, *Perhaps somehow it's <u>personal.</u>*

"Gentlemen," I said. "What can I do for you now?" after another short pause, as we looked at each other suspiciously. (It was a sort of zeugma. I mean *they* looked suspicious *to* me, and *I* was suspicious *of* them: what *they* thought of *me* God knows, but I doubt it was complimentary.) *A complaint,* I thought, anyway. *Fair enough, I've had a hell of a good run without one and I can deal with that. Always assuming that I survive.* But yet again I was wrong.

"Sir, we have a *prob-lem*," Two said, oily now and buttering me up, so I reckoned One *was* the Commissar. "The *clock* is running on its *battery*, but the aircraft was *late*" – it was – "and we both think that the power may expire *before* we reach *Gren-witch*. It is imperative, *im-pera-tive*, (they both clearly liked the sound of *cer-tain* English words, too) that the *clock* does not, *does not, stop* before we arrive."

"Yes, is true," interjected One – no 'Sir' from *him* I noted, the little shit, and said with a clear hint of *men-ace* as his command of English *dim-in-ished*, so *he was* the Commissar and unless I was *ultra care-ful*, *I* was about to go On The List – "and now we *must* re-charge. Is there a plug here, we can use?" And it was immediately apparent to me that there'd better be, because if there wasn't the alternative was a bullet in the back of *some-one's* neck, later. Or sooner.

So, "OK. What d'you need? An ordinary three-pin socket? Yes, of course," I said, in triple relief – no complaint after all, *just maybe* no atomisation either and *perhaps* even no bullet, now or in the future, especially if I didn't charge them for the juice. "Here, try this one," and I pointed at the nearest of the many sockets in the Watch House wall. Then I had a precautionary thought. "Wait a minute," I said helpfully – or perhaps hopefully, "our mains are 220-240 volts, is that – " but Two cut me short.

"*That* is *not* a *prob-lem*," he said – curtly himself this time and again without the 'Sir', the big shit, so perhaps *he* was the Commissar after all. "We have an *ad-ap-tor*," and he opened a little hatch in the side of the machine, pulled out a flex with a UK-style plug on it, inserted it into the wall-socket, switched on with an elaborate flourish and stood back. Instantly there was a load click, and as I shut my eyes absurdly to protect them for one last instant from the light brighter than the sun, I heard instead the ticking change to a purr, which slowed slowly, and finally ceased.

Then, in the deep, expectant silence that followed, I opened my eyes again, and we were all still there, and for a long moment the Numbers remained motionless, apparently frozen in disbelief before exchanging horrified glances and advancing on their charge to tap every dial, pull every lever and click every switch that it possessed in an ever-increasing frenzy of joint activity which contrasted starkly with the continued total inertia of the machine. But the latter remained lifeless, moribund at best – or perhaps just terminally ill. Anyway, it was soon readily apparent that whether or not its *tempus* had ever *venit* it had now well and truly *fugit*. And finally, in the continuing silence, One removed the plug from the socket with trembling fingers before they both turned accusingly towards me. Then Two spoke in a choked voice *and* out of turn (perhaps to show just how upset they were).

"*You*," he said, pointing at me viciously, "*you* have *killed* the *Russian Atomic Clock.*"

"Who, *me?*" I replied, giving the response of Haig's 1917 private and other complete innocents through the ages, "*I* didn't do it!" But to no avail, and it was immediately clear that they already knew who I was because they didn't even bother to ask, and manifest too that I *was* now not just *on* The Fucking List but there at The *Very Top* Of The *List Of Lists* as with final despairing, malevolent looks and rude silent internationally-intelligible gestures they disconsolately trundled their dead charge, charge-less, time-expired and now no more than an object, out of the Watch House, away through the Customs Hall and finally out of view. *It's late all right,* I reflected grimly as I watched the little procession disappear, *and in more senses than one.*

Then at last I did sigh, deeply, but now because it clearly *was* complaint-time again after all and I was envisaging the remarkable nature of the one that *this* would engender. And so I opened Two's Incident Log – it spanned the years, and was always worth a read if you wanted a good laugh on a rare quiet shift – to record my version of events because it never hurts to get in first, and I was still struggling with my entry and doubtless within the immediate blast range when I heard a knock on the door and there was our cleaner, as ever cheerful as hell. "*Hello,* love," she said smiling, in a welcome return to good old English *bonnefemmie*. "All right if I clean through now?"

"Of course, m'dear," I said and as much to distract myself from my thoughts as to play the gent I jumped up and added, "Gimme the plug, *I'll* do that for you," as I knelt down by the fateful familiar socket. "Oh *thanks*, dear," she said, then quickly, as she saw me reach out, Oh no, *no*, not *that* one, don't you men know *anything*, that one ain't worked in *years* and I don't know what it is but it's broken *more 'oovers* than I've 'ad *'ot dinners.*"

"Oh," I said humbly as I selected another socket, switched on and the vacuum burst into instant raucous non-nuclear life. "Sorry."

I never found out what happened when the two Russkis reached Gren-witch, if they ever did, nor what became of them later. Perhaps the device had unknown self-regenerative powers –

"The Thing is Dead, *Long Live the Thing*," – but anyway I scanned the papers and the TV anxiously for a while and there were no earth-shattering headlines like 'Russia calls Time' or 'Darkness at High Noon', or anything like that. And there was no complaint either, perhaps because they both took a bullet themselves as soon as they got home, if they were met by someone with no sense of humour – the Iron Curtain was like that, or so false Western propaganda and my own relevant practical experience (of which more later) told me. Or maybe just half of them did, and in that case I'd be willing to bet it *wasn't* the Commissar, who'd look after Number One all right – the Iron Curtain was like *that*, too. And of course, they might always have claimed asylum here. *Damn*; I hadn't thought of that.

So I comfort myself with the thought that whatever else happened, it was perhaps my own sole tiny and accidental contribution to the downfall of the so-called Evil Empire of its day, who knows? But if you want to confirm all this, it's fully written up there in the Terminal Two Incident Log – under the title 'The RAC' if I remember correctly, though I wish now I'd made it 'Slim Pickings' – the defensive, potted, one-sided Filthy Capitalist version, of course

DESK TOP

I was handing over one evening to Geoff, the Night Man, as he unlocked his drawer and got out a brand-new bottle of Scotch for a wee opening livener. I recall that he offered me one, and that remarkably I declined: I must have been really tired that night. Anyway I sat and watched without too much envy as he poured himself a hefty double and took a large swig. Instantly his expression changed as he blew the liquid straight out in his own personal version of a projectile stream and glared momentarily and directly at *me*, no doubt to see whether I was in on the plot (and you can't blame him, because my recent refusal of alcohol was wholly without precedent).

But thankfully I wasn't and he *believed* it, or I might not be sitting here now because I was still English and he was yet another Scot whom I'd never seen so angry, and for a few seconds he couldn't speak. Then his brow began to clear and a small grin appeared fleetingly on his craggy face before it settled again into a look which I can't describe but is instantly recognisable to anyone in the job – or anyone in the job *then*, anyway: to wit, an IS man, or woman, *on a case*.

"Cold tea, eh?" he muttered. "Bastards. How the *hell* did they manage it?" and he held the bottle up to the light. "Yep. *And* a new wrapper round the neck: *that* wasn't easy, and authentic too, so at least *one* of the buggers is in the Forgery Team. (*Again*, I thought.) And the drawer – it *was* locked, *and* not tampered with." Then he got out the office torch and crawled under his desk. After a bit, I heard him mutter, " Ah. The cunning *sods*," in a muffled, admiring tone before he emerged and sat down again. "They took the whole bloody top off, they must have," he said. "How's *that* for dedication?" But I took the question as rhetorical and said nothing. He was after all still a Celt and I wasn't sure his mood had fully settled yet, so we went round to the bar and I bought him a proper drink and after that he was fine

I don't know whether Geoff ever found out who'd done it. If he did, he never told me. It must have been another night crew because it would have taken a solid hour's work, undisturbed, to unscrew the desk-top and then put it back. So what about the spare drawer key you may ask, but they couldn't have done it that way. There was one, of course, for essential senior management security checks, but I knew that like the rest of us he had acquired that too – it was pretty basic stuff. Well, *you* wouldn't want *anyone else*, authorised or not but *especially* the former, ferreting around uninvited in *your* drawer, would you?

And what about the *quality* of the key then, I hear you say next. Could it have been *a copy*? It's not impossible of course, but most unlikely. Firstly there was nothing to copy it *from*, and secondly this was still the height of the Cold War and everyone everywhere was security conscious but most of all at Two, with all our IC flights. And it would have been extraordinarily difficult for anyone to have copied it anyway, because those locks and keys were the best that money could buy, the products of real craftsmen. Shades of Newhaven, they *still* came all the way from Leipzig.

NATIONAL INTEREST

It was rare enough to find The Assistant Chief Inspector London Airports District One, in other words the big local IS cheese responsible for Terminals One *and* Two, making even a guest visit to our Control. Still, everything was going fairly smoothly by our normal hard-pressed standards, and it could just have been your standard occasional courtesy call. But it wasn't.

"Mike," he said, without further ado – not that there'd been much ado already. "Can I have a *quiet* word?" *O-oh,* I thought, again. 'Word' was bad enough, but a *'quiet'* one? Still, what I *said* was, of course, "Of *course,* Gerald," politely, because Gerald's rank deserved respect. He was *The ACI,* high in the pecking order, he'd got there in the usual – then the only – hard way, and he was genial enough. But I didn't entirely trust him; for starters he was an Arsenal supporter, so he too had plenty to be paranoid about. Anyway we strolled away up to the far end of the Arrivals Hall where everything was as silent as the grave – it was a rare day indeed when there were enough staff to fill all the desks, and this wasn't one of them.

"Mike, I'm glad you're about, because this needs someone who can think on his feet." *Hmm. Worse still. Compliments, now?* Besides, we barely knew each other or he'd have recognised the clear contradiction in terms, and I thought, again, *O-oh,* and then, *Yeah right, Arsenal supporter, this is getting serious.* At least he hadn't called me reliable as well – well, he *couldn't,* could he, when he knew I knew he knew I was a Spurs man – or I'd have really smelt a rat.

"Anyway, I'll be brief," he said, briefly. "Sorry for the short notice, but this has only just come from ISHQ and it's red-hot. Read it and keep it," and he handed me a fax. It was marked RESTRICTED, the heading was a name, a nationality – not British, of course – and a date of birth, and *its* wording too was brief. 'Above arriving today at….. hours on flight….. from…..' – it gave a scheduled time of arrival, a Two flight number and a place of origin, but *I* won't – 'is to be refused entry in the national interest on the ground that his presence is deemed non-conducive to the public good and removed forthwith on the return flight repeat *on the return flight, without fail.* Refusal formula below.' It then gave a specific wording for the non-conducive decision on the Notice of Refusal – the very one which with a minimum of amendment you might well also use for someone, say, caught importing an atomic bomb – a decision which was not appealable anywhere, here or abroad, because it had been made personally by the Secretary of State.

"OK, Gerald," I said brightly, the way you do when you know you're stuffed and the chap telling you so is called Gerald, and at least it was something different. So back to the Watch House to check the arrivals screen, and the target's flight's ETA had come forward a little and was now due in less than half an hour but that was more than long enough to prepare. Then the ACI said, "I'll be around later, and don't worry: I'll back you all the way if things get difficult." *If it all goes tits-up,* he meant, and until then I *hadn't* worried *too* much, but now again I thought, *Hmmm. Arsenal supporter.*

Anyway, I looked down the IOs' duty list and picked Paul (not the same Paul as the one at Appeals, of course), good, calm, quick-thinking (on his feet) and with a safe pair of hands too so doubly ambidextrous – indeed, impeccable extremity-wise though not an outright goalie, and a West Ham man himself so there was no question of bias – and I took him off the Control and briefed him. "Is there a photo?" he asked, thus immediately justifying my choice – it was something *I* should have bloody well thought of.

"No," I said. (Well, it was a fax wasn't it, so there *couldn't* be.)

"*Or* description?" (Which there could have been, but wasn't.)

"Sorry, mate, no again.." *Christ, there's no need to rub it in,* I thought.

We already had a copy of the flight's passenger list so we looked for the target's name and surprise, surprise, it wasn't there – a good start and Rounds One *and* Two to Paul but then the Hammers are a one-half team, always have been. Still, the fax gave the source of the intel., and if *they* said he was on board then he *was*, because they'd have watched him embark. But even *they* weren't wholly proof against confusion or masterly devious foreigners or even the occasional prime cock-up and could well have missed a last-minute identity swap, complete with new matching ticket.

So now we were looking for the man who wasn't there, without the faintest idea of what he looked like apart from his nationality and his age; and whilst I made an urgent call to ISHQ asking for anything more they already had or could swiftly find out, to assist – "Don't hold your breath," was the honest answer, unhelpful if not unexpected and probably accurate about all top Brit teams at the time, with the possible exception of Liverpool – I took two more good, quick-thinking etc. IOs aside (both rugby men), showed *them* the fax – *How many bloody more Need to Know*, I thought – and sent all three down to the gate together.

The aircraft was indeed a little early and already on stand as they arrived, but by the time the passengers started coming up the jet-way the reserves were stationed at the top on either side, ready to do a comprehensive and apparently routine document check – routine even then for *that* flight that is, which is a distinct clue – and, having (I hoped) somehow identified the target, to point him out discreetly to Paul standing off who would then tail him back to us, and as he entered the Hall take him out of the queue for a quick fix. That way, I reflected sagely, we'd not lose him if he went to the loo, and it wouldn't hurt to see whom he walked and talked or even pissed the time away with on the way up either – all right, a slow starter, but thinking on my feet at last as specified, you see: a real Spurs man.

Well, the ISHQ advice on self-inhalation proved accurate, because reply there came none. And after a prolonged silence from the guys at the gate too, Paul finally came on the radio to tell me tersely that he and one of the others were now on their way back, his colleagues having checked every passport but found no clear suspect to tail and that they had then boarded the aircraft and confirmed that it was empty. *But*, he said, all was not necessarily lost. There *had* been another male passenger of a different name but the right nationality and of roughly the right age though not of the precise date of birth, only one. And none of them had liked the look of him though they couldn't say why, and they were keeping an eye on *him* as we spoke.

If I still believed that *they* (you know who) had been right – and I didn't have much option about that – then this could be our man, and he was at least our best and indeed our *only* bet for a removal by the same aircraft. Because if we were wrong and he *wasn't* the target at all because *he* had somehow beaten the gate check and was about to become just another face in the crowd on the grid, and if then someone somehow still picked him out albeit for the wrong reason (and stranger things have happened), it would leave us no time for an immediate turn-round. So I had to trust the instincts of the IOs, and that was easy. So I did.

The flight was in the Hall now, and I saw Paul in the grid himself, conspicuous by his lack of baggage and closing up behind the suspect – the only appropriate term for him as yet – a real Mr. Average in an expensive tropical suit. And the IOs were right, there *was* something fishy about him, but *I* didn't know what it was either. Alternative nightmare scenarios ran through my brain: *He's standing out deliberately because he's a distraction target, a conscious sacrifice to ensure the safety of the real one and we've fallen for it like the bloody fools we are. Or, No, he stands out because he's trying not to, a reclusive multi-billionaire travelling incognito, a second Howard Hughes here to make an earth-shattering multi-million ultra-secret deal with the UK Government – until we, no I, blew it, his cover, that is. Etc., etc.*

I glanced at the Embarks screen: the return flight was showing on time and it would be starting to board shortly. Then I ran my gaze quickly along the rest of the passengers. There was no-one who struck me as a likely co-national, and over the years you got pretty good at guessing a geezer's (or geezerette's) nationality purely from appearance before a word had been spoken, though that was small comfort. So I nodded to Paul, 'Now,' and in a flash he produced his warrant and hustled the startled suspect past the startled presenter, straight through the generally startled Control and into the expectant Watch House. "It *is* him," I persuaded myself, "it *has* to be, from his *lack* of reaction."

"*Get on with it,*" I hissed unfairly in Paul's ear, and listened with a flood of relief when the answer to the only question there was time for, "How long d'you intend to stay," was "One week," not, *"I want asylum,"* because that would have made things somewhat tricky. (Oh, all right, turned it straight into a right royal fuck-up, and if I'd had any sense at all I'd have asked Gerald specifically what the hell we were supposed to do in that event. But I hadn't.)

So: we'd already written out most of the Refusal Notice, in the identity *they* had provided, and now I told Paul to serve it, adding 'Also known as' followed by the name in the passport. I tensed again involuntarily as chummy scanned it, but he didn't do the simple, sensible, obvious thing and say, "What's all *this*?" or "*That's* not *me*," or "You've got *the wrong man*," or, again, *"I want asylum."* Instead, he said, "Is *this* your justice?"

And when that, and "*Help* me!" were what he yelled at the crowd waiting patiently but indifferently in the Hall, I knew we were right.

He struggled for a while as he was taken in hand by the two PCs we had lurking close by, but it was a gesture only, shades of Leon – this bloke too did not strike me as a natural man of *personal* violence – and we were all about to set off for the gate, me too, when the solitary IO left down there, whom I'd radioed to tell the airline that we were on the way with a refusal, called back to say that the flight was full and refusing to wait and due at any moment to close its doors and push back.

Shit, I thought, the other way one does, and next, *What the hell can I do now*? And I told the others to get down to the gate with the body as fast as they could to try to stall things, and then called Air Traffic Control. I wasn't too hopeful because I hadn't got any particular friends there but no particular enemies either, and this was serious and a one-off and in those days we were all still on the same side, most of the time anyway and give or take. And after I'd asked for the Officer-in-Charge I forced myself to breath slowly and deeply as I visualised the aircraft taxiing out.

Then, "Hello," said a calm assured male voice (Chelsea, perhaps?), "Duty Manager."

"Hello there," I said, and introduced myself. I told him the situation but without detail, emphasised 'National Interest', said I believed that the aircraft was about to push back and asked if there was anything ATC could do. There was another brief pause, and I could hear him muttering unintelligibly in the background. Then he came back on. "No," he said, briefly. "Nothing at all. I'm sorry. Good Luck," and I thanked him and rang off.

I didn't blame him. *His hands are tied,* I thought, as I ran after the others whilst I waited for my radio to burst into life to say that the flight had gone. But it stayed silent and then I saw them, some way ahead, and soon I began to hear the continued yelps of *"Help!"* and *"British Injustice!"* Their group progress had slowed because by now the target was being frog-marched between the two happy coppers, and although most of the crowd of new-arrivals still ignored the scene as they headed hotfoot for the Hall, I have to admit that his antics did draw the close attention of a flagging few, though whether the only responses *I* heard from *them*, and both in fluent English – *"Bugger off, mate,"* and *"Serve the stupid fucker right,"* – were as sympathetic as he had expected from proud natives of the Mother of Freedom, no-one will ever know.

We were getting close now, and the radio remained gratefully dead. So I glanced out of a side window to check on the aircraft, half-expecting an already empty stand. But there it remained, and I looked down the finger again to see the third IO still arguing loudly with the crew and ground staff and doing a blinding time-wasting job. Then I glanced sideways again, just in time to see a small white van shoot out from beneath the Terminal building, approach the aircraft at a speed normally quite unacceptably high for the tarmac (or you could say, "like shit off a shovel"), drive straight under it unseen by any of those currently in dispute, brake sharply, do a smart one-eighty and stop directly behind the starboard rear wheels.

So I stopped running, and looked more closely. The van, again unusually, was unmarked apart from the obligatory revolving light, nor when the driver opened the door and got out could I see any company logo on his overalls. Anyway he stood there for a moment, quite casually, then locked his vehicle's door, turned and disappeared from my sight, walking quickly back towards the terminal. So I moved forward again but at walking pace now, almost relaxed, and as I reached the original cluster of men, already enlarged by the group of two more IOs, the two PCs and the target, I heard the Captain say decisively, 'No'. Then he marched back down the ramp and onto his aircraft, the door was shut with a 'woomph' of expelled air and everyone else – except for the passenger, who seemed quite happy about it – turned disconsolately towards me. We had, it seemed, lost.

"Wait," I said however, apparently quite calmly and concealing my relief, and we stood there together for a couple of minutes whilst they all tapped their feet and kept glancing at me in anxious surprise. Then I went over to the window and looked out again to check and the van was still there, and I was beginning to enjoy myself. *Now should be about right,* I thought, and I walked down the jet-way and knocked loudly on the still-closed door and after a moment it opened and there was the Captain himself, oddly downcast and embarrassed, which chuffed me no end. So, "*Hello,* Captain," I said, *Clint*-like now I hoped, and I pointed down and sideways. But he didn't bother to look because he already knew what I was pointing at.

"Hello," he replied, pretty calmly himself given *his* problem, and I reviewed our comparative positions and thought, *Damn, he does a better Clint than I do.*

Anyway, "*Tell* me, Captain," I said, all innocent-like and *my* turn to rub it in, *you* know. "Am I right in thinking that you want to, um, er, (innocent pause), now what do they call it, oh yes, – *push back*?"

"Yes, sir," said the Captain, still Clint-*ish* but *extra* politely this time, and I gestured to the PCs and the now-silent, downcast and largely-knackered refusal. "All right. Bring him and put him on," I said, and to the Captain, shortly, *"Take* him," to which *he* said fuck-all, and they hustled the refusal aboard. "Now off-load whoever you like, and then you can go."

The Captain gestured behind him. "But what about -?" he asked, but by now he sounded well-beaten and more like the bounty hunter in *'Josey Wales'* who says apologetically, "I've got's to try," ten seconds before Clint sorrowfully plugs him.

"Then you can go," I repeated. But the showdown was over, so I kept my own pistols well-holstered and left him standing there, and we all walked up off the jet-way without looking back, not much anyway, and in a moment I heard the door shut again behind me.

No-one *had* got off, so I reckoned they'd just moved someone into the jump seat – not *our* man I hoped, for their own safety, but that was their business and then again I was far from sure that they hadn't known the truth about him in the first place (this, after all – another clue – was the airline strongly already reputed to have brought in hand grenades via the diplomatic bag). And then we all strolled back to the Hall and I phoned ATC from the Watch House and asked for the Duty Manager, just to give him the heads-up, because you never knew.

"Hello?" said the same voice. And that was the moment when I remembered that all their calls were recorded.

"Hello there," I said. "It's Immigration again. Just to let you know that that problem I mentioned *did* sort itself out."

"Glad to hear it," he said, after a short pause. "Sorry we couldn't help."

"That's all right," I said. "I *fully* understand," and rang off again. I didn't offer to buy him a pint as, *again*, you never knew. Then I asked Paul to sprint a little way down the finger, to check if the flight had left yet because I didn't want to report final success until we'd seen it happen, and in a moment he came on the radio.

"It's just taxiing out," he said. "It's only just pushed back. Some plonker had parked a van under its wheels, but he's moved it now," and then as the penny dropped, just, "Oh."

"Good," I said.

The ACI appeared again about an hour later (or *too* late, depending on your point of view. "Well then. All sorted?" he asked briskly.

"Yes," I said.

"No problems?"

"No," I said, "none. The IOs," – I named them – "and the two PCs did very well."

"Good," he said too, then, "Well done. I'll drop a line of thanks to Northside (police). And oh, Mike, there was *just* one *little* thing," and he picked me up on an obscure procedural point that in the heat of the moment I'd overlooked completely.

"Oh. Right. Sorry," I said.

"Oh, forget it," he said, and waved his hand dismissively in the air, flicking it away, a mere nothing between friends. *Arsenal supporter.*

GOAL!!

Which links in nicely to Autumn 1985, just another day at the office but not *any* old day because even by our normal sub-standards we were up against it, the line stretched to the ultimate limit of bloody, bulging, *bursting* hypertension. It was the date of the second leg of the England-Turkey World Cup qualifier – the lads, Robson-led, having won the first, away, at a canter – and I think it must have been an evening match because in my memory we were still hard at it in the late afternoon, frantically dealing with flights full of self-professed Turkish fans and clearing most in good time for them to get to Wembley, but refusing too a fair few who'd jumped as usual on the soccer bandwagon, after examinations which were on the thin side of short but still just long enough to get all the standard basics.

There was, you see, a real time pressure on us too, because the last flight of them to arrive had been a one-off, the biggest of several dedicated charters and unless we got all its own refusals back on the return leg leaving the same evening and on which they had seats booked anyway, the numbers were such that we'd have to remove them later piecemeal, mainly on TK (Turkish Airlines, who we'd instruct to take them although they hadn't brought them in, and which would further upset our already iffy relations). And much worse than that, in the absence of detention space we'd have to grant them overnight TA meantime and then most of them wouldn't turn up for removal in the first place, which would both further infuriate TK in terms of unnecessarily empty seats and prove by our failure to complete the job in the only meaningful way that we'd been dead right to refuse them in the first place, etc., etc. So a negative can at least prove another negative, and again, see what I mean about pressure?

So inevitably the moment came when it became clear that we wouldn't make it, that one or two of the other charters which we could have readily used for any more removals were getting slot-times which would preclude our finishing even their own inbound passengers first, thus giving rise to another

Control equivalent of Catch 22 which I have described above (an all too regular occurrence anyway but not with these kinds of numbers, and we never *did* catch most of *them*). And a solution had to be found, found *fast*, because in our world there was no facility at all for Extra Time. And it was.

"Bugger this," someone said, probably a CIO but I can't be sure. "There's no time left for proper interviews, even short ones. They're supposed to be *football fans*, aren't they? So let's just ask'em the final score in the first leg, 6 – 0 it was. If they get it right, they're in, if not, they're out." And it worked. Twenty or so passengers were yet to be interviewed and it turned out about fifty-fifty, with several a couple of goals out and one or two even getting the *result* wrong. And thus amidst scenes of great joy from those let in and of great sorrow (and rage) from those shut out, the former departed for Wembley and the latter for Istanbul, or Izmir, or wherever it was.

And thus by the time the night IOs came on duty, we were back to no more than our usual chaos, the whole thing done and dusted, and I walked back into the Ready Room just in time to hear one of the Lates telling one of the Nights all about it, ending with the eventual unconventional manoeuvre which had sorted it. "Oh aye," said the listener. "So some of them got it wrong did they, the silly buggers. Just goes to show. 8 – 0, pretty simple, you'd have thought they'd all get *that* right!"

"Er, *what* score was that?" his mate asked, as I turned on my heel and left at some speed. I didn't bother to check at the time but I did later – it *was* 8, as I'd known it would be because the Scots *never* got their scores wrong where an England match was concerned, even a win – and when, later again, I checked the departures of those we'd last landed we'd lost about fifty per cent, which to my jaundiced eye was about right and probably similar to what would have happened had we landed the other ones instead.

So overall an honourable draw, and the own-goal wasn't golden.

NOTHING IN WRITING

'Language Examinations' it said on the Interport List, and went on to give the dates for this year's sittings and their location – as usual, a Knightsbridge hotel well past its prime. *I ought to have another go,* I thought, and I'd still have time for a bit of revision – God knows I needed it. They paid extra if you spoke a foreign language well enough, written and/or oral – a pittance for French and German by then, but a fair sum for the rest with a lesser amount if you just spoke but couldn't read most of the ones that used other scripts, Urdu, for example. And to keep the gravy-train flowing, you had to re-qualify every five years.

It was in short worth doing if you thought you had the slightest chance and arguably, especially if you were only *re-*qualifying, even if you didn't, because you had nothing to lose except the cash and in any case simply by turning up you'd always meet old friends on a similar errand (and probably with the same dubious rationale), with whom you could have a drink or two afterwards to complement the three or four you'd shared beforehand, because the universal maxim was that from alcohol flowed fluency, and it was *true*. I'd qualified in French years ago but failed at the first re-sit and I'd tried Hindi and Urdu, the full bifta in both including scripts, soon after I'd joined – after all, they'd been my university subjects in which I had been truly, soberly, fluent (shit-hot in fact, so was it rather *eff*fluent) when I'd been summarily thrown out, then not too many years before – and failed them both gloriously and inevitably because I'd nervously overdone the pre-oral ports (fortified *wine* I mean) and positively *oozed* fluency from every pore and perhaps from every orifice (so perhaps it *was* *eff*luency after all) – but as Eric once nearly said to Ernie and Andre Preview, in no known language.

So I lobbed in my chit, discounting French because even at Two we never used it anymore and to pass you had to be almost bi-lingual anyway; and discounting Hindi too because for some reason you couldn't just take the oral and by now I'd wholly forgotten the Devanagari script; which only left Urdu – *oral* Urdu I mean, because I knew I'd forgotten the Arabic script also, so I simply went for that.

And having applied I promptly forgot *that* as well, so by the time the reply appeared in my pigeon hole complete with an exam date a mere two weeks ahead, it was too late for any revision anyway and I thought, as many others had thought before me, *Damn, I'll just go and have a few ports first, and then wing it.* And I did, or was going to, but even that idea proved half still-born because just two days beforehand another note arrived bringing my slot forward from 1500 hours to 1030, *before* the bloody pubs were even *open,* and it wasn't the same thing at all to swig in advance from your own bottle, *that* was just *not on.*

So I went, fully resigned to my inevitable fate and with that old familiar butterfly-fluttering in my stomach taking me back over twenty years as I waited necessarily soberly outside the door, straining but failing to make some sense of the low murmurs within. Then my predecessor emerged, white-faced, silent and trembling – and it couldn't have been the port with him either – but there I *still* waited, on and on, waited for an *eternity* until it was bloody obvious that the sadistic bastard inside was *deliberately keeping me* waiting; and then suddenly the call came: "Next! Come in please," the words all running together in a way that was somehow familiar and as I entered, the sadistic bastard inside's white-haired old head was down reading something and then he raised it, and we stared at each other open-mouthed in instant mutual recognition.

"Professor!" I said, astonished, and I wasn't taking the piss, that was his proper title because he really *was* one, my old Urdu tutor from over twenty years ago. And *he* just said, "Good God!" which showed the extent of his surprise because he was, he *had* to be, an atheist, as one of the self-avowed first hundred card-carrying communists in the UK, which latter didn't necessarily mean that he wasn't a nice person Then, as he muttered, "It's – ", he looked down at his candidate list and it came out in another half-gabbled rush, the way he'd always spoken. "It's, it's – *Clarke*, yes, *of course*, well, I've been wanting to have a word with *you* for the *last fifteen years*. Because I was on the board that sacked you, and I only agreed to it because they told me that you'd failed your exams as well as not attending lectures – you *bloody* fool – and fifteen years ago I found out that they'd *lied* to me, you hadn't *failed* at all, you'd *passed*! *Sit down*."

So I did, partly because he'd ordered it and partly because I needed to. This was a lot, a hell of a lot, to take in all at once, and I felt an instant wave of grief – wave, not pang, because it flowed and lasted, on and on – for my father, now long dead, who had never been quite the same with me or in himself after my dismissal. *Are you watching, Dad? Dad, I'm so sorry. Dad, can you see this now?* I whispered inside my head, not in pious self-righteous justification – because the professor was right, I *had* been a damn fool anyway – but just to make *him*, *my Dad*, feel better if he could, then jerked myself back to reality as he, the Professor, got down to business.

"*Right*," he said briskly – and I remembered he'd always been brisk, too – "*right*, let's get the test out of the way first, then we can address the other matter. Are you ready? OK, let's go." He broke at once into swift, colloquial Urdu, I could tell that much but little else, and it was ever-more-readily apparent from his ever-more-strained expression that my ever-more-halting replies, if they were actually *in* Urdu in the first place, had fuck-all to do with his questions.

So after five minutes, or maybe less, he stopped, looked at me quizzically and sat back. "Look," he said, " *Aapko yaad nehii he is ke baare, suc he, na?* (You don't remember it, do you? That's the truth?" – spoken very slowly now, of course.) He'd never beaten about the bush, and I honoured him for it. So, "No, Yes, professor," I said humbly, in English (though I suppose I could've managed my very own, '*nehii, jihaa, professer sahib,*' at least).

"Well, then. You *haven't got a bloody clue,* and you thought *you'd just come in here and wing* it, *didn't* you? *Like you always used to?*"

"Yes, professor," I said, still humbly. He'd nailed it all right.

"Hmm. *You haven't changed.* You know I'll have to fail you?" He was a *truly* honourable man.

"Yes, professor." Humbly still – he'd sussed me from the off. Always had.

"*All right.* Now, you were treated very badly – no,

disgracefully, by the University. So. Do you want to come back to resume your course?"

I gulped. I was sure he could fix it, but it was at least twenty years too late. "Thanks very much," I said, "but I don't think that would be too practical," and I briefly told him why.

"Hmm," he said again. "Yes, I can quite see that," and he paused for a moment, deep in thought.

"Look," he said, finally. "I've just brought out a new book on Urdu. Have you heard of it?"

"No," I said. Well I hadn't, and I could hardly lie about *that* after my recent performance, could I?

"All right. It's twenty quid. Re-sit the test next year and have it under your arm when you walk in, and I'll pass you. Does that suit?"

"Yes, professor," I said *very* humbly and I meant it, *what* a solution, and we shook hands warmly and said Goodbye. As I said, he was a very, *very,* honourable man.

Thus it was that the following year, properly *p*.m. this time, I sat totally relaxed and comfortably *extra*-ported up outside the familiar door, the professor's book in my lap. I'd never opened it and my Urdu had not improved, but I knew it didn't matter. Then the door opened and my predecessor emerged, white-faced and trembling. "He says to go in," he said this time, and I did, the book displayed prominently under my arm. There was the examiner again, his head down reading something, but I could already see that he was a much younger man, and from somewhere on the sub-continent himself to boot.

He was studying his list. He looked up and I knew I'd never seen him before. "Mr. -?" he asked me.

"Clarke," I said, then, "where's the professor?" I couldn't help it.

He looked momentarily surprised. "Who? The professor? Oh, he's gone sick today, and I'm standing in. Are you ready?"

I sighed. Sometimes you really *can't* win. "Yes," I said. I suppose it was quite useful really from his point of view because he'd been running well behind and my interview didn't take long, five minutes at most, just like before. Still, at least this time I was *fluent*.

I never saw the professor, *my* professor, again. I persuaded myself that he would be too old by the following year and I had less and less time for study anyway, so I never re-re-took the test. He's dead now, long since and I am very sorry for it. There aren't that many truly honourable men left these days, whatever cards they carry.

SATELLITES

The Curtain affected the Control in many ways. The main player was of course the USSR, and that really came down again to each night's Moscow SU. We had regular flights from other Russian airports too, Leningrad for example, but it always seemed to be the Moscow arrivals that brought the problems (the *non-Russian* problems that is, because we rarely had any with the Russkis themselves, they were far too slick for us with both their dissidents and their spies, and affairs like the RAC didn't happen every day) and that was simply because the capital was the main transit point for a number of Third World airlines from countries whose nationals wanted to wind up here but to come circuitously and on the cheap – Sri Lanka and the Horn of Africa spring immediately to mind.

And it made sense to do it that way. If your ultimate aim was to claim asylum in the UK, the more fragmented your journey here the better, because it would make your eventual removal – if, strangely, it ever came close to that – so much more difficult to arrange, even if you hadn't been primed to destroy your ticket and travel documents before you arrived and then pretend after you had that you were so confused or tired or traumatised by events that you couldn't for the life of you remember any details whatsoever of your journey, such as countries of transit or other airlines you'd used, or sometimes even your bloody name.

But there were other, wider, effects. The eventual collapse of the Soviet Empire (which visibly began soon after I'd left for North Essex pastures new) removed one of the most effective immigration controls the Brits had ever had, because on what seemed to be a passing but recurrent whim the Russians would sometimes send the UK-in-transit hopefuls back rather than onwards when they first got *there* or, in winter, give them a few weeks (or months) clearing snow off the local streets before letting them proceed here in arbitrary batches, so that we never knew whether a particular flight would bring no asylum claimants at all, or ten, or twenty-plus.

And whilst that consistent uncertainty didn't do us any favours on the busy nights, it also surely helped limit the numbers of those who opted to come that way in the first place because they or at least their handlers/agents knew that they were taking a real chance on whether they could pass straight through as planned or instead suffer an indefinite spell of hard labour half-way, sweeping snow off the Steppes or, worse still, find themselves peremptorily refused and banged up before heading off straight home again without even a passing *glimpse* of Julie Christie, whether they Looked Now or not.

Then out of that same old blue would come something wholly unexpected, and I copped two of the same kind within a month, neither oddly enough directly concerning Mother Russia but rather one of her satellites. And although I said 'come', the operative word this time should properly be 'go' instead because both situations arose on Embarks, and the first flight involved was one of the Rumanian carrier's, TAROM's.

They appeared then, the two of them, suddenly at the door of the Watch House, one IO and one passenger, both clearly and equally worried. But in fact they were three, because tagging along behind and protesting loudly at the IO's actions so far was the airline's current local top man, the Duty Manager, Rumanian himself as you would expect (though such national linkage didn't always follow, as later you will sadly – or gladly – see); and when *he* tried to enter the Watch House too, I told him, politely enough as if addressing an HMI, to bugger off and wait outside.

The story itself was a familiar one, at least if you read spy novels, but I'd never seen it before in real life. The passenger – let's call him Vlad – was young and himself Rumanian, his flight home didn't leave for another hour and he was happy enough to talk to us inside the office whilst TAROM Man paced and gestured and glowered without. Vlad, surprise, surprise, was an asylum seeker here which was the first irony since as I think I've already said somewhere, such applicants from behind the Iron Curtain, from the very countries in fact that the 1951 Convention on Refugees had been passed to protect, were thin, very thin on the ground, simply because they couldn't get *out*.

But Vlad *had*, by the only standard successful means – by

becoming a seaman, staying all at sea until he was more or less trusted and then jumping ship once here, in this case at Tilbury. He had then walked into a police station and made his claim, he was still awaiting a Home Office interview so no decision could possibly have been made on his case and he was thus in the UK quite legally – working his pieces you might say if you were a cynic or in IS or at least well-informed, though so in a way were they all, false and genuine alike – but now here he was at Two and about to go home, back to the very country which he'd been at such pains to escape. And why? Because he'd received an official telegram telling him that his young wife and child were both very ill at home in Rumania, and that they needed him *now*, needed him *badly*. That's why.

And the IO had done well: he'd got this out of Vlad in a brief exchange on embarks, where our powers were truly minimal – once we were satisfied of any outbound passenger's identity and nationality, we *had* routinely to allow him to proceed – but he'd seen the telegram himself and hadn't been satisfied that Vlad was leaving *of his own free will,* which made it a whole new ball game. And so he'd brought him round to me, and then the irate TAROM man, who'd been waiting in the wings all along, had got involved.

I had a brief chat with Vlad – he'd already picked up a good smattering of English, and that also was par for the course – whilst T Man continued to fulminate outside. And he showed *me* the telegram too, and translated it readily. It was brief – in the novels, they always were: first his surname, then *'Wife and child very ill. Come home now,'* just that, and it made good authoritarian sense. Why bother after all with a carrot or even to speak softly, when you have a big and irresistible stick?

"Who's it from exactly, Vlad?" I asked.

"It don't say," he said. It didn't.

"*Could* someone in your family have sent it?" I asked.

"No. Not like that," he replied.

"Who then?" and he said he didn't know. But I could see from his lowered eyes that he did.

"Vlad. Look. I think this is a fake," I said.

"Yes," he said.

"I think it was written by the Romanian authorities."

"Yes," he said.

"To get *you* home."

"Yes."

"Then why are you going?"

"For my wife and children. To protect them." And there was nothing more for me or anyone else to say.

But, I thought, *I can do <u>one</u> small thing for him,* and I asked him to wait and watch. So I opened the door for T Man and he came in, another Number One but louder and lesser, a small, insignificant weedy geezer with the Might of the System behind him, arrogant and blustering, full in fact of liquid shit – not that it can have taken much – and behind it all, and what I despised most in him, was his clear, sure knowledge that in the end Vlad *would* go, because he had to.

So I told Big Strong T Man that *this* was a *free* country if he knew what that meant, and that I had advised his passenger to think again. And then I just sat there for a while and let the bluster die away. And it was only when he realised that the flight could lose its slot-time that he began to half-believe me and then to think that perhaps *he'd* be on the *next* one-way trip home if Vladi-boy wasn't on *this* one, and suddenly he was crying and on his knees in the Watch House, shades of The Weeper but not worth even *one* of *his* tears, begging me as Vlad looked on, begging me, Christ, *"as a family man myself"*, not to

stop him (Vlad) going, and I said that that was up to Vlad and
he said he *would* go and then I shook *his* hand and ignored T
Man's and let the IO take them both back round to Embarks,
and he told me later that Vlad *had* finally left on the flight, as
we'd all known he would.

But as I drove home that night stone-cold sober and
heading furiously for the Windsor chippie, I was already deeply
regretting my public humiliation of TAROM Man. Oh, I
wasn't sorry for *him*, he was a contemptible little sod who fully
deserved what I trust eventually came to him, whether in the
neck or up his arse. But so far as Vlad's future was concerned
I had been nothing more than unforgivably self-indulgent, off
on an ego-trip *and* from an unassailably safe personal position
of strength.

Because it wouldn't be *me* who when he got home would
suffer the consequences of T Man's embarrassment but Vlad,
poor old Vladimir who T Man knew had seen the whole thing.
And what nagged at me most was that I should've known that
all along and that perhaps in my heart I *had*, and that all along
my vain posturing was just that, designed to make *me* feel and
look good and bound not only to fail but to make things worse
for the one I claimed to be trying to help.

So I debated it with myself as I drove, and the other side
was that for a while at least I had deflated T Man, and reminded
him of his own vulnerability. But it didn't really work because
I still doubted my own motives when it should all have been
about Vladimir, who I was sure would already be paying a
heavy and lasting price for our momentary mutual satisfaction
at the brief discomfiture I had caused his tormentor – that is,
if the price wasn't the ultimate and if so, perhaps I'd been the
cause, the fucking very *occasion*, of that too.

I didn't sleep much that night but not just through

indigestion, and in the end the only consolation I could find was in my silent vow that in the unlikely event of such a thing happening to me again – and I never *did* hear of it happening *once* to *any* of my colleagues, before or since, though it surely must have done – I would stand right back and let things take their inevitable course, however weak that might make me appear.

Well, that was the theory, and every day at work something else new would happen to distract me from brooding on it, so that after almost a month it had gone from my mind – or rather, it was still there but readily submergible beneath a sea of successive events and encounters. And that was when, on another Floor day, I took another call from embarks: could I come round, *at once*? The IO was another good one – they were *all* good then at Two in their different ways, but some of them were truly superb and he was one of *them* – and I knew he knew I had no time to spare for trivia.

So I hurried round and found him not on the control but in the Departure Lounge itself, sitting at a table by the bar with a man I didn't know, obviously another Eastern European – Balkan, I thought automatically from his skin-tone – and clearly a passenger, although he had no hand baggage. Their heads were close together and I walked over, noting without particular surprise or irritation that each was nursing a large scotch.

I approached them side-on and the IO, who seemed to be doing all the talking, didn't notice me until I was almost on top of them. Then he jumped to his feet and held up his hand – in warning, I realised later – but I had no time for any of that because I was swiftly examining his companion. He was sprawled back in his chair by now and momentarily in profile, his legs awkwardly and almost artificially widespread, his arms loose and his dark glasses well askew on his flushed face. It only took a quick glance because I have seldom seen a man so clearly, so *manifestly* drunk, and my temper rose at once. I was bloody busy on the Floor and why the hell couldn't the IO, one of the most unflappable we had, deal with this *himself?* Because pissed passengers were a daily stock in trade.

So I turned on John to blow him right out of the scotch and water. But I should've known better, and in the same instant that I saw that *his* face was flushed too and that he was shaking with anger, visibly outraged, the passenger groaned loudly as he tried instinctively to move his legs to stand up, but fell back instead. And as I looked at him again his dark glasses dropped right off his nose and now that I truly focussed and saw him properly, face-on, I realised that yet again I had jumped to completely the wrong conclusion.

Because now it was blindingly obvious that the man's eyes were glazed not with booze but with pain and perhaps with drugs, and the reason for both was readily apparent. The right side of his face was a livid blue, heavily bruised and badly swollen, and as he tried vainly and with another groan to move his left leg again, it dragged strangely below the knee and I recognised suddenly that it too, like his jaw, was broken.

So this was the moment to take charge, to assert my authority, to be cool myself. "All right, take it easy, everybody calm down," or, "John, tell me about it." or maybe "Don't move mate, stay still," anything like that would have done nicely. But *"John,"* I said instead, *"What* the *fuck?"* and then *he* sat down again and, his anger still barely in check, told me anyway whilst his companion, having himself relapsed, listened silently, occasionally grinning in embarrassed agreement despite the pain.

"*Right,* Mike. This is Georgi. He's due out shortly on

the BALKAN AIR." He stopped for a moment to clear his throat, his eyes fixed on Georgi as he carried on. *Jeez*, he was angry. "And he's determined to go, *insisting* on it, but look what the *bastards* have done to him," and then it came out in a rush, shades of the Professor, from the moment he'd seen Georgi enter the embarks hall to their initial encounter at the outbound Control and their subsequent conversation in the Dep. Lounge, once he'd got him sat down.

It was the commotion at the Security Check outside which had first drawn John's attention. He'd heard raised voices, the guards remonstrating and barring entry whilst they called their own manager, then finally falling back reluctantly at his direction to admit the two big men – always Two Big Men, I thought, like in the old black-and-whites – who were half–pushing, half-carrying the smaller man between them. And the Security Manager was right, they *had* to be let in because of their status, but the guards were right too, they knew trouble when they saw it, and John watched in disbelief as Georgi's escorts dragged him stumbling across the hall, draped him groaning over the desk, smiled wordlessly at him, patted him playfully but hard on his damaged cheek, banged down his papers, ignored John and left, still flourishing their Bulgarian Diplomatic ID cards. Diplomats? Diplomats my arse, and unlike T Man they were so fucking confident they didn't even bother to wait for take-off.

At that time Georgi still didn't speak, or couldn't, so John put the papers in his pocket, left the control to his colleagues and man-handled him as gently as he could into the Lounge. And it was only after he'd made him as comfortable as possible and they'd had a couple of drinks – by the time I got there, they were on their fourth double and it did seem to help with the pain – that Georgi told him all about it; and now John told me, and I listened to the half-familiar story with a sinking heart.

Now compared to Vlad, you might say that Georgi really *had* made it. Because just like Vlad he too had come and claimed asylum but it had been a long, long while ago, so long that not only had the Home Office interviewed him but it had even *decided* his case, and it had decided to let him remain. So here he was, legally and proudly resident – John showed me his UK Travel Document, the prized proof of it, not quite a full British passport, not yet, but the next best thing because it entitled him to stay here for another three years and was valid for every country in the world, all except Bulgaria of course, because that was the one from which he had fled to escape state persecution.

And now Georgi was working here in a steady job, and better still he was engaged to a British girl, *really* British and it was only last week that she'd told him she was pregnant. So he and his fiancée were very happy and making plans for the future when, only yesterday, he had received the proverbial knock at the door. Proverbial because the memories of the 'democratic' leaders of the Satellite countries were as long and at least as vindictive as those of their Moscow masters, and the message from the Bulgarian Embassy had again been short and simple, a minor variation on Vlad's although essentially the same. 'Your mother is alone and dying and needs you,' it said. 'Go to the Embassy at once for your papers. Then you must go home.'

Each of the Satellite communities had its own émigré network, its own bush telegraph. But you didn't need to be involved to know Rule One, which was absolute, '*Never, ever, go to your Embassy, or even Anywhere Near It.*' And Georgi was no fool and he knew that this was probably no more than a set-up, but he *had* to go – this was his *mother*, and if he was right and it *was* a set-up, then if they didn't get *him* they already had *her*, just like Vlad's family, though of course Georgi had never heard of Vladimir.

So he'd gone to the Embassy, without telling his fiancée anything about it except in a brief note saying that he loved her, gone there this very morning happy at least in the knowledge that now he probably had nothing to fear from rolled umbrellas, and they'd been expecting him just as he'd expected, and once he was inside there had been no pretence of pleasantry; the Two Big Men had just taken him into a back room and broken his leg and his jaw. Then they had splinted and bandaged his leg, very roughly, and pumped him full of pain killers and stuffed some more in his pocket and told him his flight left that same afternoon and stapled a single sheet of paper inside his UK Travel Document, a one-off one-way one-day Bulgarian visa 'entitling' him to enter the country via Sofia – they were nothing if not thorough. Then they'd taken him to The Airport in a car with DP plates which they left on a double yellow right outside Two, and handed him over to us to finish the job. It turned out that the flight was already full, but that was no problem. One official Bulgarian word and someone was simply off-loaded, just the way *we* would have worked it if Georgi had been a refusal here, but rather more efficiently.

Anyway there was still plenty of time, still thirty minutes before the last call, and John had called me round because he at least hoped that I could do *something,* or maybe simply because his conscience said he *had to*; and my recent firm resolution never even entered my mind because he was *right,* this was *wrong,* obscene and abhorrent, with the violence the icing on the repugnant cake. But there was nothing that I *could* do. John had already said all that could be said and tried every argument that could be tried, so now we tried them again together, but it was fruitless.

"If they can do *this* to you *here*," we said, "what will they do *there*?"

"Yes," he said, and smiled lopsidedly, and nodded wisely despite the pain, "and what then would they do to my mother?"

"Is your mother very old?" we asked, after a pause.

"Yes," he said, and smiled again, because he thought he knew what was coming next, but we were *trained officers*, see, and *subtle*.

"But your fiancee here, *she* is young. And what about the baby?", the unexpected low blow with a vain twist, and for a moment he frowned and looked away. But then he smiled again, apologetically.

"Yes. But *they* are safe *here*, in England," he said, deliberately half-misunderstanding. "And *she* is my *mother*."

So this time *I* bought another round, double of course, and we just sat there hopelessly and at the end in total silence whilst my inbound Control ran itself, and when the next call came we grabbed a wheel-chair and ran Georgi down to the gate, but slowly, and then we sat there hopelessly too for a while on a bench beside him and the other passengers until the final call, because although there was no point in talking any more now and to try further would have been somehow insensitive, it would not have been right either to leave him there alone.

So we stayed, and when the final call came Georgi stood up quickly, then fell forward onto his face. He was in a lot of pain and perhaps it was just that, but I wondered at the time if finally, maybe, it was fear too, and if so he was right to be afraid. Perhaps dead right.

Anyway he didn't move and just lay there, and I suppose we could just have stood by until the flight had gone and then taken him back with us. But *that* wouldn't have been right either, and he made it easier for us by saying, 'You must help me,' then realised that was ambiguous and added, "onto the aircraft,' which we'd known he meant anyway. So we did, and as we picked him up he cried out and one of the last British passengers to board turned round and asked us, 'What the *hell* we thought we were doing,' and I told him viciously to '*Shut the fuck up and bugger off*,' the poor ignorant well-meaning lucky sod.

So we wheeled Georgi down the sloping ramp and then, with great difficulty because his strength seemed at last to have fully failed him, stood him up and walked him through the door and into the aircraft, our warrants hanging from our necks as everyone looked at us in contempt and I thought to myself, *What a great Press picture this will make with the three of us half-way on and silhouetted against the light, and what an opportunity for a perceptive caption – "British Immigration thugs deport a foreign cripple, the only one they could catch."* Or something like that.

So I stayed on with Georgi, thrusting my warrant in the faces of the protesting cabin crew, who'd clearly been primed anyway. And I talked to him again, despairingly now, in the last minutes before the door closed because I couldn't help myself. And he listened and smiled and sometimes he nodded his head. But all he really wanted to do was sleep, and he wouldn't get off, so in the end I left him there and they closed the door behind me. It was easy enough for me to disembark, because they'd sat him up at the front where they could keep an eye on him.

Then John and I stood and watched the aircraft push back, and we waited until we saw it take off before walking away together in silence. I thought later that by boarding with Georgi I'd probably caused him even more trouble at the other end than I had Vladimir, because there was no doubt that the cabin crew would report it, for their *own* safety. Anyway, I made yet another entry in the Incident Log and John did a brief report, copied to Box in case when they got him home they turned him, by promise or threat, and sent him back again but against *us*. It paid to be cynical about *that*, too (we'd done the same with Vlad). But somehow I doubted it.

Still, on the bright side I found that like everything else, it was less hard to come to terms with the second time round. No doubt by the third time it would have been almost routine with all the pros and cons already thoroughly rehearsed, but the third time never came. And if either Vlad or Georgi, or even both of them, survived the years until the fall of their respective repressive regimes and chance to read this and to recognise himself or themselves, I'd really appreciate a brief if recriminatory word to say so. But, again, perhaps like them, I'm not holding my breath.

CLASH

But it wasn't all just passengers, *or* baleful regimes. All sorts of other outfits tried it on in their different ways, dodgy solicitors for example, and shady bucket shops, and not least a number of airlines – amongst which latter, one stood out. Let's call it AIR RURITANIA or AR for short, a notional national firm whose staff developed a singularly annoying habit in which they began to indulge with increasing regularity and to the growing frustration of the IOs until it reached the point where, somehow, it *had* to be stopped. 'Cometh the hour cometh the man,' as the saying goes. Or just, 'Wrong place, wrong time,' depending on your point of view.

One Friday evening due to sickness I was covering both sides of the Watch House, Floor and SEA, when the AR landed and I was soon informed that it was up to its usual tricks, having yet again knowingly brought a visa national without the UK visa essential to his entry and whose refusal was accordingly inevitable; and they (the AR check-in staff in – wait a minute, yes, that's it – Strelsau) had let him travel because he wasn't just any old Tomaso, Ricardo or Hassan but a diplomat, this time a young West African (again!) Second Secretary, just coming to London for the weekend.

But first, a spot of more personal and technical background (*his*, I mean). When, a year or so before, the young rising star in question had first been posted to his country's Embassy in the capital of what I'll continue to call Ruritania, he had opted to leave his equally young and doubtless nubile wife behind to manage the family home. And now he was clearly missing her sorely, because he'd brought an even younger and for all I know even more nubile co-national along here with him instead – no doubt just for the ride – who as I recall also worked beneath him in the Strelsau embassy, but just as a secretary there. And *she had* the mandatory UK visa whereas he, as I've already indicated, had *not*. Had he been a diplomat in his country's High Commission *here* and thus accredited to the Court of St. James, he wouldn't have needed one, but he was accredited abroad in Ruritania instead. And so, although the visa's acquisition was a mere formality, he still did.

And that was the airline's standard trick. They knew

the Visa Regulations and the Rules perfectly well, but they were relying on the good old pragmatic and flexible Brits to recognise that the passenger wasn't a threat to the Control (clearly, he wasn't) and accordingly either simply to waive the 'technicality' entirely as we sometimes did – in other words, to turn a big blind eye, but the reverse of Nelson's – and just let him in with a warning not to do it again (you put a large, menacing, 'W' inside his entry stamp, big, **big,** deal) ; or at the very worst, to refuse him entry formally on paper but then grant him TA for the weekend and direct that he stay at the very London hotel where he was already expected and report back to Two on Monday morning for removal on the very flight on which he was also already booked, thus still giving him precisely what he had asked for in the first place (although you must never forget the useful refusal statistic). Phew.

But on this occasion Chinua, as we'll call him (but don't read anything into that) came on the wrong flight on the wrong day, or perhaps he was just unlucky. Because he and his girlfriend went to an IO who was afraid neither of a bit of controversy nor of an extra bit of work in a good cause, and who had had a similar problem with AR before. And so he readily admitted the young diplomat's nubile younger companion but held *him* up, and not only referred him to me as a refusal but also pointed out that if we were double-quick, we could send him back that very evening, on the return flight, which was the last AR flight of the day.

Well. It would be tight all right since it was scheduled to depart within sixty minutes, but it would send the airline a clear signal that enough was enough, the refusal itself was child's play and when pushed to turn simple cases round that quickly, we could and sometimes did – remember *'Goal'*? So *I* said 'Do it,' – I suppose I must've been distracted, or just too busy or feeling pissed off about something too – and in no time at all, the IO was on his way down to the aircraft with the much-chastened Chinua whilst his pretty girlfriend – sorry, a slip of the pen, his *demure companion,* who to be fair did seem remarkably philosophical at the turn of events – prepared with laudable and still-smiling stoicism to buzz off all alone for her now-apparently-solitary weekend in London.

But ten minutes later Callum, the IO in question, came through on the radio. There was, it seemed, a problem. The airline's Duty Manager – why was it always Duty Managers with me – was there at the gate, refusing to let Chinua board, and could I come down? So I went, in another hurry, and at first glance everything seemed normal when I arrived. The bulk of the passengers had already embarked and the rest were straggling down the ramp. But there in a corner was a frustrated Callum beside an embarrassed Chinua who showed no sign himself of even trying to move.

So Callum rapidly explained. When he'd arrived on the scene, he'd approached the DM, who was there purely by chance. But the latter – who happened to be a Western European, albeit in current charge of the Ruritanian national airline – had immediately become excited and uncooperative, *quelle surprise*.

"The flight is *full,*" he'd said.

"No problem. Offload someone as normal," Callum said, brightly.

"Offload *who*?" The DM asked.

"That's up to you," Callum responded.

"Then *who's* going to tell *him*?" The DM asked. Tell the poor old off-loadee, he meant.

"*You* are," Callum said, which was the way it worked. So the DM tried another tack.

"And *where* is his *ticket*?" He asked. This time, he meant Chinua's.

"*Here*," said Callum, and produced it.

"A*haa*," said the DM as he examined it and then exhaled noisily in triumph, not unlike a fighting bull. "It is not for *this* flight."

"No," responded Callum, minimally sarcastic. "The tickets of refusals rarely are. So you'll have to *change* it."

"No," said the DM, "*no*, I will *not*, because there is *no time.*" And that was the impasse when I arrived.

The DM – let's call *him* Juan but you shouldn't read anything into *that*, either – was still there, standing watching the rest of the passengers as they boarded. His back was towards us, but whether that was deliberate or not I had no idea. So I took Chinua's passport and ticket from Callum and approached him. I'd seen him about a few times but I didn't know him.

"Hello," I said – I said it *extra* coolly, because I'd already decided. This time it was going to be a simple spat between colleagues, but marginally less deadly than, say, in *Magnum Force*.

"Ola," he replied, grudgingly, just that, but it was as high-plain as the nose on your face from the way he said it that he knew *what* if not *who* I was, that he already guessed my drift and that perhaps understandably he preferred *For a Few Dollars More* – The 'Man in Black's' part, I mean.

"As you already know, *this* gentleman," – I indicated Chinua – "is a refusal."

"Yes," he said.

"And as you also already know, he arrived from Strelsau, on your airline."

"Yes."

"So I have directed your airline to take him back on this flight."

"Yes." So far, he seemed a very reasonable man, albeit a little terse even for Van Cleef, and with only a slight physical resemblance (and no meerschaum, either).

"And are you *going* to take him?" *Cut to the motorbike chase*, I thought.

At which he smiled a Latin smile, and nodded vigorously several times. *He is a reasonable man,* I thought, *a veritable diplomat in his own right, and why the hell couldn't Callum have done this himself?* and when I held out my hand, he took it and shook it, vigorously. *PR*-wise, *AR* would have been proud of him. Then, "*No*," he said, simply and emphatically, shaking his head with equal vigour *and* in time, which isn't easy, and out of the corner of my eye I saw Callum smile. Clearly this was going to be a tricky Juan.

So I let go of his hand. "Why not?" I asked, and he shrugged.

"Because he has no ticket for it," he said. Again.

"You can write one now," I said, and he smiled again and shrugged helplessly. "I am too busy," he said. "There is no *time.*" Again, again. So I looked round. The flight was *still* boarding, he *wasn't* busy, there was in fact *lots* of time, and I moved closer to him.

"*You*," I said, in his ear but without particular emphasis, "don't seem to be running *a very tight ship.*" That's *exactly* what I said, I swear it.

"*What?*" he asked, apparently incredulous at the remark. So I repeated it slowly, word for word, apart from the low-key, unambiguous addition of 'I said'. At which he seemed momentarily stunned, and in the ensuing silence I thought for a moment, *What would Clint do now?* And in the absence of a white van or a spare uniform, the answer was obvious.

But I couldn't do *that,* now could I – apart from anything else I lacked even a *metaphorical* .44 Magnum, with which to blow the metaphorical punk's metaphorical head *clean off* – so instead I turned and beckoned Callum to join me and together we walked straight past him, now sullen and brooding – *him*, I mean – and I boarded the aircraft whilst the others stood just outside as I turned sharp left and went through to the flight-deck.

"Captain," I said, and nodded, and the Captain swivelled in his seat and looked up at me. Thank Christ he wasn't at all like Eli Wallach, or I would have got *totally* confused. Anyway, it was obvious that he already knew something was up but that was no big deal, there was often some minor kerfuffle or other when we boarded refusals. "Hello there," I said again, still ultra-cool and still in character. "I have a passenger outside who arrived on this aircraft and who has been refused entry to the UK. And I am directing *you*, as the aircraft's commander, to remove him on it *now*," and I handed him an extra copy of the Removal Directions which Callum had already served on the DM, for his *very own*. It was a little unusual to do it that way, but perfectly legal.

The Captain, who *was* Ruritanian, read the form carefully, his cheeks inflated (no dammit, that was Van Cleef, wasn't it? OK, so I *was* already a *bit* confused.). Then he said, "All right. Where is he?" but as I turned to get Chinua, the DM appeared.

"*You will not take him,*" he said to the Captain, rather unhelpfully.

"I am *directed* to take him," said the Captain reasonably – he too seemed a very reasonable man. "So I *will*."

"You will *not*," said the DM.

"We shall soon lose our slot-time," said the Captain, deftly half-changing the subject, but in vain.

Because the DM spoke again, this time in just the way Lee would have done, "*You will not take him*," and the Captain looked at me in just the way Eli would have done if he *had* been there too, and now it was *his* turn to shrug.

"I am very sorry," he said; but without conviction, because that wasn't Eli's style at all.

Well, I could think of plenty of other Captains from other airlines who in those circumstances would have taken a different line and told the relevant DM to fuck off – they told *us* to often enough, when they felt like it (especially the Germans). But I couldn't fault this one for doing what he was told so it was time for some other, direct, action – this was still, just, *Magnum Force*, remember? But I still didn't plug anybody because I couldn't, *or* impersonate the Captain because there he was and besides I was sussed already, *or* threaten to put the word out that the DM was an IS ear (yeah, I know that was *The Enforcer*)). So I just left the aircraft instead, brushing past him (the DM) who beamed in triumph, and addressed Chinua (*I* did, I mean).

"I am very sorry," I said. "but please be patient. There is a small problem." (Yeah, *about five feet six*, I thought, from a quick glance back). "Now. Do you understand that you are to be removed on this flight?"

"Yes, sir," he replied meekly. It was readily apparent that all *he* wanted to do if he couldn't simply take off was drop through the runway instead.

"All right," I said, and I turned again to the DM. "*Are* you going to let this man board your aircraft, so that he can be removed?"

And as the DM shook his head with renewed vigour, I saw clearly now that he was a thoroughly *un*reasonable fellow. But at least this time his response matched his height. "*No*," he said. Shortly.

So I turned to Callum. "Stay here with the passenger," I said. Then I brushed past the DM for a second time and re-boarded the aircraft. By now the Captain was in the doorway, watching the action closely. I saw him wave at the DM and point to his watch, but again Juan shook his head. Then, once on board and neatly positioned just inside the door beside my own new unwitting bodyguard of a confused Captain and two enthralled stewardesses, I pointed at Chinua outside, and addressed him (Juan, I mean).

"If *you* will not let this refused passenger board this aircraft to be removed as required by law," I said, "*I* shall not get *off* it." Which, I thought, with some self-surprise, was a bit strong even for Clint, *whatever* bloody film it was, and out of the corner of my eye I noticed the Captain's hands beginning to twitch, almost convulsively – a matter, I suppose now, of potential real concern to any passenger on that same flight who saw it. But I was concentrating hard on the DM, whose mouth opened wide in parallel disbelief.

Then the co-pilot called out to the Captain who shrugged resignedly, then remarked loudly but to no-one in particular, "*That's it*. Now we *have* missed our slot." And suddenly it was serious, and I knew I'd cocked up because it *was The Good, the Bad* etc. after all, a re-run of Clint v. Eli v. Lee – or perhaps *The Prisoner of Zenda,* with Rudolph v. Rupert v. Michael, from the DM's point of view. And that left him with just one option, an obvious or even inevitable one (his trump card in fact when you think about it, but I must admit that *I* hadn't until he actually played it, any more than he'd anticipated mine). Anyway, he took it now.

"OK," he said, breathing heavily now, and looked at one of his several aides who had gathered, all also open-mouthed, at the scene. "*You. Call the police*," and the aide stared back at him. "*I said, 'Call the police'*," he repeated, and this time the man shuffled off, muttering anxiously into his radio.

The die having now been truly cast, we had reached a temporary impasse with Lee – sorry, I mean Rupert, no, Juan – glaring passionately at me from two yards away and me looking at him coolly through narrowed *Clint*-like eyes and wishing I had a Scott's with me to complete the ensemble. But I hadn't, because I'd packed up smoking completely after I kept bruising and sometimes burning my gums as I tried to put my head out of the car window whilst forgetting my own lit pipe (still a Peterson) and hitting the glass with it, so words or other lesser actions would have to do. And as for Chinua, *he* seemed about to cry – perhaps he was visualising his wife casually reading the headlines, seconds before her eyes lighted on his picture and she formed the right impression entirely – whilst Callum looked on with ill-concealed and gleeful anticipation.

Then the impasse was broken. The police arrived in the person of a single large bearded PC, whom I recognised instantly: *no*, not as Niño, but in the flesh, I'd *really* seen him before several times, the last a year or so back when we'd both been onboard an LH (LUFTHANSA) aircraft and he'd had another of my refusals, but that time an Iranian and a completely different and violent kettle of fish, held in a regretful, almost gentle headlock as he (the Iranian) struggled in his seat minutes before take-off, whilst he (the copper) whispered in his (the struggler's) ear, earnestly advising him to '*Listen* to the Officer'. But now he gave no sign of remembering me, probably because he didn't. Nonetheless, he immediately registered my role as the local UK authority figure and so understandably made the wrong assumption, ignoring the outstretched arm of the DM as if he were invisible, passing him and coming to stand in the doorway of the aircraft to talk to me.

"Hello, sir," he said politely and calmly, making *my Clint*-impression look like an amateurish mess but then he was a true professional, at least until his next sentence. "Right then, what's all this, what's all this?" he said. So now we had George bloody Dixon, too (but at least this wasn't Newhaven, *and* he wasn't French).

"Hello *again*," I said, subtly to remind him that we'd met before, and then I pointed at Juan. "But don't ask *me*. Ask *him*. *He's* the one who sent for you."

"For *me*? *Who*?" he asked, in surprise. "*Him*?"

"Yep," I said, and added, "*He's* the AR Duty Manager."

"Oh. Right," he said and he took Juan away to listen to what he had to say, and it didn't take long. I could see the DM pointing at me melo-hispanically (whoops) as he spoke, whilst the copper stood arms crossed in an attitude that seemed to me indicative of considerable doubt if not downright disbelief (though it could have been no more than instinctive standard passive defence against foreign knife attack). Then he motioned him to stay where he was, and returned to me.

"OK," he said, "I've heard what *he* has to say. Now, what's the *Immigration* side of all this?" and I told him the bare bones of it.

"Ah. I see," he said, when I'd finished. Then he asked another question, his last as it turned out. "Tell me, one more thing," he said. "Did you *swear* at him?"

"*Swear* at him?" I responded in surprise. "*Me*? No, I bloody well did *not*."

"OK," he said again, and thought for a moment. Then he made his decision, sighed a deep and reluctant sigh, and relayed it first to me. "All right," he said. "I'm going to arrest him."

This time *my* mouth dropped open. "*What? Who?*" I ejaculated. "*Him? Why?*"

"For interfering with *you*," he said.

"But *I* don't *want* him arrested, I just want *this* – gentleman," – and I pointed at Chinua, who was looking on wide-eyed at this exchange, an example of charitable role reversal which I thought could only happen here – "to go on *that* flight."

The PC sighed again, and I didn't blame him. *Whose side am I on?* I thought.

"OK," he said for a third time, and he motioned to Juan to join us. "So then. *Are* you *going* to let this man get onto this aircraft?"

"*No*," said Juan, decisively, his head back and his chin stuck out as hard as granite in a pose so histrionically and historically familiar that I had to remind myself that he wasn't Italian. (He really wasn't.)

"Right then," the PC said, and turned again to me, one last time, to make quite sure he'd got his facts right. "And *you* don't want *me* to – "

No," I said, decisively. "I *don't*."

"That's it, then," he said. Clearly, there was after all only one sensible thing to do. "I'm going to call my sergeant," and he walked up the ramp away from all of us, talking softly into his radio.

After a short while he was back, the relief clear on his face. "He's coming straight over," he said. "He won't be long." And he wasn't. In no more than a couple of minutes the side door in the ramp opened and the sergeant, who must have come round by car, appeared with a second PC. I didn't know him already (the sergeant I mean), but I liked what I saw. He was tall, slim, young, fit, confident and energetic, in fact physically a hell of a lot more like Clint than I was, *or* the first PC, and just what we needed for a quick resolution. So, "Hello," he said inevitably, his eyes flicking coolly round the assembly at large. And we all muttered "Hello," back, including Chinua.

"Right," he said, and rubbed his hands: he was going to enjoy this. "Who's going to start?"

"*He* is," I said, pointing at Juan, my reply coinciding with his "*I* am," our first fragment of agreement for some time, and so a good beginning.

"Come with me then please, *sir,*" said the sergeant without undue sarcasm, taking him gently by the arm away up the ramp and out of my hearing once more, and I expect their conversation was similar to that of Juan and the first PC. At least, Juan's gestures towards *me* were, and the sergeant listened intently but this time with every appearance of official belief, so a *cunning* linguist (I'm sure I've used that before). Then he motioned to him to stay where he was, and returned to me.

"You *are* the Chief Immigration Officer?" he asked, just to be sure, and I could fully understand any momentary doubt.

"Yes," I said, and flipped my warrant.

"So what's *your* name, please?" and I gave it without delay, because it was way past time to try to stay in character.

"Right. I've listened to what *he* had to say. Now what's *your* side of all this?" So I told him, in detail, quoting Acts and Rules. He nodded sagely once or twice, again with every appearance of official belief, and when I'd finished he asked his final question. "Oh, one last thing," he began. "*Did* you swe- "

"No," I repeated firmly, "I did *not*."

"Right," he said again. And thought, head down, for a few seconds before he made his decision. "OK," he said to me,

"I'm going to arrest him." And he motioned to the DM to draw nigh, to be so arrested.

This time there was a multiple sigh, from Callum and Chinua as well as from me, and for an absurd moment I toyed with the idea of giving him (the sergeant) Juan. But comparative commonsense prevailed.

So, "Hang on a minute, sarge," I said instead, "*I* don't want *him* arrested. *He* sent for the police, so that they could arrest *me*," and the sergeant frowned in perplexity.

"Yeah, I *know* that," he said. "But as I understand it, *you've* done nothing wrong, whereas *he* has -" and he began to tick off on his fingers the list of offences that Juan, according to my recent quotation of the relevant legislation, had committed, ending with "…refusal to comply with lawful removal directions, and obstructing an Immigration Officer in the course of his duty."

"That's *spot on*," I said in approval, as Juan now turned appealingly to me to defend him, "but I don't want to enforce *any* of them," – Juan nodded energetically – "I just want *him*," – I pointed at Chinua, who nodded too as he grinned shyly back – "I just want *him* on the *bl-* , *on this aircraft*."

"OK, then," said the sergeant. He had nailed his colours to the mast for all to see, the options were clear and the easy way forward was apparent to any reasonable man, and now he turned to Juan. "So *will* you let this gentleman board, so that we can all get on?" he asked, nodding encouragingly, and waited for the obvious reply.

And the DM looked at me and smiled his thanks for getting him off the hook. Then, at long last, he nodded *his* assent too, simultaneously saying, "*No*," again, emphatically, and I felt vindicated – in fact I'd have laid money on it from the off. *So why the hell doesn't the stupid, obstinate bugger just give up?* I asked myself objectively, but I knew the answer anyway. Because he *was* a stupid, obstinate bugger, but I only *thought* that, mind you, I *didn't say* it. Anyway, my objectivity didn't last, and I reverted to being strictly partisan – which, after all, was what I was paid for.

Meantime, the sergeant had made *his* decision. "Right. I'm calling my Inspector," he said, and in no time *he* turned up too, with three *more* PCs whilst I silently calculated how long it would be before we got to the Divisional Chief Super. Anyway, it was obvious that numerically the cops were now ready for anything, though I wasn't sure that that addressed the main issue. Still, we went through the same routine again, virtually to the letter, and I was just preparing myself to dissuade *him* from arresting Juan and then patiently to await the arrival of the *Chief* Inspector, probably with the rest of the whole damn shift, when events took another new turn.

For some time I'd sensed a growing murmur, of seeming discontent if not downright revolt, coming from somewhere inside the aircraft, and it was whilst I'd been talking to the sergeant that two more male heads (*Mextras*?) had appeared round the bulkhead, swivelling and craning to catch sight of each successive speaker and listening mutely but with great attention. Now, one of them actually *spoke*.

"Look 'ere, mate," it said to me, as all other conversation stopped. At least it was an ultra-English head, which now spoke ultra-English. "We're gonna be 'kin late into Strelsau at this rate, and my rugby team is bein' met there. *Now.* As fings stand, there's one too many, innit? Well, we've got free or fore travellin' reserves, and one of 'em can stay be'ind, to make room. How does *that* grab you, eh?"

It grabbed me and the Inspector just fine of course, but it didn't suit Juan juan jot. I'd known it wouldn't. "*No,*" he said decisively, again, and then he upped the ante because he couldn't help himself. I'd known he would. "And *you*," he said to the craning tight head, "*you* get *back* in your seat. You will *not* get off, not *you*, not *anyone* of your team."

It was now crystal that Juan himself had totally lost the plot *whatever* film it was, and the head predictably bristled. I'd thought it would. "Now *you look*, mate," it said, as the group murmur grew to a supportive and recalcitrant team hum, the barely audible English equivalent of a mutely murderous South African rugby squad, but in a minor key. "*Don't you ever* try to tell *me* what *I* can *fuckin'* do -", and it was at that moment, when the Inspector's eyes begin to sparkle as he allowed himself to contemplate *multiple* arrests and maybe even a spot of riot control *on-aircraft* which even at Heathrow didn't happen every day, that the Captain called through in a voice of resigned despair wholly foreign to Wallach (except maybe at the very end of *The Magnificent Seven*). "*Now*," he said, "*now* we are about to miss the *second* slot." And I knew what had to be done.

"All right," I said to the Inspector, "this is getting out of hand and I don't want to muck up the aircraft's whole flight schedule. So I am getting off, but under protest," and I did, I hoped with every appearance of good grace (although I couldn't remember Clint himself *ever* retreating like that so I hadn't a clue as to how he would've done it), and in a brief flurry of onboard recriminations the Captain disappeared back to the flight deck, the two now-loose heads to their seats and the stewardesses to their multiple charges, the door shut and the aircraft swiftly backed out and disappeared down the taxi-way.

It wasn't over of course, and I got some small satisfaction as I started to walk wearily back to the distant Control with

Callum and a still shell-shocked Chinua, to see the Inspector instantly wipe the wide smile of victory – IS 0, AR 1 after extra time – *right* off the DM's face with a stern, "*Now then. That officer* was *very* reasonable. Why couldn't *you* have – " as we turned the corner, and the view and sound ceased.

"Sorry, Callum," I muttered, after I'd announced into the radio that we were returning, all three of us, and had got a curt, clearly-disappointed, 'Received' in reply.

"Can't be helped," he replied shortly (though *he* was a good six two). "You tried," and that was that.

And the next morning, bright, early and by his command, I presented myself in the office of Andy the ACI, who had by then replaced Graham. At his shoulder stood the Duty Two HMI, one rank below. They didn't ask me to sit so I remained standing too, loosely at attention. It rang a distant bell.

"Hello there, Mike," said the ACI. He looked grave, and he raised a piece of paper in his hand. "Well. This is a complaint from the AR Station Manager. It's about last night, and it makes serious reading. Why don't you tell me your side of it?"

So I did, including the previous behaviour of the airline of which they already knew, and he and the HMI listened without interruption. When I had finished, the ACI said, "And you are sure that there would have been plenty of time for the Duty Manager to have issued a ticket?"

"Yes," I said.

"Well," he said. "But he *didn't*, did he?"

"No," I said.

"So if in the end he'd let the refusal board *without* a ticket, you would've been happy with that?"

"Yes," I said, and he paused and glanced significantly at the HMI.

"Mike. Are you aware of the relevance of the Warsaw Convention of," – he named a year, which I think was 1926 (I've never bothered to check), and an anticipatory shudder ran up my spine – or down, I can't remember which.

"No, Andy, I'm afraid not," I said. Because I wasn't.

"It says that for the purposes of aircraft insurance for international travel, *every* passenger *must* hold a *valid* ticket."

"Oh," I said.

"So if you *had* prevailed, and if he *had* carried the passenger ticket-less, and *if* the aircraft for any reason had gone down, *you*, *we* and *HMG* might have been in deep, *deep* trouble." He may have said 'shit' not 'trouble', but I can't swear to it.

"Oh," I said. "Sorry." Well there wasn't much else I *could* say, was there?

"Right," he said. "You'll know better next time." He glanced again at the letter.

"And are you aware how much that lost slot cost them?"

"No," I said.

"Nine thousand pounds."

"Oh," I repeated. Again, there wasn't much else I *could* say. "And one last thing," he said. "Did you *swear* at the Duty Manager?"

I'd forgotten all about that. "*No,* Andy," I said, "I did *not*."

He glanced sideways again, at the HMI. "Well," he said, "It says *here* that you *did*, that you called him, 'A right shit.'" And suddenly I saw the light.

"Does it happen to say I said it twice?" I asked.

"Yes," he said, surprised.

"Hah," I said, in the nearest – all right, the *only* – approach to a moment of triumph I managed during the interview. "The only thing I said to him twice was that he wasn't running a *tight ship*."

This time the two managers looked at each other, and although both of them managed full facial control, it was a close thing.

"All right," said the ACI finally. "That's all – Oh, and Mike," as I turned towards the door.

"Yes?" I said.

"The sibling of the same sex. Remember?"

"What?" I asked, and he just smiled and then it came back to me. The last time we'd met had been one evening in the bar, when he was a mere divorce rookie compared to my own lengthy experience of trying to look at new-spouse-inherited children from the new partner's point of view, and I had advised that he'd probably find that his new wife would have far more problems initially with his daughter than with his son.

"Now I remember," I said. "How's it going?" and he smiled again, a little wryly, and said, "It's all right now," and I said, "Jolly good," and left.

That was it. I heard nothing more about it and I think I got particularly good markings for Initiative and Determination in my annual report that year, though I truly can't remember what I got for Judgement. But none of it mattered too much to me anyway, because what I still do vividly remember from the night before was that when we'd got back to the Control, the rest of the Late and Night shifts who had obviously heard all about it seemed to treat me differently, almost to shun me in affronted sorrow, so that when shortly we were due to finish and Callum suggested a quick wind-down drink in Raffles, the airside staff bar between One and Two, I jumped at it, bugger *Clint* and even *Groucho*, because I knew in my heart that from now on I was marked down for ever by the IOs as a blustering, bungling failure – Frank perhaps, from '*Some*

Mothers' – and I was going to need one, and more than one, often (in fact *so* often that it might prove the first step on the rocky road to alcoholic ruin already haltingly trod by more than one previous colleague), if that was how it was going to be.

Neither of us said much as we walked to the bar and then when we entered there was a small but distinct roar of welcome from one corner, and there were most of the staff who'd just come off duty with pints in their hands and ours ready and waiting on the table, and I was already beginning to feel better when with one accord they raised their glasses to me as the rest looked on and wondered. "A toast," said someone, "*AR!*" And "*AR!*" we echoed.

Bastards, I thought happily as I sat down amongst my friends and then, *Bugger Frank after all,* next. This time in the end maybe the Clint approach hadn't worked but at least, as Callum had put it, I'd tried, and so in the eyes of the rest of the staff I had achieved full Marx. Then I remembered the ACI's words: "…You'll know better next time." *Next* time? Forget it.

EACH TO HIS OWN

Which reminds me again of complaints. You'll recall that I'd had a career's worth in my first eighteen months at Gatwick but there had been nothing more, not a sniff, until I got to Two. Then they started again, thick and fast, but this time, with only the one Ruritanian exception, it was nothing personal and they were not *about* me but *at* me as a manager, or about other individual officers or about the operation of the Control at large, and dealing with them too was what I was paid for.

All the CIOs copped it that way, but it was still a decade or more before the Blame Culture crept in so most people still had the sense to recognise that cock-ups were a fact of life and that not *everything* that went wrong had to be *someone's fault*. Then too even if they thought it was, they would at least usually complain in person, on the spot and at the time, when the matter was live and fresh albeit with tempers still frayed, so that we could deal with things then and there and everyone could get their views off their chest. And sometimes, with a nominally unbiased third party – one of *us*, the CIOs, I mean – holding the ring, it would wind up in a handshake which, grudging or not, would be the end (and not the Juan-off *start*) of it.

It didn't always work that way though, and it thoroughly pissed you off when a wholly unheralded written complaint arrived weeks after the event, by which time no-one could clearly remember exactly what had happened or even if anything really *had* happened at all; or even worse, when it came from someone and about something you *did* recall, recall in detail, because you'd dealt with it at the time and the current complainant was the very same who had then professed him or herself fully satisfied, although the letter now burning a hole in your hand would make no reference whatever to *that*. Still, in that case the contemporary note about it would always already have been entered in the Incident Log. And besides, as I keep saying (and kept saying more or less every bloody day when I was still in the job), you just can't win 'em all.

But let's return to fresh, live, instant complaints, to which each CIO developed an individual style of response, all effective to some degree though some worked better than others (and you could never practically compare them anyway). At one extreme you had the technique practised consistently by The Commander, a senior CIO, ex-RN and now not too far off retirement (by my juvenile standards anyway). I still struggle to find a word or phrase for his approach: 'anticipatory'; or 'conciliatory'; or 'pro-active', as they would say now? No, perhaps 'pre-emptive' describes it best, and I hadn't been at Two long when I first saw him use it. Then, once I had, it fascinated me and after that if we were on together and if I wasn't busy when a complaint did arise, I'd just sit back in my chair in the far corner of the Watch House, saying nothing myself because he certainly didn't need any help from *me*, and enjoy the show.

That first time was typical. I'd heard raised voices on the Control but had tried to ignore them because I was the SEA man and it was as usual a Floor matter, so nothing to do with me. *The Commander is Floor. He'll cover it,* I thought. But to my initial surprise he did nothing at all, in fact he remained inside the Watch House standing behind his desk, gazing vaguely into the far distance through the glass and his glasses – perhaps scanning for enemy top-masts the far horizons of his naval past – and puffing on his big pipe, his thoughts apparently miles away and seemingly unaware of the commotion right before his eyes. Then in due course the noise outside ceased abruptly after a clear, heated but wholly inconclusive exchange of mutual insults followed by a pregnant pause, and I thought, *It won't end there. It can't.*

And it didn't. Because moments later I heard heavy steps marching purposefully in our direction and looked up to see a large purple-faced man enter the room: no, not the IO, *he* was smaller and only a little pink, though close behind. And when Plum-face started towards *me*, I silently indicated the

Commander who still stood, slightly stooped and statue-like, staring wistfully into the distance, his back turned towards us in apparent ignorance if not downright denial of the looming extra presence close by. Then, as the man burst out, "Are you *in charge?* I want to -", the Commander's right hand flew up commandingly; and instantly, magically – and I never saw it happen any other way – the voice stopped in mid-sentence, shut off abruptly as if by a switch, and only then did my colleague himself rotate slowly and precisely (as it were on his own axis), remove his pipe and for several seconds look carefully though without expression at the man whilst the world held its breath. And then at last he spoke.

"I saw (pause, replace pipe, puff,)… *exactly* what happened out there," he said, very quietly and very politely. "*I* saw… (puff, puff, puff,)… *everything*. And before you speak, allow me to apologise *sincerely*. Now, please sit down and tell me all about it. You may smoke." So plum-face did, at length (tell him all about it, I mean, not *smoke* – no-one *ever* did *that,* though some of them must surely have wanted to), winding himself up ever tighter as he continued and on several occasions pausing himself – partly it seemed to recover his breath, and partly to let the Commander respond, but to no avail in either respect, the repeated silences seeming ever more to provoke him so that by the end he had turned positively puce. Eventually he finished, and slumped back truly puffed out with every appearance of exhaustion in his chair whilst I eyed him dubiously under lowered lids and debated whether to call an ambulance.

A further, final silence then ensued, as the Commander removed his glasses and polished them carefully on his tie until they shone. Then, still in silence, he replaced them and then examined his pipe, slowly, lest it had expired or emptied (in which case he would relight or re-fill it, equally slowly, but I can't remember whether he had to do either, that time), while the silence and the tension grew and I found that now *I* was beginning to sweat. And then, when he'd finished and only then, did he speak again. "Thank you *very much*," he said, again quietly, and continued after a further long moment spent seemingly in collecting his thoughts. "And first, please accept my congratulations. Allow me to say that you put that *very* well. Now, I have already apologised, sincerely. Do you accept my apology?" He paused briefly, expectantly. "No? Oh. Oh dear. Then I withdraw it. Good-day," and he gently steered puce-face out of the Watch House.

It worked like a charm and I never saw it fail. Every time the complainant's mouth would drop open at the Commander's response, and then it went one of two ways (the scenario of course, not the mouth). Usually he (or, rarely, she – the proportions simply in strict accord with the overall frequency, per sex, of complainants, for the Commander was scrupulous in his observation of equality) would react as when I first saw it done, but after an outraged initial "*No!*", the very reaction of said puce-face, no further words ever came out because it seemed a physical impossibility, and there was instead just an incoherent mumbling as the Commander softly and sadly ushered the broken man, or occasionally woman, away.

But now and then there would be a shocked pause and then the complainant would say something like, "Well, *yes,* I suppose I *do*," in stunned self-wonder, and the scene would draw to the same conclusion except that the Commander would then break into a broad and magnanimous smile and step forward to shake his or her hand and clap him/her on the back, and they would exchange further brief genuine pleasantries before the one disappeared, made whole again, into the Customs Hall and the other resumed his myopic, absent-minded and smoke-obscured stare from the Bridge – sorry, through the Watch House glass. And whichever way it went, it was *pure magic*, like I almost said.

And so to the other extreme. I only witnessed it once – well, I can't honestly say *witnessed* exactly, because for the life of me I can't remember that I did. But I was there all right, or at least I've been *told* I was – but that doesn't mean that it never happened again (if it happened at all). And if it did, however infrequently, you may agree that it would almost certainly, no, inevitably, have been as instantly and conclusively successful. And a word for *this* technique? Again I've thought at length and again, it's tricky: 'ultimate' perhaps, or 'decisive', or 'final'. No, I think that the *mot juste* is the word itself – 'extreme': after all, that's what it would have been. Or was.

I was SEA CIO again, my Floor oppo. Geoff, he of the Desk Top and a good friend, only a year senior to myself but universally and rightly regarded by the IOs, the ones that really mattered, as the Best CIO At The Port. He's dead now, long since, having announced at the crematorium via his widow over the outside tannoy (because the crowd of Service mourners filled not just the chapel but the public car park) after the bastard cancer had finally got him, that he 'was now going for his last smoke'.

Anyway this time the first I knew was when I heard another loud voice approaching the Watch House. Now Geoff, like me, spent most of his time as Floor CIO *out* there *on* the Floor dealing with situations as they arose which was what he was doing now, so the still-raised voice should have signalled the impending *end* of an argument. But its owner wouldn't have it, and I looked up briefly from taking a reference to see Geoff walk quickly into the Watch House to answer the phone, followed immediately by *him, Mawhodikwhets,* the Man Who Didn't Know When To Stop.

Again there was no reason for me to interfere, especially as the CIO dealing was Geoff: so I told my IO to carry on with his reference and only half–heard Geoff say quietly, "Look, sirr. I just told you. This conversation is going nowhere, and I and my colleague are busy. So please leave the Watch House, and *Guidbye,"* and, briefly, Mawhodikwhets (the name sounds Iroquois to me, or maybe Kipling Burmese, but he was Anglo-Saxon all right)) did. But in a minute he was back again and still at it, so Geoff asked him to leave *again* and it went on like this for another five minutes and two more entrances and by now it was a real hindrance to me and I was trying to concentrate on another reference and paying no attention whatsoever to the exchange when I heard Geoff say, still quietly but with a clear edge to his voice, *"Look,* mate. *Guidbye again.* And this is yer *last warning."*

But back the clown came, yet again, and I was head-down giving some instructions to my IO and trying my hardest to ignore him (Coco I mean) *and* Geoff when I heard a sudden succession of new, unusual noises, a double *thump* swiftly followed by a gasp and a heavy thud, and I looked up sharply to see Geoff gazing pensively out through the Watch House glass like the Commander, and on the floor behind him and between us the prostrate apparently lifeless body of a relaxed Mawhodikwhets, on his back with arms outstretched.

So I jumped up, the way one does, went over and knelt by the figure trying to find a pulse. But I couldn't, though I tried twice, and I looked anxiously up at Geoff and said, *"Jesus Christ,* Geoff. He's *dead!"* He however (*Geoff* I mean) proved as wholly unmoved as Mawhodikwhets, and continued to stare calmly out of the window as he replied, "Naah, naah, Mike.

He'll wake up in.." – and he glanced at his watch – "..oh, three minutes." But he was wrong because he woke in barely two, sat up, looked around, staggered to his feet and rubbed his head, saying, "Where am I?" as again, I suppose, never having done it myself, you do. And since Geoff maintained his close oversight of whatever had attracted his attention outside, it fell to me to get up and go over and say, "Hello there, mate. You're in the Immigration Watch House at Terminal Two and you've had a bit of a fall, but you'll be all right now," and I guided him out and through the entrance into the Customs Hall and away. I didn't see him pick up any baggage, so perhaps he didn't have any.

We never heard any more about it, *if* it happened in the first place, and that caveat is only because this is the sole incident recorded in this book involving me directly that I cannot clearly remember myself, even in its telling. In fact, I can't remember anything about it at all – an example perhaps of nascent or of unconsciously selective Alzheimer's. Or perhaps not. But I've included it because another old Two colleague now of high rank whom I recently bumped into told me about it word for word over the inevitable couple of pints, and when I asked him how *he* knew when I couldn't recall a bloody thing, he replied, "Because *you* told *me*, a long time ago," and *he* wouldn't lie to me, any more than *I* would to him, so there you are.

Lastly, there remains my response to the only complaint (in inverted commas) ever made against me personally (Juan apart) as a Two CIO; and to find the word for *that* technique you need to understand the origins of the complaint itself. 'Well-deserved' would fit all right, and so would 'self-sacrificial' and 'invited', but they both imply a degree of intent and control that I was far from feeling at the time.

So no – or 'naah, naah' as Geoff would say. But wait, I have it: 'perverse' perhaps, or maybe 'self-*inflicted*' is the one. Yes, self-inflicted. That's it.

After all, the whole point in receiving a complaint 'live' within minutes if not seconds of its birth was that it gave you a chance to correct the simple misunderstanding which often lay behind it, at worst to make the aggrieved party calm down and reconsider and at best to kill the thing stone dead. Your role was to *fix* it, not *fuel* it – *that* would just be plain *stupid*, wouldn't it? Right. But nobody's perfect.

So. I was already dog-tired although it was only 2315 hours and already a hell of a night. I'd been there pacing the Control, the standard solitary Night CIO, since my two late colleagues, both totally creamed, had rightly left me at 2100. And I'd just sent home four of the Late IOs who should also have left then but who had volunteered to stay on to help the two Late Lates and five Night IOs out of a jam. There should have been four Late Lates, but two of them and one of the Night crew had gone sick and I can't say that I blame them, especially if they were clairvoyant.

The problems had started earlier, as they did on all such bad days. But normally they peaked at about 1900 and then slowly began to die down, so that by 2100 we had a bit of a grip on things and there was light at the end of the tunnel (metaphorically speaking, of course: you couldn't even see one end of the *airport* tunnel from the other, because it had both a bend and a dip in it) .

But tonight that hadn't happened, partly because there had been so many new cases throughout the day that we'd never even *begun* to catch up and partly because normally by around 2015 the Moscow SU, the last of the day's predictably dirty flights, would be in the Hall with the Late IOs still there to make at least a sizeable dent in it before they left. Not this time though, either because it had gone tech. or there had been a severe head-wind, I can't remember which, and it was only just entering the Hall *now*, five minutes *ahead* of the last shorter-haul flights which had also been delayed (so it probably *was* the wind), but which had still just beaten the Heathrow night-flight restriction.

Everyone used to the place always expected the SU to take a while, even its own once-in-a-lifetime third world travellers who I suppose had to be reasonably philosophical – or unaware – to travel on it in the first place. And there would probably still have been no major problem if the other, cleaner, flights had reached us first. But it was crystal clear that they hadn't, because the be-suited non-European businessmen, largely Yank, were only now entering the grid, to queue up behind the myriad crowd who had merely used Moscow as a stop-over, long or short and with or without brooms, and who had started from Dhaka or Dakar, from Lagos or Lahore; and I knew that so far they (the businessmen) didn't have a clue about what they'd let themselves in for.

So I'd started with seven IOs, six for the middle and one on the EC end, but even that wouldn't last long because the remaining Late Lates couldn't stay much longer – they should have finished at 2300 anyway, and had to have *some* sleep before *their* next days' work – and I'd had to pull four of the night-crew off ongoing cases to give some appearance of a real presence on the control and now they began picking up *more* cases, *just* – as Tommy Cooper said – *like that*. At this rate we'd still be there in the morning, handing on the still-outstanding previous night's work to the fresh – no, wrong word, the newly-arrived – Earlies to pick up *before they'd even started*, the ultimate nightmare scenario which if it ever materialised would finally and fatally *prove* the domino theory beyond any doubt and which, accordingly, simply *could not happen.*

So I humbly asked the Late Lates if they could stay on *just a bit* longer, and one of them – due to start later the next day than the other – said he could, bless him; so I asked him to stay in the middle to clear the passengers in the grid with the assistance, as soon as may be, of the EC-end IO who at present was still tied up in dealing with his *own* queue; and I told the other four to get back to their existing cases and only to re-join us if and when they'd finished sorting all the outstanding work, including the new stuff just off the SU.

OK, it sounds unbalanced – no, what's the buzz-word now, *disproportionate* – and it must have seemed that way at the time. But there were a lot of sponsors, often close relatives, of our un-cleared cases still waiting land-side – several there since the morning – and the last tube train of the day/night to London was imminent and someone somehow somewhere was going to have to suffer, so I'd do the same again today. But that predictably cut no ice (which really *is* Iroquois) with those still festering in the grid, and I knew just how *they* felt, too – it's how we all feel when we finally reach the front of the post office queue just as the grinning clerk sneers in wordless vengeful final triumph, pulls the blind down, shuts up shop and fucks right off.

So I stood there (as was my wont) out in front, between the desks and the grid with a furled black brolly to remind them that this was Britain, as the queue began to murmur. And I tried to explain but that just seemed to get them all more excited so I stood right between them and the poor solitary remaining Late Late, who kept his head down and soldiered on manfully. But now they ignored *me* and concentrated their abuse on *him*, loudly, nastily and in multiple baying packs.

And suddenly I'd had enough, and all the frustrations I felt at trying daily to do an impossible job in impossible conditions with a pitiful number of constantly-exhausted staff boiled over. And I let them have it.

They were shouting and screaming by now, so I shouted and screamed louder, which in the stress of the moment I found surprisingly easy. And I matched their abuse with my own and soon they'd all shut up, somehow I'd succeeded in silencing them stone dead. But *I* carried on for another full minute, or maybe more, marching up and down the line shouting, ranting, yelling still if not quite raving, brandishing my brolly and telling them how it *really* was and explaining that the single officer they could see was only there out of the goodness of his heart and if they didn't like it I'd send *him* home too, and then they could stand there all fucking night if they chose and if they wanted to blame someone, they could blame the bloody Home Office for getting us in this mess – not that it would do them any goddam good, because it never had when *we'd* tried it.

Then I retired for a moment to the Watch house to recover myself, shaking and breathing heavily And I looked out and saw that the first small miracle of the whole God-awful day had finally happened and that at least there were no *more* new cases, and that the Late Late man was on his last SU passenger and about to start on the businessmen. And I thought, *I've really done it now,* and waited for the complainants to start lining up outside to have a well-deserved pop at me. But only two did, both Yank males whom I saw singly with the door shut. And as each came in, to my astonishment and great pleasure he immediately stuck out his hand, apologised for *his* behaviour, said he hadn't had any idea of our problems until now, promised to write strongly to the Home Office and shook my hand again as he left.

So that was it. I never experienced a shift as bad as that again though no doubt my colleagues did, often, and I'm sure they handled things better than me. I didn't advise anyone else to take my approach, let's put it that way, and I never heard anything more about it so I don't know whether either or both of my two 'complainants' did write to the Home Office, or not. At least they can't have written in to complain about *me* because I know that *those* letters would have been on my desk, with a short deadline for a full response, by yesterday. And if they really wrote the kind of thing they'd promised to, *those* letters had as much effect as our own repeated protests had done before, because fuck-all changed.

But one other thing *had* (changed, I mean). Because as I drove home strangely muzzy-headed and very, very slowly the following morning, the coast finally cleared for my Early colleagues because all the outstanding cases[45] had somehow been sorted by the truly magnificent work of the Night IOs, I knew that if I stayed at Two much longer, much as I positively loved the place it would surely, surely kill me, which would do no-one any good, least of all my family.

And soon after that I lost consciousness twice at home, once falling noisily all the way down the stairs – sustaining no lasting physical damage in the process (this time, not even an intimidating scalp, but then I had had some practice) but sparking an instant and unusually high degree of filial interest from my two young daughters who, sensing a new game, scampered hand in hand into the kitchen to ask brightly, "Mummy, mummy, come and see. Why is Daddy lying out there with his nose stuck in the door?" – and once slumping over quite painlessly in slow, slow still-semi-conscious motion as one by one my systems shut down, but again suffering no obvious consequential lasting physical effects.

"Hmm. OK. Nothing to worry about, just faints," that's
what the consultant finally said, after a load of tests which
he seemed to think I'd passed. But he was a big heavy man
himself and went very red in the face and started shouting and
swearing and stamping round the room when I described our
absurd self-induced suicidal shift pattern (so-called, although
there was no discernible pattern at all about it), and that's
when I shut *right* up because I was scared that if I told him any
more, *he'd* be the one to flake out.

(I remembered too what Estabs. Division was rumoured
always to reply when the standard weekday Home Office nine-
to-fivers made one of their regular moans that our (the fascist
IS misfits') pensions were considerably larger than theirs, as
they were – and rightly so, given our extra payments for shift-
work, for working week-ands and not least for responsibility,
all of which, the hard way, we fucking-well *earned*. "Ah, yes,"
the Estabs. person would say knowingly, with a wink and a
fore-fingered tap of the nose – but not simultaneously, because
if you did it that way and your timing or movement was only
a little way out you could do lasting self-harm. "It's quite true,
IS pensions *are* higher. But *how long* do they have to *last, eh,
eh?*")

Because it was a recognised fact that as a body we died
young, often within a couple of years of retirement. But my
first goal, which right then seemed far away, was just to *reach*
it – retirement, I mean. And *that* was when I first began to
consider *another* transfer, away from Heathrow. And to think
of it, with deep shame and lasting guilt for those I would be
leaving behind, but quite specifically, in two related words: my
Lifeline; and my Escape.

OUT

So, reluctantly, I applied for one (a transfer I mean), and received the standard acknowledgement soon afterwards. And then it was just a question of sitting back and waiting. I expected it to take a while because I had specified Stansted and Stansted alone as my chosen destination, then still a small, a *very* small airport where vacancies didn't arise too often, especially for CIOs, because it only had one. But I knew that he was due to retire soon, and I knew too that by dint of my long continuous service at major airports, by then some seventeen years, I was top of the sacrosanct Transfer Points Table – you got so many for each year, the annual number depending on where you were based, and the one at the top always went first.

Anyway the very fact of having applied made me feel better, and Beth for that matter, and by now the Stansted incumbent was due to finish any day. So I carried on at Two demob-happy, enjoying it anew with my departure in the offing, regretting deeply and guiltily still that I had to leave but reconciled to the fact and simply biding my time because I'd checked and I was still Top of the Table by a huge margin. So it was like a kick in the teeth or even the crutch when one fine day I looked casually on the Interport List and saw that the new CIO vacancy at Stansted had just been filled – but not by me, by an ex-Terminal Three colleague now at Harwich instead, so already just up the road (from Stansted, I mean), but points-wise almost wholly bereft.

I was vexed. I was bewildered. I was, in short, *thoroughly* pissed off. It was nothing personal against Tom – already a vague friend from his Heathrow days (when he'd been in the Red Room), and we soon became close buddies after I finally joined him at you-know-where. But his accumulated points total after he'd left The Airport for Harwich some years before had then dropped to zero and must still be in single figures, whereas mine was in the roaring forties. So: a lot of time and effort had gone into a system that ensured that those with hard service should get the so-called lighter postings they wanted when, eventually, they'd had enough; and now it had gone tits-up.

So I wrote an angry letter to HQ, and in short order got a courteous reply. It said with regret that it had been felt on this occasion that the acknowledged, established policy *had* to be ignored, because Two simply could not at that juncture afford to lose 'so experienced and respected a CIO' etc. etc. and all that bollocks. But it assured me, *promised* me hand-on-heart that when the *next* vacancy arose...I clenched my teeth but left it, stifling my professional disbelief because the thing was done now and it would have been certainly futile and probably generally self-destructive to have tried to take things any further.

So I served another year at Two, whilst I watched property prices suddenly shoot up, especially in North Essex – it was the latest national boom – and in July 1988 there finally I was, at the Airport of my comparative dreams where I thought I could happily fade away amongst others of like mind, many of them ex-Airport themselves. Mind, when I say 'many' it's purely figurative, because there were only seven IOs on the place's complement. But that soon increased dramatically – and why? Because in the interim Stansted had been chosen to be Major London Airport Number Bloody *Three,* that's why, so I was going to be in the metaphorical soup *again* – but not, I thought with relief, for a few years yet, years during which I could re-charge, and in that at least I was right. In a manner of speaking, anyway.

But during that second now-frustrating wait, the grapevine kicked in – it was bound to, sooner or later – and I learned the simple truth. Which was that it was just another cock-up, they had simply forgotten me. And then, finally, it made sense.

But the next problem – the only reason why I have described this rather distasteful episode at all – is that *that* meant that the silent conclusion I'd reached whenever my earlier doubts had re-surfaced, the inevitable conclusion I had badly wanted *not* to be true, was now confirmed. Which was that the letter from HQ had been a total fabrication, a cowardly fiction to avoid the honest reality of admitting a prime balls-up, which I would have accepted wryly but instantly – God knows, we've all done it.

But that meant that the letter had been manufactured for no other reason than to hide incompetence and although we all take stuff like that as normal now, it *wasn't* then, and for the first time my belief in the integrity of the Service itself so far as its own senior employees was concerned was seriously, lastingly, dented. Anyway, *enough* of that. I'd done Heathrow, or rather it had done me, up *and* thoroughly – like, in fact, a veritable kipper. And now to Stansted, where I'd wanted for some now-considerable time to go, and where, finally, to end Slice One but not for that reason alone, I was truly going.

WANT MORE?

Sure? Because if you're already down, then Slice Two, soon I hope also to be published, will do you no good at all and now might be a good time to stop. Oh, I *want* you to buy it all right, if only because it helps fund my continued (though much-reduced) liquid research. But I ask out of kindness, because you can take it from me that things don't improve – except, slowly, for the worse.

Still it's entirely your choice, and there are perhaps compensations if you like a bit of a change, as the move to Stansted brought an entirely new element into the game, Enforcement, I mean, that's work on the streets catching the ones – by now, the thousands, the tens of thousands or hundreds of thousands, or maybe *millions* of the buggers, because *nobody* really knew then, *or* knows now – who had previously somehow beaten or simply evaded the system, and who daily still were. And are.

And enforcement itself added yet another, sometimes darker, dimension, to the comedy and the tragedy too as, if you *will* persist in reading on, you'll soon see. Because in no time at all I was right there in it (the work *and* the laughs *and* the tears) at least up to my navel, if not my neck. Or to put it another way, if you actually *enjoyed* reading this volume, you should enjoy the next. And there are still plenty of stories about Stansted *port*-life too and, then and later, a closer and more detailed (if not downright intimate) insight into the strange deeds and the perhaps even stranger minds of our ongoing closest colleagues in the strangest world of all, namely, *wait for it* – yep, the Branch (later to be joined in my *own* small world by yet *another* Branch, SO *13*, the Anti-Terrorist, until the two combined in a Met. *Command*, SO *15*, Counter Terrorism, with us in its midst and with all that went with it).

"But wait," I hear you say, amazed. "All that, and the Met too?" Well, I mentioned the streets at the start didn't I, and they (the Met, I mean) began to figure – albeit *en passant,* in uniform and only now and then – whilst I was still at Stansted, and loomed necessarily larger when I first found myself in and (dimly) through the Smoke, running PATT, the London Port Absconder Team (to learn more of which as I said just now, you'll have to read the second book, anyway). But as far as the junction of two Met Branches is concerned, not only will you have to *begin* to read it but, I'm afraid, *finish* it too, because it was only towards the end that I somehow wound up, as a strictly-temporary HMI, running the small, elite, discreet and, though I say it myself, *ultra-fucking-effective* IS's *own* Anti-Terrorist Unit. So. *Surprised?* Then how d'you think *I* felt?

★ ★ ★

And now: a brief opening excerpt from Book Two, whether to whet your appetite to proceed, or stiffen your resolve to refrain.

"STANSTED. So, made it, there I was, home at last. Even now when I say it out loud, *'Stansted'* like that, an involuntary grin creeps over my face and only some of it relates to the old terminal where I started in 1988. Because when the new, the present one opened in 1991, our IS staff, already expanded in anticipation, remained largely the same – and so in particular did SB's, and at the end of the day it's the people who make or break a place. That said, the old Stansted *was* special: a true, a splendid anachronism at the best of times.

And Stanstead, with the extra 'a'? Now *that's* somewhere else entirely in another county, and besides the wench is dead. But *we* are talking about the place *without* that second 'a', now a *real* major London airport albeit deep in the rolling North Essex countryside, pastures new and I *mean* pastures, in the middle of nowhere to be precise until the opening of the M11 and after that much easier of access but still in the middle of nowhere much, which is a comment of affection, not derision.

And when I pulled into the staff car park that first sunny July morning – our *very own, restricted* Control Authority staff car park, ring-fenced (albeit with holes) *for us alone,* just SB, Customs and the IS for Chrissake, and a mere *fifty yards walk* from the entrance because there, we still *mattered* – and peered dubiously at the front of the old terminal, I was struck forcibly by two things: first, the general absence of an ever-present bustle of passengers – well, the absence of anyone *at all* to be precise, because the whole place seemed deserted; and second – as if neatly to punctuate the complete lack of anything human – the noisy, jostling host of house martins in their spittle and daub nests in the eaves directly over the entrance, eagerly awaiting my passage below – as regards which and in all fairness let me make it quite clear that there was nothing truly forcible about *them*, not *physically* anyway, because the shrapnel-like patter of bird-shit on your head and upper body, though persistent and corrosive, didn't really hurt.

So: pass through various unmarked gates and winding mossy ways, or time it carefully and sprint the *wrong* way through the automatic doors outside Customs (of which more later[46]), and you came eventually to the Immigration Control itself, and beside it, our and SB's offices. They adjoined anyway, but in terms of the constant flow between them they might just as well have been one. The Control itself was by Heathrow and Gatwick standards very small but nonetheless perfectly formed, and fronted straight onto the tarmac whence passengers arrived directly on foot or occasionally by coach. And I can see it now, echoing hollowly in its emptiness the first time I walked through it to our office door, to be met with a thunderous, rumbling, welcoming roar by the multitude of

IS staff on duty who Tom had kindly lined up to greet me, the whole shift in fact, all three of them, (including Tom himself, of course).

Then I met SB – *Essex* SB, but I do not propose to go again through all the damp detail of the events of that opening day[47]. Suffice it to say that it was memorable in terms both of its alcoholic intake (staff) and of the slickness of the removals procedures (passengers). Routine refusals arrived and left again almost before their feet had touched the ground, and asylum claims were as rare as tigers' eggs. It didn't always work that way of course but it mainly did, and especially on the day I started, and it took me back almost twenty years. But let's get straight down to a few, just a few, of the Stansted stories, which could fill a further book or two, all on their very own[48]."

Appendices

1. *British Caledonian Airways.*
2. *Until the end of 1972 the IO's landing stamp had two flanges, one at the top and one at the bottom, each inclined upwards at an angle from the main flat date-and-port pad, and worded 'leave to land for three months' and 'granted admission for six months' respectively. The former applied to Aliens and the latter to Commonwealth Citizens (to show that they were different and thus advantaged), and all the IO had to do was to apply the basic stamp and then incline his wrist one way or the other (i.e. 'roll' it, forward or backward) as appropriate and the job was done, the real significance being that no record whatsoever of either endorsement would be kept centrally by the Home Office, so you only ever used the 'roll' on those passengers in whom you had complete confidence, yeah, right (and not many people know that).*
3. *The Commonwealth equivalent of refusing 'leave to land' to an Alien. (See page 14 for more on its practical application.)*
4. *Special.*
5. *To find out why, where, when and by whom, see 'Satellites,' page 242.*
6. *Put crudely, if on a foggy Friday morning in a dark mean sea-town street straight out of Dickens you had the low cunning first to find, then to corner and finally to extract real dosh out of a young single mum debtor who had only put the kids' grub on the table for the past week on tick, courtesy of you, in the first place – and especially if the extraction could be effected violence-free (if she or her bloke didn't bash you, I mean) – then you were probably just what the Branch's doctor had ordered. That's my theory anyway, but who knows? Perhaps it was just the cricket.*
7. *For Aliens, your average, standard, perpendicular cross. But for Commonwealth Citizens, a diagonal, Saltire-like, instead, to show that they were different and still somehow advantaged!?*

8. *The media's everyday reference to the 'deportation' of foreigners is almost always wrong. Deportation is a formal legal process that has always carried with it extra time sanctions on any return here that simple refusal of entry or, internally, the 'service of papers' on an individual as an immigration offender did not involve. Such passengers/offenders were, simply, 'removed'.*

9. *A UK screening operation of immigrant DPs (displaced persons), intended to identify communist agents and sympathisers.*

10. *British Airports Authority.*

11. *Inspector.*

12. *The Department of Health and Social Security, the DSS or BA of its day.*

13. *To check that all the passengers had all the requisite jabs.*

14. *Dai Lemmer, who Bernie invented.*

15. *Moths', I mean, the first intrusion by Sellars/Cluseau. There may be more.*

16. *Gibson, of course, although he's really American/Irish. Anyway, I'm sure I don't need to identify the films, the ones where the English are all cowardly conniving shits who can do no right and the rest, of whatever other nationality but mostly courageous ex-colonials, all altruistic saints who can do no wrong.*

17. *It's said that as soon as she'd finished her part in recording 'Gimme Shelter' with the heavy strain on her that it involved, Merry Clayton went straight home and promptly miscarried.*

18. *By a remarkable chance, in my foreshortened stay at university I <u>had</u> studied a number of oriental languages, to wit Hindi, Urdu and Sanskrit; but never Bengali, and when you come to the appropriate section, on page 237 of this opus, it may come as no surprise to learn that I could remember fuck-all about any of them anyway (and even went so far as to prove it).*

19. *Technically speaking he would actually have been the Sixth, because the real Fourth Man was (the then Sir) Anthony Blunt and the fifth John Cairncross – not that their existence or identities were known publicly at the time – and those two didn't physically defect, anyway. The first three did though, and if you don't already know who they were or even what*

the hell I'm talking about, you should feel fucking ashamed and turn at once to page 136. Does <u>no-one</u> know what they <u>do</u> need to know any more?

20. Playing 'Merry Xmas Everybody', and that year everybody <u>was</u> having fun. Well, almost everybody.

21. The North Vietnamese (regular) Army.

22. The largest was Richard Criel, 'Jaws', and contrary to first Bond impressions the nicest man you could ever hope to meet. But that was later at Terminal Three, and now I've told you anyway.

23. A paper requiring the recipient to submit to further examination under the I.A. 1971 and thus, then, in proper, constant, use.

24. 'Victor Charlie', the Viet Cong.

25. Read the next story and you'll understand.

26. Ditto.

27. Ditto.

28. See the last story.

29. The 5/6 referred to the French boat, either the *Valencay* or the *Villandrie*, which left Newhaven at c.1830 each night and came back in at c.0530 the next day, and which was notorious for cheap refusals because the connecting train from Paris had the lowest fares. It was also a common belief amongst those very same refusals that just as at every UK port on Christmas Day the IOs on that crossing would nightly be both pissed and pissed off, and that as a consequence they would be reluctant to involve themselves in all the work attached to a refusal And just as with Christmas, they were generally half-right.

30. In fact her apparent final surrender was simpler, quicker, more sudden and infinitely more despicable than that. See 'Sound of Fate', page 119.

31. It turned out that the passenger had stuck stamps over the Visa Officer's hand-written signal in the passport, so I had missed <u>that</u> too.

32. By then the Service did have an Enforcement Arm, comparatively primitive though growing, but there was no detachment at Gatwick and by the time they'd arrived from anywhere else, it would have been far too late…

33. And before you start going all Christian forgiveness and bleeding hearts on me, try reading 'The Naked Island' and then 'End of a hate', or if

you want something more recent, 'The Forgotten Highlander'. Russell Braddon earned his right to forgive, earned it the hard way; just as Alistair Urquhart earned his right not to. And you? Unless you were there, or your son or your father or your brother or your husband, what the hell do <u>you</u> know about it?

34. *The Iranian Imperial Secret Police.*

35. *Though I see it's back on the standard medical agenda now.*

36. *Ask any well-informed Rugby man about that in the context of the '74 tour, and he'll tell you its significance, especially over a pint or six.*

37. *Of course I remember really – at least now and then – and the reason is on page 3- page 3, that is, of Slice Two.*

38. *Broken down.*

39. *Refusal report face-sheet.*

40. *After the gradual and long overdue demise of industrial-scale MPs' representations – see the opening to 'Two Excursions' on page 178.*

41. *'The Beguiled'.*

42. *Excluding asylum seekers of course, I nearly forgot them because this was still a little before their true main time. But even then they could tell you any goddamn lie they liked, and often did, however absurd, and all you could do was sit there, clock it and take it.*

43. *Old Barnes's final, biggest bomb, built not for the dams but for railway viaducts, bridges and the Nazi supergun, (itself a predecessor of the later and late Gerald Bull's) and equally successful – to Upkeep the bouncer I mean, not the doomed Project Babylon.*

44. *Deighton of course, not...-in.*

45. *They were mainly asylum cases naturally, and to be fair our by-now relatively small part in their completion had recently diminished further, thus enabling us to finish things a little quicker. But that was only because the Home Office no longer required our input, our view as highly experienced interviewers – it was, after all, what we did for a living – on what you might reasonably think was a matter of at least as much (if not more) import and relevance as it was in every other sort of case: to wit the claimant's personal credibility. But all we did now was to complete a Pro Forma, recording the answers, however palpably ridiculous, without*

comment. And forgive me, I should have been more precise. It wasn't simply that HO no longer required our conclusions on an applicant's truthfulness; it had specifically, positively, instructed us not even to make, still less to justify, any such conclusions in the first place, on the grounds that they were likely to prove 'unhelpful'.

And Oh, I almost forgot. The ultimate recourse to avoid a hang-over of cases was to reschedule any outstanding for another day – or, by now, another month. Which only left two problems: firstly, it gave the lucky recipient a hell of a long time to rehearse his story, true or false and with or without his specialist solicitor; and secondly, if he (the passenger I mean, naturally, never ever the honest brief) still wasn't happy with it (his story, I mean) he had again ample time to take a hike, join the swelling ranks of port absconders (but at such an early stage in the process as routinely to preclude any real attempt ever to re-find him) and thus not return at all.

46. See 'Gatecrash', just ahead in Slice Two. The title may just give you a clue.

47. You'll find a fictionalised but factually wholly accurate general account of it in my novel 'Dog Strap Five' (always assuming it's ever published) if you turn to the Chapter on 'Friends'. It provides no details of the refusals, which – barring the speed of their departure – were unexceptional, but is otherwise a comprehensive description, albeit seen through amber-coloured glasses (pint-sized).

48. Just say the word and I'll write one, and with a few more Branch stories too (but nothing you don't Need to Know, naturally).